John Boyd Kinnear

Principles of Reform

Political and Legal

John Boyd Kinnear

Principles of Reform
Political and Legal

ISBN/EAN: 9783337297374

Printed in Europe, USA, Canada, Australia, Japan

Cover: Foto ©Suzi / pixelio.de

More available books at **www.hansebooks.com**

PRINCIPLES OF REFORM:

POLITICAL AND LEGAL.

BY

JOHN BOYD KINNEAR.

LONDON:

SMITH, ELDER AND CO., 65, CORNHILL.

1865.

PREFACE.

It need hardly be observed that the title of this work is not to be understood as implying that an attempt to discuss every important question of Reform, now agitated, is to be found in the following pages. But there are certain cardinal and primary subjects, alike in politics as in law, to which Reform must first be directed, and in which it must secure success before any further advance can be made. Thus, in Politics, the great objects of Peace, Retrenchment, and Extension of the Franchise are recognized as the very motto of the party of Reform ; while in Law, the simplifying of its provisions by the adoption of a Code, and the abolition of needless discrepancies between the legal systems of the several parts of the realm, are shown, by the discussions of jurists, to be the fundamental improvements to which all others are subordinate. And it seems to me not inopportune at the present moment to recall attention to the Principles on which our true policy, in these leading and essential questions, ought to be based. For it has happened that both in Politics and Law the prosecution of Reform has fallen in some degree into abeyance, chiefly because the party which supports it has been content of late to take its impulse rather from the exigencies of mere Parliamentary contests, than from deliberate conviction of the truth of its principles and a steady determination to make them prevail.

Therefore, first dealing with the question of the Extension of the Suffrage, which is often understood by the single word Reform, I have sought to show the principles upon which the franchise truly depends, and by regard to which it may be arranged so as to concede the just claims of the unenfranchised without danger and without unfairness. In the Appendix will be found the rough draft of a measure for practically carrying out these objects. I have next endeavoured to point out, in regard to our Foreign Policy, the principles which must be adopted by us if we are to hope for either an honourable, a just, or an enduring state of Peace. In regard to Retrenchment I have been obliged, in order to make the discussion practical and fruitful, to go more into detail. But I trust that this fulness of examination will be held justified by the magnitude of the interests at stake; and that the difficulty of combating the increase of expenditure, forced upon us of late years by our rulers in the name of mere safety, in any other way than by consideration of each allegation they have put forward, will be thought to warrant the minuteness of the inquiry, and the copiousness of professional authority, which I have adduced to support my conclusions on each point.

The second branch of the subject, that of Legal Reform, belongs more peculiarly to my own profession. As a practising member of both the Scottish and English bar, I have had better opportunities than fall to the lot of those whose knowledge is restricted to only one of our legal systems, for comparing the effect of their different provisions. Judging that want of simplicity and of brevity are the worst defects in both, I have first pointed out whence they arise, and how they might be most fully remedied. I have then discussed the important and interesting question of the assimilation of our Law, indicating some necessary conditions of the problem which have not generally been recognized. Finally, I have devoted some space to an examination of the Marriage Laws of the two parts of the kingdom, believing that I could offer some suggestions on that most important branch of our jurisprudence which would not be unworthy of being taken into consideration, while being at this time of more than usual interest.

But if the leading subjects thus embraced in the following work extend over a wide space, too wide, it may be perhaps thought, to be fully dealt with in such restricted limits, I may be allowed to point out the one guiding principle which throughout the investigation I have sought to keep in view, of which indeed the discussion on each topic is only an application. It is that in all questions respecting the Policy of the Nation, we are to take, as the sole test of its propriety, the influence which that policy will have on individuals. Thus to enable us to ascertain if in any case there is any rule of moral right, we must bring the question down from abstract heights of expediency to the level of individual duty and capacity, and refuse to look on " nations," or " classes," or "interests " as the means by which, or the subjects for which, we are to legislate. But if no rule of moral right can in the special case be suggested, then we turn to experience of individual convenience for a guide, and demur to accept any theories of civil law as furnishing unbending forms and systems to which human nature ought to be forced, in spite of itself, to conform. I have therefore referred the question, What is right? to the individual conscience of those who have to solve it, applying their reason to the individual circumstances of the men and women whom their decisions will affect. I have made theories of social propriety yield precedence to facts, and have sought to discover in the laws impressed on humanity by its Creator, in each separate country and race, the guidance which must supersede all artificial rules and all arguments of what might be more seemly or more consonant to our own notions of legal accuracy. That such is the true method of dealing with all national problems I cannot doubt. How far I have been able to apply it correctly I must leave to my readers to determine.

It is proper to state that the substance of Chapters II., IV., and V. of Part I., and of Chapters III. and IV. of Part II., appeared in the *North British Review* a few years back. But they have been to a considerable extent re-written, and much new matter has been added to adapt them to the present time and to their place in this work. It may, perhaps, also prevent some possible charges of plagiarism if I add that I have, as opportunity offered, urged, in other organs of public opinion, but in the anonymous form which custom requires, many of the facts and arguments which I have here re-produced.

June, 1865.

CONTENTS.

PART I.—POLITICAL.

PART II.—LEGAL.

APPENDIX.

PRINCIPLES OF REFORM.

.

POLITICAL.

CHAPTER I.

THE FRANCHISE ON THE BASIS OF EDUCATION.

A PHRASE dropped almost casually in the heat of debate in the House of Commons last year, revived all the old disquisitions on the rights of man and the fundamental compact of Government. When Mr. Gladstone declared that every man was entitled to share in the franchise whose exercise of such rights was not proved to be dangerous to the community, he uttered one of those elementary truths which, obvious to men capable of admitting them, spread amazement and dismay among those who have supported an artificial system till they forgot what nature is. To such as these, who boast of our Constitution as something not amenable, because superior, to principle, it is nothing less than shocking to hear a principle announced as one which our Constitution embodies and to which it should conform. And yet, after all, the question only is, whether, when every one confesses that we must advance in the direction of extending the franchise, we shall make that advance hap-hazard, by mere blind guess-work, or whether we shall try to find out the reason why we ought to advance, in order that we may judge as accurately as possible of the extent and direction towards which the advance should be made. It is only a question whether we shall yield to brute force, or be guided by reason; whether we shall let the State drift helplessly in the currents of surging democracy, or stand by the helm to guide the vessel towards the clear light that beacons the course of safety in the intricate channel.

And if we do not accept the principle that the franchise is a matter of general and natural right, to be restrained only by proof that its full concession would be perilous to the State, where shall we find any principle at all? Some say that there is no principle in the matter, and that those, and no others, have a right to rule who are born to rule. But is it at all likely that this will satisfy the ruled? If there is no

Heaven-implanted mark by which the right of the rulers is stamped on their brow, if they are, after all, mere ordinary men, distinguished from their fellow-men by nothing else than accident of birth, is it even possible that their fellow-men should acknowledge the title a moment longer than suits their own convenience? Nor will the plea, sometimes stated, that such is the Constitution of our country, and that those who do not like it may emigrate, at all avail to support exclusive pretensions to authority. Our Constitution is not Heaven-given; it has been slowly built up and fashioned by the successive efforts of generations of Englishmen. And as it has thus been modified from time to time, it affords no prescriptive title to those who chance to be, under the last modification, (one yet only thirty years old,) in exclusive possession of privileges under it.

But though the case had been otherwise, and the sanction of ages had hung around the Constitution, it would be futile to argue that its provisions are unalterable. Men are guided by their own opinions and wishes, not by those of their forefathers. If it happened that A's father agreed or permitted B's father to be his ruler, nobody can pretend for a moment that the arrangement descends, so as to make it criminal in A to refuse to be subject to B. Such a doctrine would be nothing else than undisguised slavery. But if A and

B are thus free to bargain with each other as man with man, it will plainly never do for B to say to A, that if he does not like the slavery arrangement he may leave the country. It is clear that the retort on A's part would be just and unanswerable, that if B does not like the system of free bargaining, he may leave the country. And the retort will have a greatly enhanced force if it should be made by four millions of non-electors to the one million who, by the Constitution of our fathers, exercise rule over them.

This terrible proportion forces then the question upon us as one of fact, if we refuse to make it one of principle. It is clear that what the four millions positively demand, the one million can never be able to deny. But if the one million can point out that what is demanded would be dangerous to the whole body alike, it will stand on a very different footing. Appealing, then, not to its abstract right, which does not exist, nor to prescriptive right, which is of no avail against a new generation, nor to force, which is wholly on the other side, but to reason, it has a title to be heard; and if it can make out its case, it certainly will be heard. Were it not wise, then, to accept the principle that the safety of the State is, after all, the only limitation we can assign to the inherent right and might of the majority of the people to govern, rather than, by refusing to accept it, to drive them to the argument of force in default of that of reason.[1]

It is, of course, possible to resolve to abide as we are without giving any reason for it, and thus to obviate any reference to principle at all. But that is a course which no one, Whig or Tory, now ventures openly to advocate, however willing the leaders and the bulk of both these parties may be, tacitly to adopt it. Nevertheless, nothing can be more certain than that it cannot be much longer maintained. In a very little time we shall have the recurrence of a general election, when, as usual, each of the closely-balanced parties will be trying to outbid the others for support. Now, even if it be granted that there is comparative indifference among the actual holders of the franchise in regard to its extension, and that there is no fervent anxiety on the part of the unenfranchised to attain the privilege; still, it will not be denied that there is some anxiety, and, little as it is alleged to be, it may turn a contest. Beyond a doubt, then, on the lowest estimate of the public interest in the question, it will again, and ever and anon, be the subject of rival promises and

---

[1] I defer to a later page the consideration of the argument for the restriction of the franchise to those having property, because, as that is rested on the idea that it would be dangerous to property to allow others to have any power, it involves the admission that the general safety is the sole ground for restriction.

pledges; and it is not to be supposed that English gentlemen will, during a second period of seven years, absolve themselves from performance of their pledges on the pretence that they are not absolutely compelled to fulfil them.

But it would be a very great and serious mistake to rate the public interest in the question at this minimum point. The electors, by the fact of having sent to Parliament a majority of members pledged to reform, have proved that, at least, their convictions on the subject are decided. The non-electors, though they do not enter on an excited agitation, prove unmistakably, whenever the question is put to them, that they do deeply value the privilege of sharing in our common government. What holds them back from agitation is a twofold motive. In the first place, they do not care to present humble petitions for what they conceive to be their mere rights. In the second place, they know that, though it be unconferred, they actually have and actually exercise, the power in the State to which their numbers and their intelligence entitle them. They look back to Catholic Emancipation, to the Reform Bill, to the Repeal of the Corn Laws, all yielded by Lords and Commons in despite of very recent overwhelming majorities in both Houses on the other side; and they recognize in the fact of the rapid conversion of the rulers, the confession of the supreme power of the ruled. They see, also, that in the present day questions are not decided by bare majorities, but by the sense of public opinion; and they know that in the formation of public opinion they are not left out of account. They see, in fact, measures passed or rejected by Parliament on the avowed ground that they are urged, or not urged, by "pressure from without;" and they accept, in this established phrase of modern statesmanship, the acknowledgment that the power of those without is so great, that when it is exerted those within must inevitably yield, and that it is only when not expressed that Parliament itself can dare to act on its own judgment.

But although the real depositaries of power may be very indifferent as to their possession of its badges, and those who know they can sway the nation irresistibly on all questions in which they care to make their wishes known may be very willing to leave to others the trouble and responsibility of managing the routine affairs of the State, it by no means follows that that is a wholesome arrangement. The fitful exercise of supreme power by those who do not train themselves to its steady exercise, is full of peril. And the withdrawal from responsibility in the measures of ordinary government, on the part of the majority of the community, not only deprives them of education in the qualities of statesmanship and self-government, in the capacity to look before and after, to weigh slight influences, to yield to the natural prejudices of others, to sacrifice the less for the greater, to maintain principle while adjusting details, all tending to the formation of a habit of mind without which political power cannot be safely exercised ; but it directly encourages indifferentism and carelessness of principle, not more among those who hold back from active concern in such matters than among those to whose care they are left. For no class or body of men, indeed no single individual, can abandon duties and avoid responsibilities without breeding, by the contagion of ill-example, a wide-spreading evil reaching far beyond the consequences of their personal neglect; an indifference to principle and disregard of right and wrong, which, when it infects the State, is fatal to its life.

All, therefore, who care for the true and highest interests of their country must desire that the real and the nominal authority should be harmonized, and that those whose will is the ultimate guide should be subjected to declared and constant responsibility for its exercise. They must desire that the great public, which rules the nation, should be impressed with a sense of the duties belonging to the possession of such power, should be habituated to consider political questions of every description, should be directly appealed to by statesmen, and not left to exert, only when their own interests move them, that "pressure from without" to which, when exercised, all our statesmen confess they must bow.

This may be called the argument of necessity. But there is another, of not less weight, which may be called, in no invidious sense, the argument of expediency. It lies in this, that no man can rise to the full dignity of which human nature is capable, unless he is self-governing. To leave the regulation of affairs which concern his temporal and spiritual welfare to another, is to be content to be a child or a slave, to be content to surrender, for a mess of pottage, the birthright of reason and of self-guidance.

Nor is it merely self-guidance which is the heritage of man. Within a State, whoever exercises the right of self-government, must also of necessity exercise with it the right of sharing in the government of others. Wielding an influence that cannot be discarded over the affairs of his fellows, he learns, in the only way in which they can be learned, the duties of self-sacrifice combined with independence, of self-restraint combined with dominion; he perceives that the weal or woe of his brethren, perhaps to remote generations, depends upon his conduct now, and he is taught, as no other method can teach, that great lesson, the denial of which was the excuse of the first crime recorded on earth : the lesson that we *are* our brothers' keepers, and that we dare not and cannot shake off that responsibility for them which our Maker has imposed upon all as a condition of social existence.

These reasons furnish the answer to the arguments, very favourite ones at the present day, of those who tell us that we have nothing to do with abstract rights of men in politics, and that good government is the sole object of all systems. For it is not good government, but an essentially bad and dangerous government, when on great questions we are ruled by the " pressure from without " of the mass of the people, whom we yield to because they are irresistible, but to whom we accord in the ordinary matters of policy neither responsibility nor opportunity for learning. It is not good government which tells four-fifths of the nation that they shall have what they demand when their passions are angry, but shall have no part or lot with us when we are debating matters that do not rouse their fury; that on questions that affect their interests deeply they shall do as they choose, but that on questions in which their judgment is calm they shall have no say; that on the turning-points of national existence their votes shall be counted, not in the polling-book or ballot-urn, but by the shouts of excited mobs and the measured march of threatening feet, while in the ordinary management of the national affairs they shall be allowed no opportunity for gaining experience, wisdom, or self-control; which makes them as aliens in the state, till the moments come when we bow to them as its masters; which deals with them as bastards of national rights, till they seize the whole inheritance as their own. Nor is that good government which teaches its subjects that they have no concern in each other's welfare, that they are neither bound to exercise the duties of self-guidance, nor in any way interested in the guidance and improvement of their fellow-citizens. It is a miserably blind policy which accepts a quietude and apparent contentment in such circumstances as evidence that we are well governed, and have no need to look to the future till the future is upon us.

Regarding thus the extension of the franchise as a matter, firstly, of mere necessity, and secondly, as of infinite value in itself alone, it is needless to take count of those who tell us that we ought not to allow it because we cannot point out important measures which we desire to obtain by its means. Only the fact that there are no such measures, may at least be suggested as a conclusive answer to the fears which the same objectors inconsistently express, that the result would be to " swamp" the present constituencies, and reverse our course of legislation. If the unenfranchised are content with our present laws, there is no danger of their altering such laws for the worse on their obtaining legal power; while nothing is more certain than that if they were discontented with any of our laws we should have to alter them, whether we extended the franchise or not. They desire the franchise, not to carry any favourite measures, but in order to be on an equal footing with the rest of their fellow-citizens, to have a voice in the management of affairs that concern them as well as the rest of the community, and to obtain the sense of self-government, without which they are not men. And we are bound to grant the demand because it is irresistible, because it is just, and because to delay it is to continue in a position of incalculable peril to the State.

Yet though there is no pretence for asserting that the demand is made with revolutionary intent, or that the granting it would be followed by objectionable legislation, it may justly be urged that it would infuse an element of invaluable influence in the general direction of our policy and the tone of the national councils. No one can have mixed in any degree with the working classes without becoming aware that they unconsciously and unpretendingly have, in many matters, a different and a higher standard of moral judgment and action than those have who in worldly position are above them. Indisputably, for example, they are more charitable. They contribute readily, and as matter of

mere course, to the succour of a distressed brother or
sister, in a proportion to their own income, which if a
Rothschild or a Baring were to adopt, the world would
stand still to gaze at it as an unprecedented and scarce
conceivable act of magnificent liberality. And in
adopting any principle or course of conduct, they are
more directly swayed by what they think right, inde-
pendently of the present profit it offers, than the
majority of those immediately above them. These
are qualities for which they are not to be flattered, but
which also are not to be ignored. They spring from
the position, not from any difference in the nature, of
the classes that display them. For it is the blessing
of poverty that those who only from day to day receive
their daily bread, feel inevitably a more intimate trust
in Him who gives it, than those can do who are able
to build great barns in which they may lay up store
for many years. Seeking also as a rule no more than
daily bread, they are free from that grasp of mammon
on the soul which those inevitably succumb to, who,
striving to rise in wealth and position, have constantly
the thought of money-making in their minds. Therefore the poor have this peculiar help in faith and
prayer, that they have no other trust and no worldly
object, and by daily experience their faith is confirmed
and their prayer is answered. And thus it is that with
more faith they have more hope, and more charity.

Ought we not to desire an infusion of such influence as this in our daily political life? Although it may not suggest great measures to be adopted, will it not beneficially affect and modify the details of the measures we do adopt? Can we not see at a glance that when in our legislation we have to deal so much with questions relating to pauperism, to crime, to education, to the social relations—nay, even when our government has to deal with our colonies and with foreign alliances—the influence in some measure of those who habitually think less of money, and more of what is right and true and brotherly, may be good for the whole nation?

Let me not, however, be misunderstood. In doing justice to the particular virtues of the poor, I am not for a moment blind to their peculiar faults. Poverty that brings blessings brings curses also; and human nature is so mixed in quality in each individual, and yet so uniform when man is compared with man, that we shall deeply err if we attribute to any class whatsoever more than a superiority in some qualities, balanced by an inferiority in others. But while this would be an unanswerable reason against making any class supreme, it is an equally unanswerable reason for excluding none. And if we hear it said that the poor would be sometimes misled by their prejudices and their interests, let us not forget that confessedly so have been also the rich. Every party now, for example, admits that the corn laws were a gigantic blunder, as well as crime : yet for thirty years they were imposed on this nation, because one class was predominant in power, and that class had a supposed interest in their maintenance. It would, indeed, be wholly wrong to say that the landlords deliberately maintained a system for their own benefit and for no other reason. But at least this must be said, that their own benefit did so bias their reason, that they could not see that they were hurting their fellow-citizens, and that they actually came to entertain a firm conviction that the good of the whole public was bound up in the preser-vation of their own artificial profits. Now if such is the effect of prejudice and self-interest on the class which esteems itself the best educated and the most reasonable, can we find any ground for excluding another class because it would not be always exempt from similar influences ?

True, if that other class were to become, as the landlords once were, supreme, there might be reason for excluding it. And this point raises the question which most of all disturbs men's minds in regard to an extension of the franchise—the fear that there is a class—what are called the "lower classes," or the "working classes"—which would be supreme, and "swamp," as the phrase is, all the rest.

But the true answer to this fear is found in the

very words in which it is expressed. It is not "a working class" that is to be admitted: it is "the working classes." The distinction is everything; and it is as real in fact as it is plain in language. The working classes do not, and never can, form one class, except in the single point in which we make them one class, by excluding them from the franchise. But other bond of union they have none. If we go among them and converse with them on any question of the day, we shall find them holding as great a diversity of sentiment as their superiors in station. There are Whigs among them and Tories; there are Federals and Confederates; there are Churchmen and Dissenters; there are some for, and some against, compulsory education; there are supporters and opponents of the Permissive Bill; there are approvers and disapprovers of foreign intervention; there are peace-at-any-price men, and there are *Cives Romani;* there are adherents of Mr. Bright and admirers of Lord Palmerston. In a word, there is not a single question on which they are united and form "a class," and they will, in consequence, when admitted to power, merely add to or turn the majority in each locality according to its particular circumstances, leaving us still governed by the prevailing sentiment in all classes, and distinguished into parties much the same as at present. And this simply and necessarily because the working classes are composed of *men*, not of electric clocks, all worked by a central battery, and because each man among them thinks as much for himself as the average of those above them do, while they contain a full proportion of those who follow their own judgment in each separate question of the day with as positive confidence that their own particular reason is better than their neighbours', as does the most independent or obstructive member of the House of Commons.[1] We should lose all our fear, and escape half the folly that is uttered on this topic by very estimable persons, if we would only turn our minds to the practical details of the question, and try to remember that we really have not to deal with any huge vague image of some unknown and awful power, but only with a certain number of individuals who act and think under the same rules as ourselves.   More than anything, the terror of the change is, perhaps, traceable to a source so simple as the use of that most misleading and pernicious term, "the masses," suggestive as it is of only brute force, and the inertia of unreasoning matter.   But unless we combine the unenfranchised into a "mass" by the sense

---

[1] Since these pages were in the hands of the printer, I have had the pleasure of seeing this argument, which I had urged last autumn in a speech on reform in Fifeshire, eloquently enforced by Professor Fawcett of Cambridge, at the meeting of the unenfranchised at Bradford.

of injustice done to them as a body, nothing is more certain than that they have no intrinsic element of coherence, and will on every question be moved by the same infinite variety of motive and reason which influence the minds of those whom we call the "upper" or the "middle" classes, but whom we do not find forming, in virtue of their names, any distinct body, or endowed with any of the characteristics of a "mass."

There is indeed one, and only one point, on which it can be suggested that there might be a unity of interest among the working-classes, adverse to that of the rest of the public. As we may roughly describe the upper classes as those who have realized money, and the middle classes as those who are making money, we may assign to the lower classes the designation of earners of wages. We have certainly not found that the admission of the money-makers to power has injuriously affected the monied, yet it is urged that the admission of the earners of wages would be dangerous to the payers of wages. The example is worth a moment's examination that we may see how impossible in practice a combination with such a result would be. It is assumed that an attempt would be made to raise wages by the enactment of a general law. This would, if successful, have exactly the same effect as a general strike. But if a law would be passed, why is a strike not attempted without law ? The idea is familiar enough. Every now and then it happens that one trade strikes, and that one or two other trades help it. But the whole body of working men never do. And why ? Because there is always a proportion of them that sees clearly that it is not for their interest. So would it be with 'legislation. There would be no such fools as to legislate for increased wages to shoemakers, when the obvious result would be to make every man's shoes dearer, or to bricklayers, when it is plain it must raise every householder's rent. And the idea of a universal rise of wages in every trade is not merely a thing that the trades would never be able to adjust in rates which each would accept as fair to itself, but it would be too palpably taking money out of one pocket to put it into another, minus the charge of transfer, when it would be clear that everything would be made dearer in order to afford the enhanced wages of manufacturers.

Thus even in the most critical and general question it is idle to talk of unity among the working classes. There is no object or motive that can be suggested which we shall not see at a glance would affect them all differently. And since this is the case, it is certain that any partial policy favourable to one class,

but injurious to the rest, would, the moment its
bearing was discovered, be put down by the majority.
As we have got rid of the corn-laws by admission of
other interests to a fair hearing, so in the widest
possible admission of different classes lies the greatest
security that no one among them shall hereafter gain
predominance. Taking the whole nation together, it
is impossible to point out a single unjust measure
which would not be opposed, firstly, by a large body
whom it would immediately injure ; and, secondly,
by that overwhelming proportion of the public, which
having no interest either way, would have clear heads
to guide them in adopting and enforcing the policy
of reason and equity.

But while necessity, prudence, and expediency
thus all counsel an extension of the suffrage to the
utmost limit compatible with safety, they do not
solve the question, What is safe ? They point out,
indeed, that since it is that element in the population
which is capable of reasoning and of being reasoned
with, that ought to be admitted, our effort should be
to distinguish it from the unreasoning portion. But
where are we to find a line that will even roughly
effect this distinction ? If we adhere to property
qualifications, at what point are we to fix them with
this view ? Nearly all admit that a ten-pound rental is

too high; that there are many who cannot afford such
a rent who are in every quality worthy of the franchise.
Would a six-pound rent be sufficient and safe? There
are some who say it is too low, some who say it is
too high. If a five-pound, a three-pound rental, even
if a "household" suffrage be suggested, there are still
some who take opposite sides as to its propriety.
Who is to reconcile such variance of opinion?
Neither reason nor experience avails, for reason
affords no abstract rule to tell us the intelligence of
the inhabitants of a certain class of houses, and all
parties appeal to their own experience in support of
their own views, and refuse to accept any experience
differing from their own. How shall we, amid these
differences and disputes, arrive at a satisfactory solution of the great and inevitable problem, What is a
safe extension of the franchise?

It is obvious at once that while we adhere to a
mere property qualification the difficulty is insurmountable. There is no possible line of demarcation
capable of being expressed in rental, between the
ignorant and the educated, the reckless and the
thoughtful. Nobody can pretend to say that a six-
pounder is of a class at all essentially different from
a seven-pounder or a five-pounder. The selection of
a rental point to confer the franchise is therefore
mere guesswork. Nobody can support his opinion

as to what is safe with any better proof than his
mere assertion. In every different town the character
of the class occupying houses of a certain rent varies,
depending not on the intelligence or morals of the
men, but upon the accidental circumstance of the
comparative dearness or cheapness of accommodation.
Between individuals in each town the distinction does
not establish that the one in the higher-rated house is
better than the other, but only that he has a smaller
family, or gets better wages, or is not so saving and
provident for old age, and therefore spends more in
present comforts. Now none of these are proper qualifications for the franchise, and it is impossible to make
those who have not the franchise think that they are.
And the absurdity of them is so gross that we now
find that the working-classes are becoming utterly
disinclined to an agitation for the franchise based on
expenditure in house-rent, and are, in default of any
more reasonable proposal, plainly announcing that
they will have "manhood suffrage" or none. Only
this spring their delegates in London declared that
this was their positive and final resolution.

But we cannot afford to run the risk of being
obliged to concede universal suffrage merely because
a rental suffrage is absurd. At least, before we do
this, let us try whether we cannot discover some
method of reconciling common sense with constitu-

tional principle. Let us ask ourselves what is the purpose of a limitation of the franchise at all, in order that we may discover what is the true distinction on which it should be founded.

There are two theories on this subject. The one is, that the suffrage is for the protection of property, and, therefore, that it should be limited to the holders of property; the other, that it is the right of intelligence, and therefore should be granted wherever intelligence exists.

The former is a modern and an unconstitutional doctrine. Far from recognizing wealth as the chief object of constitutional protection, our old law recognized only those on whom it laid the duty of doing service to the State. It selected in counties the lords and freeholders who, holding lands, were bound to aid in the public defence, and in boroughs those who were the freemen, or all who " boiled a pot" within their limits. Nor to this day is wealth admitted as the real ultimate cause of a limitation of the franchise. We do not hold votes proportioned to the amount of our property, as we do in a joint-stock company, and as we should in the nation, if the management of its wealth were all our concern. And we admit to the franchise the members of the Universities, not in virtue of their property, but in virtue of their being educated and intelligent men.

Nor can any one pretend that it is property which is chiefly to be considered in government, and, therefore, that only its holders should share in the government. The poorest man is concerned just as much as, perhaps more than, the rich man, in the laws that affect his domestic relations, such as the laws of marriage and divorce, of guardianship of children; or the social relations, such as those of master and servant; or the civic relations, such as those of pauperism, of education, of the church, of the punishment of crime, of taxation; or the national relations, such as those of peace or war, alliances or treaties. Where expenditure at all enters into these questions (and it does into only very few of them), the poor man's interest is, in proportion to his livelihood, almost the same as the rich man's; for, while he is relieved of only a small proportion of taxation, such as the income and assessed taxes, he pays beyond his due proportion of the customs and excise duties, which form the bulk of our revenue. And any error in our fiscal system, or extravagance of expenditure, while it only diminishes the rich man's profits, is liable, by injuring trade, to deprive the poor man of his livelihood altogether. His stake, therefore, being that of life, is undeniably at least equal to the rich man's. And, therefore, neither on the ground of legislation being only, or even chiefly, concerned with property, can we find any just reason for excluding universal suffrage.

How, then, can we exclude universal suffrage, by any other than an arbitrary, irrational, and unconstitutional test, such as that of rental is ? There is but one way, by taking that test directly which the other method proposes to take indirectly. A property test, indefensible on the plea of property being more entitled to regard than human bodies and souls, is accepted as a rough method of gauging intelligence. But when we speak of intelligence in this question, it must be distinctly kept in view that we mean, and can mean, nothing but education. There is no heaven-bestowed difference in mental capacity between the poor and the rich. Give both an equal education, and, man for man, the one will display identically the same intelligence as the other. Therefore, education making the only real distinction, why cannot we make education itself the test of fitness for the franchise ?

There is no answer ever given to this question except that the proposition is " impracticable," and that it " could not be worked." A very sufficient answer if the experiment had ever been tried and had failed, but a very insufficient answer if it has never been tried, or if it has in any place been tried, and found to work successfully. And this experiment has been tried in some of the States of America, and is there found to work so well that it is continued in use to this day. No doubt, in applying it in this country we must cease to look at it as a theory, and turn our minds to the consideration of practical details. But this ought not to form an insurmountable difficulty with a practical people like ourselves. We have found of late years that an education test can be usefully applied, under circumstances very much more complex than need disturb us here, to the determining the fitness of candidates for offices. Why, then, should we still argue that the simplest of all tests is inapplicable to determine the fitness of men to hold the office of elector?

The simplest of tests—for let us consider what is the character of that education which we really can demand as a fair and reasonable test in this case. There are obviously two limiting considerations. It would be useless to try by examination the amount of attainment in branches which have nothing to do with the science of government. This principle excludes all that are commonly called the higher branches of education — Latin and Greek, or mathematics, or metaphysics, or physical science. All these are pre-eminently useful in their place, but that they are unnecessary for political purposes is proved by the fact that every one in turn, and often all of them together, have been wanting in the education of some of the greatest of our statesmen.   Next we must take care not to ask, under an educational test, even knowledge in political science, which the majority of existing electors and elected have not.   It might, perhaps, be highly beneficial to institute an examination in the works of Adam Smith, of De Lolme, and of Hallam, which should be passed by all members of Parliament before taking their seats, and by all voters before approaching the polling booth.   But the result of its application without warning would certainly be to disqualify ninety-nine in a hundred of the legislators, and to disfranchise nine hundred and ninety-nine in a thousand of the present electors.   So we cannot for very shame, if for no other reason, demand of the unenfranchised a degree of knowledge which the enfranchised have not got.   What, then, is practically the education which the present electors have ?   It is the faculty of reading, and the habit of reading the newspapers.   It is in these organs of information and discussion that they find from day to day their knowledge and their opinions.   And by the application of an average common sense to that information and to these discussions, they govern us on the whole very tolerably.

Thus, then, it is a power of reading (to which we may add as a cognate test, easily applied at the same time, the power of writing,) that forms the amount of political education now qualifying for the franchise, and to which, therefore, we must look as the only fair test for its extension. Nor, if it seems at first glance a low standard, let us forget how much it really implies. It means that its possessors are not dependent on merely what they hear, on the talk around them, or the speeches to which they listen, for the information and arguments that make up their opinion. It means that they can, if they choose, inquire as deeply of the wise men of old, and of the thoughtful men of the present day, as any of their wealthier brethren. And since we have now cheap newspapers as well as dear ones, and the cheap often as good as the dear, and since nearly every one who can read now reads his paper, and talks with his fellows about what his or their papers contain, it means that he goes through exactly the same education in politics—the same in kind and in degree, as the rich man who takes his threepenny morning paper, and therewith is content.

How, then, ought such a franchise to be looked upon by those without, and those within the pale of the present franchise ? By those without it ought to be, and there is reason to expect that it would be, accepted heartily as sufficient and satisfying. For it would make the privilege not dependent on any external circumstances, but upon intrinsic fitness, and few would be found to argue that if a man could not read and write, he is a safe man to be trusted with control of his fellow subjects. By those within it ought also to be, and there is growing reason to hope it would be, accepted as fair and beneficial. It would at once and finally obviate all danger of an "ignorant mob" over-ruling the educated classes. It would set the question of extension of the franchise for ever at rest, for it would adjust itself to the progress of the nation. And while every successive lowering of a property qualification will admit a larger and larger proportion of that class which at present makes the worst element of our constituencies,—men who are making good wages, but who are unable to read, and therefore the prey of demagogues or of corruption, the adoption of an educational franchise would at once and permanently obviate that danger. And, lastly, it would present a motive for acquiring education, in the honour and privileges which it would confer on the educated, such as would be of priceless value to the moral progress of the nation.

Nor would the increase to the constituencies by this measure be so great at present as some may imagine. In England and Wales we now have, in round numbers, one million of electors and four millions of non-electors. But of the whole popula-

tion the Registrar-General tells us that 25 per cent.
of the adult males cannot write their names, and of
course this class is to be found almost entirely among
the present non-electors, and therefore would deduct
1,250,000 from the number admissible. And if we add
to the number thus disqualified those whom change
of residence, or indifference, or age would prevent
from registering themselves or presenting themselves
for examination, and all those who, though they do not
sign by a mark, would yet fail to come up to the test
of intelligent reading and writing, we shall probably
find that the remainder would be under a million,
or a smaller number than many of the rental qualifications now talked of would admit; but with this
difference, that while many uneducated men would be
admitted by any lowering of a rental franchise, none
could, in the nature of things, be admitted under a
direct educational franchise.

If, then, an educational franchise is commended
to us by such potent reasons, and, we ought also to
remember, by so many thinkers of the highest authority, why is it that it is not distinctly adopted as the
" cry " of any political party ? The chief reason,
probably, is that it has as yet scarcely been put forward as a practical measure, capable of being enacted
by Parliament. And, therefore, in the hope of
making its discussion more easy and more fruitful,

I venture to submit in the Appendix a draft of a bill for carrying out the principle. There is no better touchstone of the practical in legislation than to reduce the proposal under consideration to the language of an Act of Parliament. Yet it is fair to keep in mind that no bill on a new subject can be perfect at once. It is only the experience and suggestions of many minds, viewing the subject from every different point, that can so mould it as to make it suitable for the variety of circumstances in which it will be worked. I offer, therefore, this draft as no more than the rough framework by aid of which may be built up a safe and complete system of most desirable Reform.[1]

In the draft bill it is assumed, for the reasons assigned above, that the capacity to read with understanding (a point which any examiner will ascertain in two minutes), is the main part of the test. But as the power of writing a few words to dictation in such a way as (whether or not the spelling be strictly orthodox) to be understood, is a matter as easily ascertained, and as it will generally imply an educa-

---

[1] It is proper to state that the draft, and some reasons for its adoption, were published by me six years ago, in a letter which appeared in the *Daily News* of 31st May, 1859. Subsequent reflection, and the opinion of others, have confirmed me in the belief of its practicability.

tion continued long enough to ensure that reading is easy, it has been added as an additional test. Further, it is suggested that an age somewhat more advanced than twenty-one, say twenty-five, would be a reasonable and useful requirement of those who are to be admitted to a privilege so important, and to the fit exercise of which some habit of reflection and some knowledge of the world would be so desirable an aid. It would also materially limit the numbers admitted.

The details of the machinery for ascertaining the degree of education demanded are simple. The Committee of Council on Education—a very competent and, for such purpose, a perfectly impartial body—are to appoint a sufficient number of examiners, and to assign to each a district. Within his district each examiner is once a year to hold an examination at every polling-place in a county and in every borough. Thus in a year each examiner will go over a very large district. Probably, after the first year or two, ten or twelve examiners will be found sufficient for the whole of England. The applicants are to send notice of the place where they wish to be examined, and the examiner is thus enabled to fix the days of examination at each place, and to give ample notice of them. To prevent favour or partiality, the agents of the political parties are to be present at the examination ; if they are not, at least three other persons must be present. A person rejected by the examiner may present himself in any succeeding year till he is at last able to pass. And to obviate accidental admission of one not really competent it seems proper to allow an objector to call for a re-examination, in a future year, of any one admitted, the admission under such second examination being finally conclusive. Persons who have obtained certificates of sufficient education make their claims to be registered as voters in the ordinary manner. A six months' residence in the county or borough for which they claim is thought a proper requirement. On changing their residence they will be subject to the same necessity of being again registered (but without anew undergoing examination, the original certificate being still valid) as attaches to other voters.

The bill I have suggested does not in its present shape make any alterations in existing property franchises. But while the rights of all electors now on the lists may be reserved, it would probably be right to make, ere long, the educational test the sole one for the registration of new electors. There would otherwise be an awkward, and on both sides an invidious distinction, between persons of privilege by virtue of property and by virtue of education. And it would not be wise to deter any from claiming a

right, granted to them in virtue of the latter qualification, by the false shame which they might perhaps
feel in thus announcing themselves as forming
members of a poorer class. The purpose, indeed,
of the measure being to obliterate class distinctions,
it would clearly be advisable, as soon as the first
novelty was overcome, to place all persons indis-
criminately on the same footing under its provisions.

Very sensible of the difficulty of the problem, and
above all anxious to induce others to bring greater
abilities and wider experience to attempt its practical
solution, I therefore lay before the public this effort to
advance beyond the stage of barren theory, and to
settle by discussion the details of machinery by which
a sound principle may be reduced to simple and convenient operation. Whatever may be the value of the
suggestion I have offered, something will be gained if
it shall aid in defining the field of future discussion,
and either by indicating what is possible, or by
showing what is erroneous, shall make it a little
easier to establish, on a firm and enduring basis,
a measure of value so incalculable to the future of
our country.

CHAPTER II.

.

A VERY great and increasing difficulty has of late years beset the direction of the foreign policy of this country. It arises from the general adoption, on the one hand, of what is called the doctrine of non-intervention, while, on the other hand, the interest taken by the public in the affairs of our neighbours has every year become more marked and more warm. The professed principles and the irrepressible tendencies of the nation are thus in conflict, and the painful result follows that we constantly encourage what we regularly disclaim, that we are often on the verge of war, and not always very honourably recede from it, and that, by an inconsistency born of irresolution, we bring on ourselves the charge of treachery, of selfishness, and of cowardice.

With the instance of the conduct of this country in the Danish war last year so fresh in memory, it is hardly needful to cite examples of the operation of this unhappy divergence between our theories and our practice. Yet it may be well to remember that that case had no factitious interest or peculiarity of feature. We felt and expressed sympathy no less strong in the Hungarian insurrection, in the Italian revolution, in the Polish revolt. In the case of Italy, indeed, we actually broke through the limits of neutrality, for we sent large sums of money and a considerable force of volunteers, to succour the party of liberty, conduct amounting to an actual *casus belli*, and which, had the King of Naples or the Pope possessed the power of France or Austria, would undoubtedly have led to a declaration of war against us. Nor can it be disputed by any one who has watched the spirit of the times, that if our government had actually declared war in behalf of either Hungary, Italy, Poland, or Denmark, it would have received the eager and enthusiastic support of all but a section of the aristocracy and a section of the trading classes in the nation. When, for a whole week of ministerial deliberation, the question was in suspense whether, after negotiation had failed, we should draw the sword for Denmark or not, there were no meetings held, no agitation commenced, scarcely a voice was raised for peace ; and when at length peace was resolved upon, the public rather sullenly acquiesced in what its recognized leaders told it was right, than rejoiced in the sense of danger escaped or fatal error averted.

For it is after all an entire delusion to think that
we are a purely prosaic nation, a nation of shop-
keepers, moved by no thought or hope save what is
capable of money appreciation.   There are, indeed,
feelings and aspirations to which we are as a nation
slow, and perhaps somewhat ashamed to give expression ; for it is our pride to call ourselves practical
and unromantic, and we accept, with the satisfaction
of superiority, the taunt that we never "make war
for an idea." Yet our actions belie in this our
words, for no nation in the world has more often
shaped its course by the loadstar of romantic motive.
And though we are apt to turn a cold ear to the first
who suggests such a course, yet no sooner does it
seem to be not universally contemned, no sooner does
it attract the support of one or two of those on whose
judgment we are accustomed to lean, than with eager
and united ardour we follow it, and suffer no check
in the pursuit, no difficulty in the attainment, to damp
our energy, or to withhold us from the sacrifices which
we are ready to make to bring our hope to fruition.
The spirit which sent army after army into Spain to
back what we felt to be a patriot struggle—which
carried the eyes of the nation in eager gaze after that
English nobleman who gave his life and his fame to
the cause of the Greeks—which rejoiced over Navarino,
and, by the strange revulsion of opinion, was thirty

years later stung to frenzy by Sinope—which bestowed on a plain Italian seaman, chief of an Italian revolution, a welcome transcending all that royal potentate ever had at our hands—which gave English gold to purchase West Indian manumission, and has since a dozen times approached the verge of war with the most powerful peoples on the earth in the effort to annihilate the slave trade,—is undeniable evidence of the deep hold which an "idea," and a purely "romantic sentiment," may take in our northern blood.

Therefore we must take into account, as a vital national force, the sympathy which the people of this country have, and every day feel and express more strongly, in favour of the advance of liberty, the deliverance of the oppressed, and the recognition of the rights of nationalities abroad, however little be our material interests in these objects. And no statesman of any weight or position has ever ventured to lay down the principle that this sympathy is to be always limited to words. Even when proclaiming non-intervention as a general rule, and applying it to any particular case, they have always admitted that there might arise cases in which adherence to it would be criminal or impossible. Unhappily, however, they have never attempted to define what these cases are. And thus it comes to pass that our statesmen, of all parties and all characters, are driven by the force of public opinion to utter reproofs, encouragements or warnings to foreign parties and powers, while at the moment when it is expected that deeds should support our words, they suddenly grow terrified at the responsibility, tremble for their party supremacy, and remind us that our policy is one of non-intervention, and of considering only ourselves; and we accept the admonition because we know that sometimes it is true, and we do not know in what circumstances it is untrue.

But if the promptings of an undefined popular instinct be perilous, surely more perilous is their restraint by an undefined principle. The one may, in a sudden fit of passion, urge us to irrevocable error, the other makes us at every moment uncertain whether we do right. Nor can foreign nations be expected to understand what we cannot explain. They cannot comprehend how we can reconcile it to our consciences to give only barren sympathy with right or ineffectual reprobation of wrong. They cannot conceive how, holding the opinions we so strongly utter, we can be content to stand still when the time has come that, by a blow, or even a threat, we could ensure the triumph of these opinions. Nor certainly is it easy for us to submit patiently to the taunts which our conduct draws on us, or to that which is worse to bear, the knowledge that the charge of failing to back by action the cause we espouse in words has been the source of its disastrous failure. So there arises on all matters of foreign policy a deep sense of uneasy trouble, a mental swaying backwards and forwards between the generous desire to act and the prudent remembrance that our supposed principles require us never to act; a mixed sentiment of shame and haughtiness, of real ardour and assumed indifference, which makes us feel, we know not why, at enmity with ourselves, and dissatisfied with the position in which we force ourselves to stand.

There is but one way of escaping from a position so false and dangerous. It is to examine the character of the instinct which prompts our sympathy, and the nature of the rule which seems to forbid our acting upon it. We must try to find out why, and when, the one or the other is right or wrong. We must give the true meaning to words, and apply the strict test of principle to actions, since so only can we strengthen the national conscience or enlighten the national reason. And, as always the first step towards discovering what we really ought to do, is to discover what is our actual position, and how we got into it; and the first step towards discovering the meaning of any plausible phrase is to find what ideas originally gave it birth, let us cast a backward glance over European history, so as to ascertain the nature of that species of foreign intervention to which it has heretofore been witness, and under what circumstances arose the present cry for " non-intervention."

Used in its modern sense, the phrase intervention is of modern date. We understand by it an interposition supported by armed force, with a view to compel submission to a certain form of government or dynasty, or to aid in the overthrow of the established rule and the setting up of a new rule. It is, therefore, something quite distinct from any species of conquest for the purpose of colonization. It is not a transfer of population; it is only the repression or the support of the existing population by a force which continues to be foreign. Therefore the wars of the dark ages, when tribe after tribe overran and settled in fresh districts of Europe, either exterminating or amalgamating with the aboriginal inhabitants, were not instances of intervention proper. Each nation took what extent of land it required and could hold; if it attempted oppression on its neighbours, they migrated; nor could it, while either the patriarchal, or the purely feudal systems of warfare prevailed, long spare from tillage and hunting a body of men sufficient to retain any foreign people in permanent subjection, without actually occupying the territory. As the Highland armies of the Jacobite leaders used to melt away after a short campaign, because the soldiers were compelled to return home by the exigencies of seed-time or harvest, so while military service was personal, there was no chance that there should be, from without, any prolonged interference with the rights of other nations. But when wealth gradually accumulated, and advancing skill enabled each cultivator to extract from the soil more than enough for his individual support, and so to set a certain proportion of the population at liberty to devote themselves solely to war and other non-productive pursuits, a new danger dawned upon Europe. Taxation of the cultivator now supplied pay for the mercenary. So it was possible to maintain armies at a distance from their homes, and to subdue, without colonizing, a foreign territory. Then taxation could be extended to this new acquisition, and the elements of farther conquest acquired. Thus each extension of the bounds of the nation became a source (within certain limits) of increased strength; and as there was once more danger of universal empire, the independent spirit of modern Europe invented for its safeguard the theory of the " balance of power."[1]

---

[1] It is necessary not to confound the introduction of the principle of paying troops in time of war with the institution of standing armies kept up in time of peace. The latter did not take place, in this country, till the period of Charles II.; but the former practice

From this moment intervention, in its modern sense, became inevitable. And as it was the danger to be feared, so it was the only weapon that could be used in defence. As it was now possible for one nation to conquer another, it became necessary to forbid, or to regulate conquest, by the interposition of a third nation. And thus, for one reason or other, most nations came to be held in subjection, not, as under the old Germanic rule, by the frank submission of freemen, but by the domination of an external force, which was able to wring from their industry the means of its own perpetuation. So now also dynastic inheritance became a method of transmitting authority as irresistible as conquest itself, because it was supported by the very same method. Hence, to prevent the accumulation of power in one man's hands, it became necessary to oppose it by the same principles. Territories were parcelled out, under the authority of Europe itself, so as to give an equality to the strength of the leading states ; and a gain made by any one in one direction was redressed by an abstraction of territory on the other side. The effects of family alliances

---

was in force in the invasions of France by Edward III. See Hallam, *Middle Ages*, vol. i. pp. 315, 492. Although the establishment of standing armies increased the probabilities of intervention, yet it had become possible, in the sense explained in the text, so soon as the progress of wealth permitted soldiers to be hired and kept steadily on foot during the period of war.

were counteracted in some cases by treaty, in some by
force, in some by other alliances of a similar nature.
But throughout all these changes no regard was longer
had to the inclination of the people who were dealt
with.   They had become as so many pawns on the
chess-board—base pieces that were little worth counting, save as an addition to the aggregate strength of
the players—valuable chiefly in that, if skilfully played,
they might, after infinite loss of their own number,
furnish a force of a higher character, fitted to carry the
sphere of conquest over wider and more ambitious
fields.   So through long generations men saw successively strange and unnatural unions effected—sometimes between England and large provinces of France,
sometimes between Spain and the Netherlands or Germany, sometimes between Austria and Italy, sometimes
between France and Naples, or the Germanic provinces
of the Rhine, sometimes between the Russian and the
non-Slave populations on her borders, sometimes between Prussia and a Swiss canton.   No slice of territory
was ever too remote to be thrown into the balance of
power, for every scrap yielded money, and all money
bought soldiers.

Nature, indeed, was for ever at work sapping the
foundations of these proud edifices of man's construction.   The inextinguishable vitality of the principle of
race ever and anon broke out, and wrested from alien

governors and soldiers the provinces which they oppressed. So, after many ages of conflict and bloodshed, it resulted at last that the several great European nations were confined pretty much within their natural limits, and that the accessions of strength which, by treaty, marriage, or force, any among them had striven to win, were reft away. Then came the French Revolution to explode whatever dangerous combinations had yet been left. First gathering up the whole French race in one overwhelming and all-embracing sentiment of unity, it broke its proper bounds, and spread the infection of freedom over every oppressed people in Europe. At the call to throw off their yoke, to assert their nationality, rose Pole, and Italian, and Fleming. For a space it seemed as if nature was again supreme, and the reign of artificial arrangements of territory under dynasties had for ever passed away.

The hope was indeed premature, for the military power of France betrayed her. But the spirit it had evoked was even able to triumph over its own recoil. When from being a liberator, France turned to be a subjugator, the nations whom the electric shock of her example had fired were not slow to league together for her overthrow. Spaniard and Portuguese, Prussian, Austrian, and Russian, flung back her conquering armies, and, reducing her once again to her old limits, proclaimed once again the sacred principle of national independence. Old traditions, however, still survived. In the new partition of Europe, the claims of dynasties, and the persistent theory of the balance of power, received more regard than the rights of peoples, or the recent proof of the vanity of all treaty arrangements. But, in the interval since then, these family and political pretensions have one after another faded away. Holland and Belgium have separated—Greece has successfully rebelled—Prussia has lost Neufchatel —Italy has become united—Poland and Hungary, though not yet successful, have shaken Europe by their convulsive struggles.

In all these changes of system and policy England bore her share. Her early wars with France were struggles for conquest by the help of mercenary armies; her final defeat and expulsion were the triumphs of nationality. Under the Tudors and the Stuarts she took a regular part in those alliances by which it was supposed that the peace and stability of Europe could alone be preserved. But when William III. brought the continental ideas into closer contact with the English nation, it hesitated not to throw the whole weight of its power into one or other of the scales of European equilibrium. All those territorial arrangements by which opposing forces were expected to be neutralized, without reference to national rights,

were, through the eighteenth century, sealed with
British blood and ratified by British diplomacy. The
traditions of such a policy prevailed after the French
Revolution had given it its death-blow. Regardless of
the will of the French people, it seemed natural that
British statesmen should send fleets and armies to
support a war avowedly undertaken by the Continental
Powers in the interest of a dethroned dynasty.

The mad ambition of the French victor soon,
indeed, changed the issue. When he abandoned a
policy of liberation for one of annexation, the opposition of Great Britain, already declared, was placed on
a different, and now a just and sound basis. She now
became in the Mediterranean and the Baltic the
friend and succour of oppressed nations. But because
she was guided in this by her spirit of hostility to one
people, even more than by her sympathy with others,
and influenced by the accident which had turned her
enemies into traitors to their own principles, rather
than by a hearty recognition of the principles themselves, which, when thus abandoned, she adopted for
her own, she failed, when her gigantic efforts were
at last crowned with peace, to secure for them that
respect and observance which alone could make peace
perpetual. So the great war of the nineteenth century, though it really was waged for, and brought to
an ultimate triumph, the independence of nationalities,

left the map of Europe still blotted with many a stain
to mark the spots in which the rights of nations were
utterly violated.

But since that time public opinion has greatly
advanced. Even during the intoxication of the war
with France, there was a large party that, with more
or less of clearness, denounced any attempt to interfere with another people for merely artificial objects.
Though silenced by the din of battle, and glad "to
clap this royal bargain up of peace," without too
critical an inquiry into the doctrines which it embodied,
this party never ceased to have influence with the
nation. The terms of the peace, indeed, in so far as
they were adverse to its principles, were rather forced
on the public by our diplomatists than carried by the
force of their own intrinsic popularity. Then, as now,
there was a strong sentiment among the bulk of the
people against the forcible cession of Lombardy and
Venice to Austria, and against the perpetuation of
the crime of dismembering Poland. But the sentiment
has gained prodigiously in intensity by the events
which have since occurred. All the successes achieved
by the principle of nationality in Europe have met
the hearty support of the British people. More and
more they have grown to ally themselves in feeling
with whatever nation may raise the standard of revolt
against foreign masters. A unanimity, such as internal

political questions have never known, has, as to its foreign policy, animated of late years the British public, and that unanimous opinion has been invariably ranged on the side of the assertion of national independence and popular rights.

But though such is the unquestionable tendency of opinion, the accident of events has given a singular turn to the phrase in which it most commonly finds expression.   Because the interference of our statesmen in foreign affairs has generally been hostile to the principle which we have now chiefly at heart, we have come to demand most earnestly the simple policy of non-interference.   And because a small knot among our leading public men, and a small section of that wealthiest and highest-born portion of the community which naturally furnishes most of our statesmen, are believed to retain still the traditional respect for dynasties, and aristocratic indifference to the rights of subjects, which once animated our policy, we have united in the aspiration that they should not meddle at all in the arrangements between foreign rulers and subjects, and have declared strenuously that the policy of this country is henceforth to be "non-intervention."   And finally, because that same aristocratic section of the community sees for itself that it can no longer commit England to connivance in a system of repression or misgovernment, and that if England strikes at all, it will for the future be with all her might upon the side of so-called rebels, therefore that section has adopted, as the closest attainable approximation to its own desires, the policy of holding England aloof, and it echoes with cunning vehemence the cry, that England is now committed to the policy of "nonintervention." Thus is swelled the cry which none truly mean, save that very small party of comfortable traders, wholesale and retail, who actually do object to every step that is not directly in the interest of trade, and who, to save trade a shock, would yield to every nation but ourselves the right of intervention. And so it strangely happens that there is in sound a unanimity, where there is utter discordance in sense, and that from opposite motives, from mere mutual dread and distrust, Tory and Whig, Catholic and Protestant, the men of the past and the men of the hour, all unite in proclaiming the formula of "nonintervention." Only, being a formula adopted not from conviction, but to attain a limited and special purpose, it is in reality believed in by none, and it is set at nought by the acts of the very men who, for the protection of their own principles, were the first to invent it.

Such is the origin, and such the meaning—or the want of meaning—of this universal cry. But there can be no doubt that it is now kept up chiefly by mere force

of authority, in despite of conviction.   The people of
this country have beyond all others a reverence for the
authority of their own statesmen.   It is a great and
admirable quality of the national mind—it contributes
stability to a democracy, and forms the check that
keeps popular impulse from affecting the counsels of
the State with sudden and causeless change.   But it
has also its disadvantages.   When our statesmen, who
have through a generation secured our respect, are for
the most part old men, with the stereotyped ideas of
a former period, our respect for them is apt to make
us untrue to the newer principles which they cannot
understand, but which are the faith and the hope of
the present generation.   Age is prudent, but prudence
is not always wisdom, or justice, or honour; and as in
the operations of active war we generally find that the
prudence which well and carefully guided us through
the routine of peace, must give way to the energy,
and daring, and enthusiasm of younger men, so in
politics, the prudence which is suitable for a period of
quiet and of smoothness, may not be the safest guide
when new combinations arise, and new human problems
press for instant solution.   And such is the present
position of the nation in regard to its foreign policy.
It is guided by Lord Palmerston, Lord Russell, and
Lord Derby.   These men have all in some degree
liberal sympathies.   But they were all educated in

4—2

the school which taught that the "balance of power"
was the sole object worthy our fighting for, and that
the balance of power was to be maintained by maintaining the rights of dynasties and the territorial
equality of states, without any reference to the tendencies of the populations.   So these statesmen, while
readily professing every sympathy with foreign liberal-
ism, declare plainly and positively that we must not
aid it by arms.[1]   And thus, though the great bulk of
the British nation is impressed by an opposite desire,
though it would eagerly respond to a call to arms in
a justifiable cause, and though it would lift into the
highest popularity the statesman who should venture
to utter such a call, yet it is so much more deeply
impressed with reverence for its ancient counsellors,

---

[1] A nominal exception to this proposition ought, perhaps, to be
made in favour of Lord Russell.   In the debate on the question of
recognition of the Confederate States, on 23rd March, 1863, Lord
Russell declared his abhorrence of the idea of intervening in favour
of a Slave State, and in very noble words recalled the fact that we
intervened in favour of Holland to rescue it from the tyranny of
Philip II., in favour of Portugal to deliver it from Spain, in favour of
Greece and of Belgium ; and he added, that all these were just and
laudable interventions, because "they were in behalf of the independence, freedom, and welfare of a great portion of mankind."   He then
expressed his hope that nothing would ever induce us to set an example
different from that of our ancestors, but that any interference we may
hereafter be bound to make, should be " in the cause of liberty, and to
promote the freedom of mankind, as we have hitherto done in such
cases."   But it is to be feared Earl Russell's words rather express his
historical theory than his practical purpose and fixed principle of action.

and so accustomed to mistrust its own judgment when opposed to a unanimity among its statesmen, that it falters, looks back, and, in sheer doubt what to do, does nothing.

Nor ought we, in reviewing the influences that have affected the determination of our recent foreign policy, to leave out of account the fact that the first effect of war would be disastrous to our gigantic trade. There is, indeed, no reason to believe that this fact would induce the public to hold back from a just war. But it at least inclines a large portion of the public to listen favourably to those who on every occasion when war looms up, insist that its causes do not concern us, and that our participation in it would be a blunder and a crime. And when the leaders of parties tell us that in their judgment our honour and duty are not involved, we are then ready to take their word without inquiry for ourselves; the rather that we know well that our immediate interests all lie on the side of peace.

This spectacle of a whole people held in voluntary restraint by the opinions of those whom it respects, may be, in one view, a very great and noble one. But it may also have a different aspect. Diffidence is praiseworthy, but utter sacrifice of principle is base. To pause in forming a resolution, to weigh with anxious care the arguments on the other side, to ascribe even more than their apparent value to the opinions of men whom we honour, is true wisdom. But to give way utterly to the decision of another, to renounce the privilege of private judgment out of mere deference, or to hand over to another, out of mere idleness and lassitude, the duty of forming our convictions and carrying them into action, is to fail in our highest duty as citizens of a free state. No man can thus throw off the responsibility which attaches to him —no man can divest himself of influence in the progress of events; for even his self-seclusion strengthens one side or other. He who withholds himself from active interference in the affairs of the nation, flings the weight of his support into the hands of those by whom they are actually conducted. If even the inclination of his opinion be on their side, it may well be doubted whether he is justified in abstaining from a close investigation into the reasons by which they support their policy. But if the inclination of his opinion be against them, terrible indeed is the responsibility belonging to a weak or lazy acquiescence. Dare we think what this responsibility actually means? —dare we picture to ourselves that England's foreign policy means, to many a human being, life or death, prosperity or famine, peace and happiness, or a country desolated, towns sacked, savage murder of innocent men, brutal violence to women, eternal perdition, as far as our human sight can reach, to human souls? Can we free ourselves of these things because we see them not—or will turning away our eyes wash the spurts of blood from off our garments? Or will it, to our consciences at the moment of final trial, prove any solace that we can say, *we* did not murder, nor spoil, nor violate? Are we not taught by the Judge Himself that the demand on that day will not be,— What did ye? but, What failed ye to do? And shall we now lay unction to our souls with the thought that though men and women elsewhere are dying, are captives, are tortured, are sick and in prison, yet it is no concern of ours, for they are of another race, and are beyond our range of vision, and we have handed over to some one else the duty of thinking whether we could conveniently, and without too much cost of comfort, feed the hungry or clothe the naked, or give so much as a glass of cold water to those who are writhing in agony?

Vain indeed is such delegation of responsibility. As free citizens, as intelligent beings, we *must* think for ourselves. Our statesmen may have the excuse of the prejudices of an olden time, of an early education under a different state of European society. The mind grows rigid as the limbs stiffen, and it were as idle to expect the ideas of a life to change at seventy, as it would be to look for the lithe activity.

of the lad in the bent frame of the greybeard. But
we who are of the time must try ourselves by the
tests appropriate to the time. We must seek by our
utmost endeavour to find what it is that is demanded
of us by our brethren now living. We must measure
our responsibility by our own power, not by our
fathers' power. We must examine for ourselves
what is the nature of the struggles of which, in this
middle of the nineteenth century, this world is the
scene ; we must discriminate the evil from the good ;
we must demand what are our means to help the one,
to abate the other ; and then, when we have satisfied
our minds, we must be prepared, under the awful
penalty attaching to him who knows what is required
of him and who does it not, to affirm our convictions
with our deeds.

But in thus seeking to know in order that we
may do our duty as members of the great family of
mankind, where shall we turn for instruction and
direction ? There are men who tell us that law, and
politics, and international right are sciences apart,
resting on their own basis of reason, and having
principles discoverable only from the common consent
of civilization. If they admit that such principles
ought at least to be consistent with morality, they
affirm that it is sufficient if they are merely not
opposed to morality. But those who thus argue

would, in truth, build their house on the shifting
sand of the sea-shore. If there be no other standard
of public right and wrong than common consent, it
is a standard varying in every continent, and in
every generation. True, there is much of law,
which, being concerned only with the convenience
of the regulations which give uniformity to our social
life, is referable tô no higher principle. But can it
be said with truth, that because the forms of law are
determined merely by convenience and consent, the
fundamental principles of law are subject to the
same fluctuating rule? Consent properly regulates
the manner of transmitting property from one owner
to another; but does it follow that the right of
holding property rests upon no higher principle?
Consent of the nation directs the most suitable local
forms of contracting marriage, and the period during
which parents shall be liable to support their children;
but does it follow that we have nothing to quote
but general convenience in declaring the sanctity of
the nuptial tie and the doctrine of parental obligation? Are not these great rules of conduct fixed
for us in our consciences and by our religion—do
we not instinctively appeal to these judges to try our
conduct, and to approve or condemn our legislation?
For when we come to be actual legislators, or in
any way to recognize that we have an influence in

legislation, the fact itself sweeps away all sophisms
respecting the origin of law.   Then we feel that in
acting we must perforce take our own consciences
into council, and that we inevitably subject them to
responsibility if we wilfully do what we know to be
contrary to the precepts by which they are enlightened.
And so, individually, we do reduce law to the test
of religion, and do, because we must, endeavour to
accommodate every enactment to the dictates of
Christianity, in so far as Christianity furnishes direction for the case.

Nor is it otherwise with international law and
policy.   All its forms, modes, special rules, are
ascertained by the consent of nations, and delivered to
us in the writings of its great jurists.   But we cannot
be content to refer the *principles* which should animate
nations in their dealings with nations to nothing more
than conventional convenience.   We cannot, in bearing
our share in the direction of national policy, divest ourselves of our individual consciences, or free ourselves
from the obligations by which our consciences are
governed.   So, then, when we are in doubt, not about
questions of convenience, but about what, if they arose
between individuals, would be felt to be questions of
justice or injustice, of right or wrong, we must, when
acting as component parts of a nation, seek to solve
them in no different way.   We must bring them to be

judged by that Book to which Christendom appeals when it would determine what is commanded or forbidden.   True, we shall not find there aught to supersede human research and reason.   Its purpose is not to supersede, but to guide.   It lays not down definite rules for every act, but its spirit may inform every act.   It lifts up before our eyes, in whatever transaction of life we may be occupied, a banner, whereon are inscribed, in no doubtful characters, the principles for which we must contend, and to which we must conform.   The application of these it leaves to human discrimination.   But first let us humbly seek for the principles, and then, with what clearness of judgment and strength of will we can, strive to apply them to the eventualities which present themselves, or to give them effect in action.[1]

---

[1] To show the very insufficient character of the arguments usually adduced against the idea that international law may be founded upon a primary divine law, it may be instructive to refer to two instances suggested by a recent writer under the name of "Historicus," who has cited them to show the absurdity of such a test of law.   It is, he says, a necessary element of war, that the belligerents may injure each other "to any extent they can, within certain limits, which the habits of the civilized world have agreed upon,"—but that "to found this right upon some law directly emanating from God, would be preposterous, not to say profane." But surely, if war, defensive or protective, is ever justifiable by divine law, we are right to take every means by which its end may be attained, and its horrors abated most speedily ; and, therefore, even the *modes* of warfare may, without profanity, be tried by the spirit

Now, it certainly cannot be pretended that Christianity has nothing to do in regulation of our transactions
as individuals with men of another race, and subject to
a different government. Between Jew and Gentile it
knows no distinction. All the tribes of earth are in
its view as one people. All mankind without exception are embraced within the all-pervading maxim,
Love thy brethren. When a Jew had fallen among
thieves, the Levite who passed him by was condemned,
the Samaritan who succoured him was commended.
Though of hostile race, of different faith, set apart
from each other by the wide chasm of religious
intolerance and of political rivalry, we are bidden to
recognize that each was to the other in the eye of duty
as " a neighbour." Now, the command to love our

---

of divine law. " Historicus " next asserts that this principle would
apply to even municipal law, " a standard to which law is not
amenable." It is morally right, he tells us, to keep our promises, but
the law only compels us to keep those which are made for a valuable
consideration; " yet the law is not therefore unjust, it only shows
that the provinces of law and morality are not co-extensive." The
illustration is accurate, if we regard only the law of heathen Rome
and of modern England; but " Historicus " being only an English
barrister, is ignorant that the canon law, expressly on Christian
grounds, disavows the distinction between promises, and makes all
pacts equally binding, whether for or without consideration, and that
this law has been adopted in most of the States of Europe, including
Scotland. His demonstration, then, is unimpeachable, that English
law is not co-extensive with morality; but it entirely fails to establish
that law *cannot* be co-extensive with morality, or consistent with " a
primary divine law."

neighbour, when translated from mental disposition
into practical rule of action, means no less than this,
that we shall do such good to our neighbours as may
be in our power. We are bound, then, as individuals,
to succour and comfort them without distinction of
people; we are bound, in so far as we can, to advance
their individual temporal and spiritual interests, if by
any means it be in our power. This obligation none
can dispute, and it is one which we daily confess in our
actions. But if such be our unquestionable duty as
individuals to individuals, is it affected by the circumstance that our act must be done in a corporate
capacity in unison with others, and in favour of a
large class of persons? In practice, our duty may be
affected by this wider range—in principle, it certainly
cannot be. It is possible that what one individual
might rightly and beneficially do for a portion of his
fellow-creatures might fail to have a beneficial, might
even have an injurious, effect upon them if done by a
larger body. It might in such a case " o'erleap itself"
by the very additional vigour with which it was
performed; it might, from help, grow into oppression;
or it might raise an opposition which would not have
been excited by humbler aid. All these are practical
questions relative to the application of the principle.
But as to the principle itself being sound, there can be
little hesitation. To do such good as we can, is

obviously an even more imperative duty if it can be done at once to many. It is as evidently a duty if it can be effected only by uniting with others to effect it. And this obligation also we admit by our numerous societies and associations in which numbers of our people unite to do good to a number of persons either in our own or in foreign countries. Then to proceed a step further, if we, as a nation, see *unanimously* how we can do good to another nation, there cannot be a question that Christianity binds us to make the effort. Our effort must be guided by prudence; it must be preceded by careful and anxious investigation as to whether the object we propose is really beneficial, and is really greater in advantage than the drawbacks which attend it, as they do every human good; but, when we are satisfied on these points, our duty is clear, and we are bound to spend fortune and life, if need be, in carrying it out.

All these are propositions little open to contro-versy. But it will be answered, that they fail to carry us to any conclusion on the point really at issue. For it will be urged, that they settle only the course of conduct proper to bodies incorporated and established for the special object of rendering such benevolent services as are here in question. Now nations and governments are established not for mere benevolent purposes, but for strictly useful and necessary purposes.

They are social leagues, primarily for defence of the whole body, secondarily for protection of the individuals composing them.   To use a power, acquired by association for these limited purposes, to effect other external purposes, however laudable and lofty in themselves, is to assume, it will be maintained, a false position, to employ a weapon for a purpose for which it was not designed, and in a manner which consequently can result only in mischief.   Moreover, it will follow that a breach of this principle of government must necessarily work a vast amount of positive evil for the sake of a doubtful good.   It can scarcely ever happen that the nation is unanimous in desiring to interfere in foreign affairs; and therefore, if it does interfere, it will be by the exercise of a tyrannical power on the part of the majority over the minority. This is objectionable in all cases in principle; in the present instance, it is fruitful of evil and suffering. The minority cannot escape the miseries of a war into which it is thus forced against its will.   War, however holy and just, is an agent of uncountable suffering. To compel soldiers to die on a battle-field, to perish of the wounds and diseases of a campaign, or to drag out as cripples a maimed and wretched existence,—all in a cause which they personally disapprove, and in which they are forced against their will to fight,—is, it may be argued, an indefensible infliction, unless

justified by the immediate objects of national existence.
But a wider injury is done by war than any to which
the actual combatants are exposed. There is inevitable dislocation of industry, and this means infinite
private suffering from which there is no possibility of
escape. It means loss of capital to the rich, starva-
tion to the poor,—words which find their plainest
equivalents in robbery and slaughter. All these, we
have been told, are the consequences of departing
from the fundamental principles of national existence,
and taking part in sentimental foreign conflicts in
behalf of races with whose cause we have no personal interest.

Such is a fair statement of the arguments urged
against national interference on behalf of foreign freedom. A very brief examination will suffice to show
their sophistry. It partly lies, in the first place, in
a confusion raised between sufferings that are directly
caused by a course of conduct, and sufferrings that are
merely consequential upon it; partly, in the second
place, in the assumption, as proved, of the very points
in dispute; and partly, in the third place, in a perver-
sion of the opposing propositions, so as to educe from
them conclusions to which they do not truly lead.

For, in the first place, when it is asserted that
the majority of the nation has no right to impose on
the minority the burden and sufferings of a war not

directly involving its own interests, the proposition must be taken with very great limitation. So far as our soldiers and sailors, the primary sufferers, are concerned, it is to be remembered that they are neither slaves nor conscripts, but volunteers. They are not forced into the trade of war: they embrace it of choice. And while this is the case as regards war in general, it may be very positively asserted that if the question of any special war, approved by the majority of the public, were left to the arbitrament of the two services, it would be instantly declared by universal acclamation in the affirmative.

And as this consideration excludes all idea of a tyrant majority inflicting death and wounds on the reluctant servants of its will, it also excludes all responsibility for the sufferings of the widows and orphans or other relatives of the actual combatants. The choice has been made for them not by the nation, but by their own fathers or husbands. No responsibility for their grievous sorrows can lie on the majority of the public, when the fact is that the sufferings would not have come to them had not the profession of arms been deliberately selected by those for whom they mourn.

Again, when we consider the sufferings caused among non-combatants by the stagnation of trade and other secondary results of war, we shall see on

the slightest reflection, that these, though very proper
to be taken into account in balancing the propriety
or prudence of a war, cannot be taken as results
which make a war necessarily unjustifiable.   The
nation lies under no compact to secure a fixed rate
of profits to those engaged in any particular trade.
The majority has not forced the minority into trade,
nor guaranteed the prosperity of any trade.   War,
indeed, if it makes some trades worse, makes others
better.   But neither consideration makes a war just
or unjust.   The question to be weighed is whether
a war will do most good or harm, and if the majority
of the nation think that the good it will do to our
fellow men, either at home or abroad, exceeds the
amount of harm it will indirectly inflict on a certain
portion of our countrymen, it is not only justified,
but clearly bound, to strive for the larger good.   This
is not doing evil that good may come; it is doing
right, at the cost, inevitable in all human actions, of a
certain, but smaller, proportion of secondary suffering.

There is, indeed, one point on which it must be
admitted the majority has no right to act inde-
pendently of the minority, except for purposes tending
to the benefit of the whole nation.   This is the raising
of taxation.   For taxation is, in fact, a direct seizure
of property; and though justifiable when necessary
for the maintenance of civil institutions, by which all

take benefit, or for defence or security which accrues
to all, and without which society must dissolve into
barbarism, it would not be justifiable merely to enable
the majority to carry out its own ideas of benevolence.
Thus, if it were established that a war in aid of the
independence of a foreign people did not tend to the
advantage of our own nation, we should be bound to
admit that though we might as individuals volunteer,
or subscribe, to support it, we should not be warranted
in imposing taxation on a recusant minority for that
purpose.   On this point, then, we have to consider
the proposition, the assumption of which as proved
constitutes the second branch of the sophism in the
argument of the opponents of all intervention, the
proposition that intervention is never necessary or
expedient for the mere ultimate defence or protection
of the realm itself.

It is clear, in the first place, that if we concede
the assumption that it never is, we must be prepared
to admit also that all treaties of alliance with foreign
states are indefensible.   For treaties of alliance cannot be one-sided : if they are to ensure to us support
in the event of attack, they must guarantee our support in the event of attack made on our allies.
Here, then, is a case of possible intervention result-
ing in war, in which, nevertheless, it may happen
that a large minority of the nation are unconvinced

of its propriety. Nor can this dilemma be eluded
by maintaining with Bentham (who wrote, however,
on this head before the experience of the wars and
combinations which followed the French Revolution),
that we need no alliance of any kind. All experience
is against such a doctrine. Were it indeed possible
that over the whole globe alliances and conquests
could be simultaneously abolished, we might allow
ours to go with the rest. For then we should have
reached the point to which all just alliances are
instruments to bring us—the complete independence
of nations. But, till that millennium arrives, what
would be our position if we alone were to renounce
alliances? We could not prevent their being formed
against us, and we should speedily be left alone
against a world for our foe. Who would stand on
our side after we had explicitly announced that we
should never stand by any one? What motive would
remain to attract to us help, after we had declared
that we should never give help again? Who would
not look upon us then as the common enemy and
the common spoil of mankind? Who would not
join in extirpation of a state whose utter and avowed
selfishness held her aloof from every interest but that
immediately her own? and who would not join in
seeking a share of the rich booty which the combination of all other powers against her would speedily

hold out as a certain prize? Nor let us flatter ourselves that such a combination is impossible. If
despotism gains in Europe as it has done during the
last ten years, if Russia, Prussia, Austria, France, all
hate us because we are free and prosperous; if Italy,
Switzerland, Denmark, at the same time are taught
that we never will move to help them to resist the
absorbing influence of their more powerful neighbours,
is it so very unlikely that we at length shall be marked
out for destruction? And do not let us dream that
we could alone defy the armies of all despotic Europe.
Against such a combination we have never yet had
to struggle. In the darkest hour of the war with
Napoleon we had always at least one European
power on our side. In 1805, Austria drew off from us
the troops destined for our invasion; Spain and
Portugal made the next diversion in our favour;
Prussia, Sweden, and Russia took up by turns our
support. When, finally, Europe combined on our
side, even the genius of Napoleon wielding the mighty
warlike power of France could not resist its overwhelming approach. Would our single strength
prove greater than his, if we should isolate ourselves
by selfishness as completely as he did by ambition?

So, then, it is obvious that on the straitest theory
of the functions of government, there must be alliances
between us and other states; and such alliances, as a

necessary condition, involve us in an obligation, under certain circumstances, to go to war, subject to all its terrible results to ourselves, in behalf of interests not immediately our own. Therefore, now, the only gap yet existing between the conclusions to which Christian principles and political principles lead is this, that while both sanction in some cases foreign intervention, the former bid us compute the benefit to others as well as to ourselves, the latter take account, so far as we have yet seen, only of the benefit to be wrought to ourselves by means of the benefits done to others.

But does this make any real discrepancy in our course of action under both? It does not, unless we grant the third branch of the sophism to which the opponents of intervention have recourse. When they say that the supporters of the Christian theory would have us fight for a merely sentimental object, they use a phrase of double meaning in the sense in which it is untrue. All objects are in one sense sentimental, for the opinion of their value to us is merely a sentiment. But when by " sentimental " is meant fanciful, intangible, or unattainable, we may flatly deny that Christian principles lead us to struggle, or to help in a struggle, for anything of the sort. That freedom which alone ensures the physical and moral wellbeing of a people is not fanciful or intangible ; that

national independence which is an instinctive desire in
every people is not always, nor often, unattainable.
Where freedom would yet be unsuitable, because
civilisation has made too little progress to permit its
real development, or where national independence
would be impracticable, because the people aspiring
to it are too few, too weak, or too divided to be able
to profit by it, there were no kindness in forcing these
boons upon any community ; and Christianity nowhere
bids us to act, where by acting we cannot effect any
good.   Therefore Christianity never does require us to
interpose on behalf of a merely "sentimental" desire.
It is most thoroughly practical in the ends it proposes,
and in the cautions it enjoins.   So it goes hand in
hand with the strict doctrines of selfishness, at least
thus far, that both recommend such alliances only as
are positively feasible, and such as will, to one or
other of the contracting parties, work definitely an
unquestionable degree of benefit.

And, therefore, we now come only to ask, whether
the alliances so recommended are different, or are not
in truth the very same ?   To answer this question,
we must advance a step further than we have yet
gone.   We have determined that Christianity bids us
to do the largest amount of good to foreign nations
which it is in our power to do.   We have determined
also, that policy bids us make to ourselves friends of

those who are able to do us most good. Let us see
what course each line of motive would lead us practically to take.

And first of the two, let us see what is the most
good we can do. Here we may exclude at once—
taught by a bitter experience—all question of forcing
a hypothetical good, according to our own notions,
upon a reluctant or indifferent people. This course
is not to benefit, it is to tyrannize. We cannot make
men happy, any more than we can make them
virtuous or religious, by compulsion. They must
teach themselves by their own experience, advance by
their own efforts, adopt their own systems, and carry
into action their own ideas. Foreign interference
with natural development is never other than
disastrous. Therefore no such interference falls
within the scope of Christian precept. On this head
it is at one with the maxims of the most ardent
preacher of "non-intervention."

But in this exclusion, it must be kept clearly in
view that we are supposing the case of a people free to
follow the bent of its own inclinations. If there be
a nation not free to this extent, but held in subjection
by a foreign power, which prescribes to it rules not of
native growth, and imposes on it restraints against
which it rebels, then intervention against the conqueror, and in favour of the subdued, becomes of a

totally different character. It is in such case no longer an interference with the laws of nature, but an effort to procure them free play. It is not a forcing of alien ideas upon an unwilling population, but a procuring of liberty to them to follow their own ideas. Therefore it is conferring on them the highest benefit which man can bestow on man. It is giving them opportunity and means to elevate themselves, socially, morally, and intellectually, to the utmost extent to which the faculties bestowed upon them may reach,— so fulfilling in the highest degree the destiny which has been laid out as possible for them on earth.

Yet again this boon must be understood in its rational and practical sense. To aid a population to achieve independence when it is so intrinsically weak that, to preserve its independence from a foreign oppressor, it must always be dependent on foreign succour, would go beyond the limit of duty, because beyond the limit of real benefit. Active succour could not always be given; and when not at hand, the condition of the weak state would be worse than it was before. Therefore the principle of Christianity does not require us to help indiscriminate revolution of petty districts, or declarations of independence on the part of sections of a population, between whom and their neighbours there is no substantial difference of blood or thought. It points out that aid should be given to distinct and considerable races,—a phrase which it may be very difficult to define in words and numbers, but which it is always comparatively easy to apply to any case that practically occurs. It would refuse help to a local and partial outbreak of passion, but would give help to the wide-spread, deep-seated repugnance to amalgamation on the part of a well-known and recognized people.

Nor is this rule materially affected by the question, whether the people, which claims our aid towards achieving freedom, has been recently, or for a long time, subjugated. If a long-continued subjugation, with all the influences which under an identical government tend to make unity of sentiment among its subjects, has failed in any case to produce that effect, and leaves still two distinct nations, of which one is dominant and the other enchained, the prescription of injustice cannot obliterate the right of freedom. Neither does any degree of recognition by foreign powers of a certain territorial arrangement establish a perpetual bar to its modification. It is quite possible that it might be proper, under certain circumstances, to allow the experiment to be tried, of placing a district under the control of a neighbouring government, in the belief, for instance, that there was no fundamental antipathy between the two populations, or that the one was so feeble that it could not resist the operation of gradual amalgamation. But if facts belie these expectations; if the subject race retains obstinately its nationality, and grows to such strength as to be evidently capable of asserting and maintaining independence, no treaties or course of diplomacy can bind us to the perpetuation of a manifest evil and injustice which we did not foresee. Whether, then, the assertion of nationality may fall under the category of revolt against a recent conqueror, or of dismember-ment of an ancient empire, we are bound by Christian principles to grant it, and to aid it, provided only it is the result of so definite an existing repulsion, and affects so considerable a population, as to place beyond a doubt that the happiness of the world would be enhanced by its success.

Now, let us turn and see what mere selfish policy would counsel. Its aim is to make for us the strongest, the truest, and the most profitable friends we can obtain. Let us try to divest ourselves of the prejudices of the map of Europe, and ask who, in this sense, would form our natural and best allies. Is it the despots, whose overgrown armies waste the sub-stance of the people, and whose apparent strength is a mockery, because it is eaten away by internal discord, and by the necessity of binding their hostile provinces with garrisons and standing camps? Is it the dull nations who submit placidly to be held under domina-

tion, wanting the energy and self-control which are
needful to the character of freemen? Can there ever
be real sympathy between such as these and ourselves;
can we ever depend upon them as friends; can we
even expect them to prove profitable customers in our
trade? On the contrary, between the Briton and
either the despot or the slave there is an insuperable
antipathy. Circumstances may make us for a time
league ourselves with them; but there can be no
hearty and enduring alliance, where on the one
side there is mingled hatred and envy, and on the
other contempt and pity. We can neither depend on
their external policy continuing the same with our
own, nor, even when it is, can we be sure that, when
we most need their help, they may not be paralysed
by internal disaffection. Nor, in time of peace, is the
trade much worth to us which is carried on under such
restrictions as powers of a tyrannic type always impose,
and with a people whose enterprise is broken down by
the enervation of political slavery. On the other
hand, between ourselves and free nations there is the
lasting bond of community of feeling and of interest.
Being free, they are as a consequence industrious,
energetic, and strong. Their unshackled vigour opens
up to us new markets, and yields us new supplies; the
intercourse of unrestricted and profitable commerce
strengthens the ties of regard; identity of aim and

interest makes them our fast friends; the wealth and internal union of freedom exalts them into powerful supporters. In every way it is obvious that free nations are our natural, most reliable, and most advantageous allies. Can there, then, be a doubt whether our true policy does not bid us aid in the establishment of their independence, and does not tell us that better far for us would be a Europe permitted and aided thus to shape herself into the states into which the inclinations of her population would naturally arrange her, and in which they would find their full development, than a Europe mapped out into artificial and incongruous principalities, whose discordant elements need the maintenance of enormous armies to keep them from shaking asunder, and to subdue that internal energy which alone can give happiness and prosperity?

The doubt, if it exists, cannot be as to the principle, but only as to the degree of help we should give to such a new reformation, and the expediency of going to war on its behalf. To judge of this, we must turn to the page of experience, and seek there what our acquiescence has cost us, in war itself. Let us take two examples. We abstained from more than remonstrance when Poland was partitioned, and when time after time she struggled for liberty. What has that cost us in tangible penalty? It cost us the

enlistment of the gallant Polish cavalry in the ranks
of the French army, when France promised them
something more than cold sympathy — that cavalry
whose charge up the fortified pass of the Somosierra,
after the flower of the French infantry, directed by
Napoleon himself, had recoiled, laid Spain a second
time at the feet of the conqueror, and directly brought
about the retreat of Sir John Moore, the carnage of
Corunna, the evacuation of the country by the British
army, and the years of subsequent campaign under
Wellington. So the fortune of a future deadly war
was turned against us by one little incident springing
as an immediate consequence of the policy which held
us back from going to war in a just cause. It would
be an endless task to enumerate the other exploits of
Polish leaders and troops in the French ranks. Let
this plain question suffice. Would it not have been
cheaper for us, in money and in blood, to have
despatched an expedition to help that nation in resisting invasion at first, or in throwing off oppression
afterwards, if by so doing we could have secured them
as allies, and deprived our enemies of their succour,
in the future wars of the French Revolution? But
the lesson closes not with that passage of history.
Since the re-establishment of peace, the disturbing
fear of Europe, and chiefly of England, has been the
stealthy but giant advance of Russian power. To

curb this, we invaded Afghanistan ; still later, we were
compelled to go to war on behalf of Turkey; and
after we had repelled the invasion of Turkish territory,
we deemed it sound policy to make a descent on the
Crimea, with the object of crippling more effectually
Russian powers of aggression.   What these conflicts
cost us, lives fresh in our recollection.   Was it less
or more, let us ask ourselves, than would have been
needed, if in 1830 we had sent an expedition to support Poland when she had all but recovered her freedom — when she had beaten, single-handed, the
Russians in more than one pitched engagement—when
Diebitsch was dead, and Paskiewitch was gathering
up his forces to cast the last die for Russian supremacy ?   And would not a Poland, liberated then, have
proved a far more sufficing and impenetrable barrier
to Russia than the subsequent destruction, with infinite
waste of life, of a single arsenal on the Black Sea ?

The next test instance shall be by way of comparison.   Italy and Western Germany have had this
point of resemblance, that they have both for many
ages been separated into numerous small political
divisions, with merely local jealousy, but not ethnological repulsion, between the component parts of
each.   But their fate has been different in this respect,
that, while the Germanic States have been kept for
the most part free from foreign interference, and

though generally subject to nominal despotisms, yet despotisms voluntarily accepted, maintained by purely native force, and therefore not individually oppressive, Italy has had her fairest provinces subjected to a wholly foreign power, maintained by foreign bayonets, and crushing the spirit of the people by foreign violence. Which of the two has been our best friend? Germany, broken up as she is, has always been on our side. She might be for a period overrun by Napoleon, but it was against her will; and he drew nought of permanent strength from his nominal tributaries beyond the Rhine, while German troops formed constantly a large part of our armies. But Italy sprang to arms at the first glitter of French bayonets levelled against her oppressors; she remained the faithful friend of her French deliverers; she was one vast recruiting ground for French troops; and her legions were, with those of Poland, to the last the trusted auxiliaries of the French armies. Such was the actual difference to us, in time of war, of a prior support of, or contempt for, national rights. In time of peace the contrast has been as striking. Between ourselves and self-governed and contented Germany there has been ever a large and profitable trade; between ourselves and an enslaved and revolutionary Italy there has been next to nothing in the shape of trade. Now that Italy is again free, we begin to experience her riches, and the value of her friendship. But it is well we should recollect that, had our friendship been a little less hesitating, there would have been no cession of Savoy to France. That iniquitous bargain and perilous precedent was the immediate result of our leaving Italy without a friend in time of need except France, and without a supporter in time of success still unconsolidated, except a power which was strong enough to exact a rich price for that support. Have prudence and selfishness proved themselves in this instance, then, real wisdom?

From the history of every people in the Old and the New World, we might, did space permit, draw corroboration of the truth which these two European instances suggest. But these are enough for the purpose. They establish, in striking but different cases, that when Christianity bids us do what good we can, by interfering to procure the free development of national life, she counsels us to no other acts than the most enlightened and far-seeing policy would direct—a policy the neglect of which is ever avenged speedily and heavily, by unlooked-for loss and peril to ourselves.

But if the two principles thus lead to identical results, why, it will be asked, press us to take for monitor that religious teaching which is less obviously our guide in temporal matters, than the dictates of earthly policy ? Why not leave us to the guidance of reason, without seeking to supersede it by the admittedly similar precepts of faith ?

The answer is this. Because, though Divine Wisdom has ordained that true religion and true reason shall never be at variance, yet of the two, religion is infinitely the longer sighted. Reason is but human wisdom ; religion is the Divine Wisdom itself. As we grow in knowledge and in enlightenment, our wisdom approaches nearer to God's. But it is still subject to partial prejudice—to temporary error from imperfect information, from inaccurate deduction. We know by experience that when these are removed, it leads to the same conclusions as religion at once prescribes. It were folly in us, then, longer to adopt the weaker and less perfect guide, when we may at once resort to the clearer and wholly perfect. For it is of the very nature of human aberration that we cannot tell when we have fallen into it. Only afterwards we discover it by its consequences, and know that we have drunk poison by the agonies we endure. But if we accept divine teaching, we take a guide that cannot err. No doubt, even in this we may mistake the application of the precepts we receive. But the danger from this source is infinitely small, compared with that which we run when we ask, not what is the duty commanded, but what is the profit to be gained.   The one is plain, and simple, and near at hand ; the other involves all the complexity of human affairs, and all the uncertainty of the unknown and distant future.   The one is the Sermon on the Mount ; the other is the record of diplomacy for a thousand years.

Thus, then, we have established that Christian precept is, after all, the wisest director of our foreign policy ; and that to do the evident good which we can do to our neighbour, at whatever present and apparent loss, is our most certain ultimate gain.   And now, before we leave the subject, let us consider, as we have done in some instances in the past, what would, in the present and future, be the course of policy which this direction would enjoin.

First of all, it would bid us hold back from inter-ference with any states wholly ruled from within, because it would warn us that, while a nation is satis-fied with the government it has selected or permitted, foreign interposition would be not only useless but injurious.   So, however strange it may seem to our notions that men should choose to live under such a rule as prevails in France, in the Germanic States, or in Russia proper, our intervention can have no place with them.   They form great and united populations, whose determined will no army raised from their own bosom could resist ; and, therefore, though a scattered

minority of enlightened men may desire an advance
in the path of liberty, yet, till that minority can leaven
the mass, it must be content to submit to the will of
the majority, which really, though without express
acknowledgment, is the foundation of the subsisting
despotic and military rule. We may indeed, when
occasion offers, give friendly counsel if it should seem
likely to be of service; but as our mission is not to
force but to help, we ought to abstain from action, and
as decidedly from unwelcome and irritating counsel.
We are at liberty, however, to choose our own friends;
and if the governors of any state shall, even with the
implied sanction of a sufficient portion of the population, commit acts unworthy of humanity, we may justly
mark our detestation by withdrawing from fellowship
with them.   So we rightly recalled our minister from
Naples when it was ruled by Bomba; and so we might,
had we thought fit, have been justified in breaking off
our relations with Louis Napoleon on the morrow of
the massacre which followed the *coup d'état.*

Neither have we any concern with insurrection,
while it remains purely internal. It is then the struggle
between two parties to ascertain which is the stronger,
and as such entitled to direct affairs according to its
own ideas. No doubt it is a very rough and cruel
test; but so are the strikes which in our own country
form as yet the sole ultimate mode of ascertaining the

balance between the supply of, and the demand for, labour.   To interfere with the weight of an external authority in either case, would only be to mislead the parties, to give a victory which probably could not be sustained, to introduce a new and most irritating element into the struggle—and so most effectually to prolong it.   The sole remedy is that which nature provides—the stronger must overcome the weaker ; and the weaker must become sensible that its struggles against force are bootless, and that, if its principles are really true, it must first, by reason and persuasion, gain for them a wider assent.

These are the considerations which have wisely formed our guide in accepting, of late years, whatever government in any foreign nation the apparent will of the majority establishes, and in refraining from help to the minority, even where it seems to combat for principles nearly akin to our own.   And they formed in a different sense, the reasons which forbade our recognition of the Southern States in America as an independent people.   For these States broke off from their Northern brethren, not because they were of different and incompatible races, for their blood was the very same mixture in both ; but because, on a single question of municipal law, they could not agree.   Whether slavery should be extended or not into new territories was the sole question at issue between North and South, at the date of President Lincoln's election; and that election, which indicated that the question would be determined in the negative, was the signal on which the rebellion broke out. Now, such a question might be of immense importance; but on the principles of the South itself, it was one of property only, or of pecuniary advantage. And to hold that a regulation affecting only a question of property would justify revolt, and call for foreign recognition of the revolt while it is yet incomplete, would be to break up the principles upon which all political institutions rest. If, on any ground whatsoever, a portion of a nation had succeeded in establishing its independence, we must, of course, then have recognized the fact; but no principle called upon us to favour dismemberment on a question put at the highest as one of title to property and of freedom of trade, because it was evident that no permanent good can be effected by interposition in such a quarrel.

But passing from cases in which Christian precept has no mode of operation, let us now glance rapidly at those in which it has. It bids us, we have seen, support the freedom of nations against the domination of aliens, and it does not regard whether the domination is so recent as to be called conquest, or so ancient as to be called union, provided that in either case the nationality survives, distinct, hostile, and self-sustaining.

On these principles it would bid us be ready to help either Poland, or Venice, or Rome, when any of them demonstrates, by resolute and nearly unanimous effort and sacrifice, the strength of its convictions.   For the one is capable of being, and long was, an independent nation; the other two are set upon forming part of a kindred nation which is independent; while all three have proved by the experience of years that they are wholly discordant from the dominant races who hold them in chains.   The case of Hungary is in a great degree different.   At present it is engaged in protracted negotiations with its own monarch, a matter with which we have no concern.   It is also so very large a portion of the empire to which it is united, that, if unanimous in itself, it can scarcely be overpowered by the troops of the other provinces. Therefore we ought to leave it, in case of revolt, to assert its own privileges by its own force,—sufficient if the will is sincere and general.   But the position of affairs would be changed if Austria were to call in foreign auxiliaries to put down a revolt which she could not stem of her own strength.   Then our clear duty is, not to intervene, but to prevent intervention. By so doing, we should secure the rights of the Hungarians, and not interfere with those of the Austrians; for no nation has a right to enforce a tyrannical power by foreign force.   Therefore, in

1849 we ought to have forbidden the Russians to cross the frontier, and have left Austria and Hungary to adjust their own future relations. A word from us would have checked Russia; and a check there, as we have already seen in Poland, would have saved us the coming Crimean war, and possibly another war yet to come. For it seems as if Nature herself had placed between these barbarian Scythian hordes, ever pressing onwards, and the civilization of Western Europe, a chain of ineffaceable nationalities for our bulwark. Poland, Hungary, the Rouman States, Greece, are the outposts of Europe. That on the southern flank has constituted itself in independence under every conceivable difficulty. But the three on the north we have suffered to be divided, surrounded, and captured. When shall we be wise enough to aid instead of resisting nature? When shall we be Christian enough to help our brethren, even if we cannot see distinctly at the moment that we are benefiting ourselves.

The recent case of Denmark and the Duchies illustrates the principle in both ways. The Germans claimed that by race the inhabitants of the Duchies were their countrymen, that their desire was to be severed from Denmark, and to be united to Germany. Had this been true, German intervention would have been justifiable, and no ancient treaties would have been valid against a sacred right. But, in fact, it was not true. A small portion only of the southern part of the disputed territory was German, the rest was either mixed or Danish. And though the German element had, fifteen years before, sought to annex itself to Germany, that feeling had so far ceased to operate, that in 1864 there was no insurrection whatever to justify foreign interference.. The German interposition was, therefore, really an attempt to coerce a smaller nation, and to acquire territory on the entirely false pretence of protecting nationality. It would, therefore, have been just and right in us to define the line beyond which German arms should not be allowed to penetrate. And no one who considers German history, and the insecurity of German governments, can doubt that, had we done so at once and decisively, there would have been no war, and no popular acrimony engendered. But our statesmen showed themselves " willing to wound, and yet afraid to strike," and thus drew on the British nation all the reproach of treachery to Denmark, while yet believed, by Germany, to be restrained from war by cowardice, or weakness, rather than by principle. It need not be observed, that such a reputation is simply a provocative of war hereafter, which no sacrifice of principle will then enable us to escape.

Such suggestions, and the policy to which they point, have not the demerit of being new. But I must leave them for the present to stand on their intrinsic truth, rather than on the authorities which might be adduced in support of them. There are, however, two thinkers, among the greatest by whom our country has been adorned, whose opinions I cannot resist the temptation to quote. The notes which Sir James Mackintosh drew up as the basis of his Lectures on International Law have fortunately been preserved, and the two first propositions he laid down were these : " It is the interest of all men, 1st, that every nation should exclusively direct their own affairs, and should enjoy, undisturbed by others, all those advantages which nature and situation have bestowed upon them ; 2nd, that every nation should defend by arms their independence, their natural advantages, their safety, and their honour, which is one of their greatest advantages, and one of the chief bulwarks of their safety." [1] The thought, which Mackintosh doubtless expanded, has been carried to its legitimate conclusions by Mr. Stuart Mill. That clear and profound reasoner, in whom strictness of logic only confirms generosity of sentiment, thus (in his essay entitled *A few Words on Non-intervention*) sums up his argument :—

" With respect to the question, whether our

---

[1] Inaugural address on the Law of Nature and Nations in the University of Edinburgh, by Professor Lorimer, 1863.

country is justified in helping the people of another
in a struggle against their government for free institutions, the answer will be different, according as the
yoke which the people are attempting to throw off is
that of a purely native government or of foreigners ;
considering as one of foreigners, every government
which maintains itself by foreign support.   When the
contest is only with native rulers, and with such native
strength as those rulers can enlist in their defence, the
answer I should give to the question as to the legiti-
macy of intervention is, as a general rule, ' No.'   The
reason is, that there can seldom be anything approaching
to assurance that intervention, even if successful, would
be for the good of the people themselves.   The only
test possessing any real value, of a people's having
become fit for popular institutions, is that they, or
a sufficient portion of them to prevail in the contest,
are willing to brave labour and danger for their
liberation . . . .

" But the case of a people struggling against a
foreign yoke, or against a native tyranny upheld by
foreign arms, illustrates the reasons for non-intervention in an opposite way, for in this case the reasons
themselves do not exist.   A people the most attached to
freedom, the most capable of defending and of making
a good use of free institutions, may be unable to
contend successfully for them against the military

strength of another nation much more powerful. To assist a people thus kept down is not to disturb the balance of forces on which the permanent maintenance of freedom in a country depends, but to redress that balance when it is already unfairly and violently disturbed. The doctrine of non-intervention, to be a legitimate principle of morality, must be accepted by all governments. The despots must consent to be bound by it as well as the free states. Unless they do, the profession of it by free countries comes but to this miserable issue, that the wrong side may help the wrong, but the right must not help the right. Intervention to enforce non-intervention is always rightful, always moral, if not always prudent. Though it be a mistake to *give* freedom to a people who do not value the boon, it cannot but be right to insist that if they do value it, they shall not be hindered from the pursuit of it by foreign coercion. It might not have been right for England (even apart from the question of prudence) to have taken part with Hungary in its noble struggle against Austria, although the Austrian government in Hungary was in some sense a foreign yoke. But when, the Hungarians having shown themselves likely to prevail in this struggle, the Russian despot interposed, and, joining his force to that of Austria, delivered back the Hungarians, bound hand and foot, to their exasperated oppressors, it would have been an honourable and virtuous act on the part of England to have declared that this should not be, and that if Russia gave assistance to the wrong side, England would aid the right. It might not have been consistent with the regard which every nation is bound to pay to its own safety, for England to have taken up this position single-handed. But England and France together could have done it, and if they had, the Russian armed intervention would never have taken place, or would have been disastrous to Russia alone; while all that those powers gained by not doing it, was that they had to fight Russia five years afterwards, under more difficult circumstances, and without Hungary for an ally. The first nation which, being powerful enough to make its voice effectual, has the spirit and courage to say that not a gun shall be fired in Europe by the soldiers of one power against the revolted subjects of another, will be the idol of the friends of freedom throughout Europe. That declaration alone will secure the almost immediate emancipation of every people which desires liberty sufficiently to be capable of maintaining it; and the nation which gives the word will soon find itself at the head of an alliance of free peoples, so strong as to be able to defy the efforts of any number of confederated despots to bring it down. The prize is too glorious not to be snatched sooner or later by some free country; and the time may not be distant when England, if she does not take this heroic part because of its heroism, will be compelled to take it from consideration for her own safety."

Nor let us, while daring to bring others under these tests, shrink from the proof of applying them to our own conduct. We, too, have had hostile provinces —we have dependencies. What, by the same principles, ought to have been, and to be, our conduct to them? Assuredly none other than what we recommend, and should be justified in helping to enforce, elswehere. When, either because of difference of race, or of distance, our dependencies cease to feel as one with us, and have gained strength enough to stand alone, we ought to bid them go, in God's name. Thus we have done with the Ionian Islands, because they desired to unite with Greece, and Greece seems now able to keep them without peril to Europe. Thus we are ready to do with Canada, or the Australian colonies, when any of them shall desire to part from us. We hold India on a different footing. Whatever our original title, we are now the governors chosen by the people. If doubtful before, this fact is ascertained by the late mutiny. When our hired troops revolted, and had all but expelled us, the population, as a rule, remained faithful. So, anomalous as our authority may be, we cannot doubt that it is voluntarily submitted to ; and therefore we do right to hold it, exercising it always under a solemn sense of its responsibilities. Lastly, let us apply our tests to Ireland. Of our rule as it once existed there, they are the absolute condemnation. We were conquerors and oppressors, being also aliens. The population was large enough to be able to maintain independence if dealt with as independent. Therefore we were not justified in resisting the demand of the people to be free from our tyrannical yoke, and France was justified in aiding their revolt. Nor is it indeed doubtful, that during last century they cost us far more than the gain they brought. Happily the circumstances are altered now. We have repented, we have done penance, we have borne our share in making amends. Ireland, therefore, seeks no longer to separate; even the cry for repeal of the legislative union has died out; and her angriest remonstrance of late years was that excited by the proposal to withdraw the representative and emblem of English royalty. The lesson is an important one for ourselves and for Europe.

So now, with clean hands, with the sad but fruitful knowledge in our own consciences of the errors we have heretofore committed, let us turn our faces to the future. We live in an age that calls upon us to discard the traditions of wrong, and to apply to our conduct the guidance of new and higher principles. Theories are everywhere giving way to facts, and the most cunning projects of men are being burst asunder by the instincts implanted by God. One generation has seen Greece freed and Italy united. It has seen powers compacted only of discordant elements torn with the throes of internal conflict; it has seen everywhere the sentiment of identity of race drawing closer those whom political divisions still hold separate. Meanwhile, the extreme case of all in the problems relating to the domination of race over race is hastening to solution before our eyes. African slavery, abolished already in this age by every European power except Spain, is in the course of inevitable extinction in the nation that has profited most by it, and to whose industry it was deemed most essential. There, as everywhere it must, the sin is indeed bearing bitter fruit. The penalty which we had to abide for it was mercifully restricted to loss of property. But in America the life of a white man has been paid down for that of every black man who has perished by the lash or by disease in the cotton lands or the rice swamps, and the wailing of a bereaved white mother or widow rises to expiate the agony of every severed domestic tie of the unregarded slave. Yet out of all

evil springs good at last, and, now that the contest is terminated, it is seen that the end of slavery
is come. Alone, this mighty event would stamp
our age as an epoch in the world. But it is not
alone. It is consentaneous with the advancing
knowledge of God in all the world, with the new
deference to divine law among every people, with
the clearer working of the Spirit in the hearts of
mankind.

Shall we not, then, take the lesson of the age to
ourselves, and give our help to make the Gospel
triumph, by helping to make peace and goodwill
prevail in the only way they can ? The whole history
of the world proves that there can be no happiness
save with freedom, no assured peace save between
freemen. Shall we not do well to let this experience
warn us, and to take for our guide henceforth that
law which has been confirmed by our sufferings
whenever we have broken it ? Shall we be held back
by timid fear for our fortunes when we would dare
loss for the sake of acting on Christ's precept and
example ? Shall we not rather, if our faith is true,
take for our motto the noble words spoken by one
himself in former time a slave, and believe that, even
in this world, " one man, with God, is a majority."

The lesson calls for humbleness and prudence, indeed, as well as faith. We must not mistake our

7

own fancies or wishes for the commands of God's book. But, applying diligence to inquire, reason to investigate, modesty and self-distrust to decide, how can we find better law to apply to our national conduct than that which we apply to our personal conduct? Where shall we find better diplomacy, better guide in foreign policy, than in the one simple command, " Thou shalt love thy neighbour AS THYSELF."

CHAPTER III.

REDUCTION OF TAXATION.

RETRENCHMENT and economy have always been pre-eminent among the distinctive principles of the Liberal party. Yet that party, having been in power, with intermissions of only a few months, for nearly twenty years, has in that space of time raised the national expenditure to the highest point it has reached since Waterloo. And though during the last three years it has taken credit for moderate reductions, our annual outlay is still, after every allowance for charges of collection, twelve millions more under Lord Palmerston than it was under Sir Robert Peel. This anomaly is certainly remarkable enough to deserve consideration by the party, and inquiry by the public.

It is true that during the same period taxation on many articles has been lowered or remitted. And it is thus possible for the government to compute what has been taken off, and excluding from view all the other conditions of our position, to assert that it has

7—2

relieved the nation of a great part of the load which it formerly bore. But whatever the benefit from mere re-adjustment of burdens, it is idle to claim merit for reductions on some branches of revenue, when the fact is, that sums greatly larger are extracted from other branches. The broad fact remains that the nation pays more than it did, although it happens to have enjoyed such continuance and increase of prosperity, that the additional sum is drawn from a larger consumption of a restricted class of articles, or from larger payments under certain surviving taxes.

But the growth of the nation which thus furnishes the increased revenue does not make the burden less an evil. Trade may have expanded, but its expansion is still hindered by the remaining fiscal fetters laid upon it; and the injury to the country is always far greater than the mere sum abstracted in taxation represents. For surrounded as we are on all sides by competition, the difference of a fraction per cent. in the cost of production, which a tax may amount to, signifies often the suppression of an important branch of industry. It signifies in any case a more limited production, and this means diminished employment, lower wages, less diffusion of wealth, less capacity to purchase other articles, the product of other branches of industry. Every man in full employment not only supports himself, but creates by his labour a surplus of valuable material, which is so much addition to the wealth of the country, and therefore every check on employment not only throws a certain burden of pauperism, more or less definite, on the rest of the community, but deprives the community of the gain which would have resulted from the labour which has been displaced.

The manifold manner in which every removal of burdens adds to the public wealth, is very clearly shown in practice by that phenomenon which is familiar to us under the name of " the elasticity of the revenue." It is taken as a condition in finance, about which there can be no dispute, that every judicious reduction in taxation causes an ultimate loss to the revenue of greatly less than the proportion which the part remitted bears to the total tax. But every year the Chancellor of the Exchequer has the agreeable task of being able to announce that the loss has been less than his anticipations, and that the income drawn from the lowered duty has been larger than, with all past experience of the matter, he had ventured to calculate on. This arises simply from the fact that the lowering of the price has multiplied itself in benefit in several different directions. It has, firstly, caused a larger consumption of the article. It has, secondly, given rise to a larger production, or importation of the article. It has, thirdly, increased the production of other articles, either exchanged for the article imported, or produced by its aid.   It has, fourthly, by thus increasing the employment and the wealth of the country, afforded increased means of purchasing the article itself as well as all other taxed articles.   Hence the recovery of the revenue is an index and a result of the wide-spread advantage which all classes of the public have indirectly reaped from the reduction of the single tax that was dealt with.

We do not, however, quite represent to our minds the full gain from public economy when we think of it only as expressed in figures, or as augmenting the wealth of the nation.   It is well to remember it also as an incalculable personal and individual benefit to thousands of our fellow-countrymen.   Life is a thing no less delicate and sensitive than trade.   That fraction of a per cent. of additional charge which injures or annihilates trade is also indirectly the cause of suffering and death in many an English home.   A penny a day better wages may just supply the difference in amount of food, in quality or quantity, which saves the father from being struck down by fever, the wife or children from pining away under the various forms of the disease of innutrition.   The cup of additional tea which the poor sempstress can afford herself because it is sixpence a pound cheaper, may be exactly the stimulus which saves her from sinking. These are questions of life and death. But how much of happiness does not cheaper food and better wages everywhere diffuse, even among those whose lives are above peril? How much of physical comfort, how much relief from the presence of torturing anxiety, how much time for relaxation and for thought on higher things, how much facility for education of children, for reception of the good seed sown in the heart, does not the cheapening of necessaries, and the increase of employment and of wages, allow? And therefore the question of taxation is not a dry matter of statistics and political economy; it is instinct with deep human and spiritual interest, and we must look upon the sum abstracted for the uses of the State as contributions, to be given ungrudgingly indeed so far as they are needful, but not the less to be jealously watched and counted out as in truth the very lifedrops from the heart of the people.

It is, then, no light matter that the so-called popular party has, while in power, abandoned the principles of retrenchment which it professed when seeking power. But when we ask for an explanation of this abnegation of its ancient faith, we are brought face to face with causes which not only operate to produce this result, but which are silently changing the whole system of our representative government. For we have to look at the fact that the House of Commons, which used to consider itself as the special guardian of the public purse, now turns to the country for its guidance, and when the country fails to furnish it with explicit directions, holds itself absolved from responsibility. Thus Government is left without a check, and hence it happens, as in all such cases, that finding itself practically without supervision or restraint, it indulges the tendency to spend, which is sure to be urged upon it by all to whose benefit the expenditure accrues, and by all those influential classes whose interests and friendships lead them to think the maintenance of large civil, military, and naval establishments indispensable for the benefit and safety of the realm.

The reason of this singular state of things is to be found partly in the greater diffusion of education and the wider interest consequently taken by the public in affairs of state, and partly in those marvellous material facilities of communication which late years have seen introduced. When intercourse between town and country—between a member of Parliament and his constituents—was a matter of weeks, when, also, the number of the constituents who cared at all what their member was doing, was very limited, he naturally felt himself a distinct power, and therefore was sensible of personal responsibilities.

All that the public could do was once in several years
to elect representatives of their general opinions;
during the subsequent period the furtherance of these
opinions in any fresh circumstances that might arise,
was perforce left to the representatives, and any
failure on their part drew no excuse from the default
of their constituents to exercise a control which in
the nature of things could not be exercised.

But cheap newspapers, railways and telegraphs,
have altered these conditions of the representative
system. The constituencies are now larger, they
include a greater number of persons who take an
eager personal interest in the politics of the hour, and
that interest is fed by information as full and rapid as
that which reaches their representative himself. Thus
their control over him is now strong and immediate.
What he has said in the House over-night is known to
his constituents before he rises next morning. Perhaps
it is made the text of a leader in the London journals,
and if the matter is of importance he probably receives,
before he leaves his house for his committee-room, a
telegram from some leading supporter approving or
blaming the course he has taken. The following
morning at least brings him shoals of letters, and
the comments of the local papers, which disseminate
and unite public opinion. Thus the current of every
protracted debate is sensibly affected by the direct and

avowed external influence which in old times was so vehemently disclaimed and deprecated. And thus it comes to pass that the country at large is becoming the immediate ruler and director of its own affairs. We are passing out of the period of representative institutions, and are, through the strange operations of material discoveries, reverting to a state of things more nearly resembling that of the ancient republics, when all questions were submitted to the general vote of the people assembled in the forum or on the sacred mount. Only with this most essential and most hopeful difference, that they are now submitted not through the rosy or murky haze of oratorical eloquence, but through the calm judicial medium of printed documents, and with a full investigation, from every point of view, at the hands of the ablest men of the time, placed within reach of every one who has learnt to read.

But a state of things so novel, whatever may be its ultimate results, is attended in present practice with some grave inconveniences. Parliament considers itself divested of responsibility, while the nation does not yet feel itself inclined always to take the place of Parliament. For as yet it is only upon great and important questions that the nation is disposed to interpose its direct influence, and the exertion is then so great that it sinks unnerved after the struggle, and remains more than ordinarily apathetic to what it deems matters of less pressing consequence. The House of Commons, however, cannot or will not distinguish between these moods. Admitting that it has fallen from the position of a House of Representatives to that of a House of Delegates whenever the popular mind is seriously agitated, it refuses to incur trouble and responsibility in directing the affairs and controlling the expenditure of the nation, when it receives no positive impetus from without.

By the operation of this cause, the power of Government, which in one respect has been so greatly diminished, is in another as largely increased. In the general direction of the State, it has come to abdicate all its functions. It has surrendered them to the House of Commons, which again passes them on to the people at large. But when the people have determined upon any general line of policy, they do not attempt to superintend the details. This they expect their representatives in Parliament to do, but their representatives despise such humble duties, and since they cannot control, cease to affect to guide. So it happens that when Lord Palmerston, whose utmost astuteness is given to the detecting the popular under-current, accepts it with apparent frankness for his own, and gives it expression in plain and vigorous English, the public and Parliament leave him to adjust the channel in which it shall flow very much at his own pleasure. It does not seem worth the while of the whole nation to interfere in details, and its representatives here also apply the national confidence to excuse their own negligence. They allege as sufficient reason for a lavish and unchecked expenditure, that the public desired efficiency, and does not demur to expense. But the result is, and it is daily becoming more apparent, that either we shall have a very large amount of folly and jobbery in carrying into effect the national will, or the nation itself must undertake some supervision of details of the executive, as well as the determination of the great lines of policy. It must, in short, educate itself in details, else it will suffer from the combined evils of a democracy in power, coupled with an irresponsible aristocracy in administration.

There can be no doubt that these remarks are applicable to every department of the national expenditure. In every branch of the public service there is a necessary absence of the motive to economical supervision which exists in a private establishment, and there is a natural inclination to extend its duties and to increase its patronage. But in the civil service, there are at least some reasons to be given for augmented expenditure. The nation is expanding in population and in interests, and the regulation of its increased business involves increased labour. It also

takes on itself some cares which it did not formerly
provide for. A vote of nearly a million for education
is an entirely modern source of expense. Then there
are inspections of trades, a more efficient police, new
courts, and additional judges; besides the necessary
growth of the old public offices. And, therefore,
though there is beyond a doubt much waste and some
fraud in disposing of the nine millions a year which
is spent on the management of our civil affairs, it is
not in this quarter that we are to look for the main
explanation of the needless increase in our sum-total
of expenditure, or at least it is not here that we are
to expect to be able, by careful economy, to effect
any very material reduction.

But when we turn to the military and naval outlay,
we shall find, in its contrast with that of former, and
not remote, years, matter for the gravest reflection.
Our actual outlay on the army in 1864 was 14,382,672*l.*
On the navy, 10,898,253*l.* In 1846, under Sir Robert
Peel, the former department absorbed only 9,061,433*l.*,
the latter, 7,803,464*l.* On the two services, therefore, we now spend between seven and eight millions
a year more than we did eighteen years ago. Indeed,
the lapse of time since the alteration took place, is not
so great, for the sums voted were scarcely increased
till the commencement of the Crimean war, only eleven
years ago. Nor can it be said that the growth of the

nation justifies, as in the case of the civil service, this enormous increase. The defence of a country is not more difficult by reason of its being more populous; the reverse is rather the case. We have no material augmentation of colonial territory, we stand in no more peril of war than we did. The Syrian war, the Spanish marriages, the Canadian rebellion, the Chinese difficulties, the Affghanistan expedition, were all then recent embarrassments, quite as formidable as any European or colonial troubles we have to encounter at the present day.

To what reason, then, are we to attribute the increase of seven millions in annual warlike outlay within ten years ? To this only—that the Crimean war found our establishments in a position of disgraceful inefficiency of organization, that the country declared its will to be that they should be reformed, and that its rulers took advantage of that resolution to the extent not only of improving organization, which was all that was defective, but of augmenting numbers which were already large enough, if only made efficient. The nation desired to be secure, and declared that it would not grudge money for that object. Thereupon Lord Palmerston and the heads of the services declared that we ought to have more troops. Parliament declared that whether the number was too great or not, was an affair for which only the public and the

Government were responsible; and the public has not yet addressed itself to the consideration whether it has been wisely served, or only cleverly duped. For to answer that inquiry, details must be gone into, and it has not yet risen to the necessity of considering details. But nothing is more certain than that the seven millions a year of increased taxation for naval and military purposes, for which the Liberal party is responsible, will only be reduced when the public, after careful examination for itself, determines that it is excessive, and that the purposes it is designed to serve can be as amply attained by a judicious use of far smaller sums.

Nor is there any reason why the public should not examine and decide for itself on these questions. They involve only matters to which its own common sense is fully adequate. It must, indeed, turn to professional men for technical information. But when the information is given, the nation is perfectly competent to apply it to existing circumstances; and this is, indeed, the fundamental theory of our Constitution. It is Parliament that fixes the strength of the army and navy in each year. The Ministry, which proposes the strength of each force, consists of civilians only; nay, even the responsible heads of the services are civilians. The Secretary for War is not a soldier; the First Lord of the Admiralty is not a sailor. The Premier himself, who undertakes to arbitrate between all the conflicting schemes of military and naval defence, does not profess to have directed his mind to these matters for more than a dozen or fourteen years. Thus every one of the important questions on which expenditure turns is decided, in its final stages, by men with no professional education, but with only that amount of information which any member of the public may derive from the like sources of general knowledge which are open to all.

I propose, then, in the following chapters, to enter in some degree into the military and naval details which for these reasons it seems to be indispensable that the public should consider if it is to obtain any material reduction of taxation. But details must themselves be regarded as constituent parts of a whole. One of the most successful of the devices by which we have been persuaded into so great an increase of our force, has been the taking of each department separately, and presenting its claims without reference to its connection with other departments. Thus, when the naval force is under consideration, we are informed that the number of sailors voted—immensely increased as of late years it has been—is not too large to man our sea-going fleets, and yet leave enough to render the Channel secure. But when we come to the Army Estimates, the increase in them is justified by a picture drawn of the abolition, by steam, of the Channel as a defensive line, and the consequent necessity of relying now on our troops on shore, instead of, as formerly, on our sailors and ships. Then, when fortifications are the question, both navy and army are ruthlessly sacrificed, and we are called on to picture the consequences of our volunteers and raw militia encountering the enemy's regular forces in the open field on our own soil. Now it is undisputed that all these contingencies are proper to be considered. But it is at least equally clear that they should be considered in connection and not in isolation; that we should put ourselves into the position of an enemy who, meditating an attack, measures the total strength of the accumulated defences which he will have to overcome in order to attain his purpose; and that we shall only be misled if we listen solely to the arguments of either military, engineering, or naval authorities, or to the statements made in Parliament by their representatives at the periods when votes are demanded for their several services.

But above all it is desirable to avoid the error of mere theorizing on subjects of such moment. Assertions of opinion on either side of a question are valueless, unless they come from authority of irresistible weight. And it can scarcely be said that any such authority has spoken on the subject of the necessary strength of Great Britain, at least since the increased strength was resolved upon. In these circumstances the safest course is to resort to the great authorities of older days, and to apply to their opinions the modifications which any alteration in the strength of other nations, or the advance of science, has introduced into the problem. Happily we have now very full means of obtaining this guidance in our deliberations. We know the opinions of Napoleon on the prospects and necessary conditions of a successful invasion in 1805. We also know the opinions of the Duke of Wellington on what was necessary to our security in 1846. I shall first lay these before my readers, and compare the position in which we stood at both dates with our present position. I shall then endeavour to estimate the nature and influence of the subsequent alterations which new warlike appliances have introduced. When this is done we may be able to see more clearly what is really essential to our security, and what is the amount of excess in our present outlay beyond what is really required to maintain our safety and our just place among nations.

CHAPTER IV.

BRITISH ARMAMENTS FROM 1805 TO 1865.

A SOURCE of the fullest evidence we can desire regarding the opinion of Napoleon on the chances and conditions of a successful invasion of England, has fortunately been supplied to us within the last few years by the official publication of his *Correspondence*. In part, indeed, his letters and despatches had already been published in well-known works.[1] But the series contained in the ninth, tenth, and eleventh volumes of the *Correspondence* shows the unbroken chain of thought of the great Emperor on the project, as it grew day by day into shape beneath his eye. Here is evidence of the profound anxiety with which, even when, on the one hand, his life was threatened by conspiracy, and on the other he grasped, it might be thought, the summit of his ambition in the combined sceptres of

---

[1] DUMAS, *Précis des Evènements Militaires.* Paris, 1822. THIERS, *Histoire du Consulat et de l'Empire.*

8—2

France and Italy, he devoted himself to the scheme of humbling England by carrying the war within her own borders.   Nothing that could be done by a strategy embracing both hemispheres in its scope, by a personal attention which superintended the most minute detail of the fitting of a mortar-bed, or the teaching his troops to handle oars and boathooks, was omitted from the chances of success of the great design.   Therefore we have here the final, and it may be said almost the experimental, conclusion of the most daring and brilliant military genius of modern times on the possibility of invading England, and on the requirements of such an enterprise.   An outline of the schemes which Napoleon thus meditated and built up to all but completion, cannot but be in the highest degree instructive to us, for most persons will agree in considering that what that mighty commander considered essential, will still be so in weaker hands, and that what foiled him may, subject to due allowance for later modifications of science, be still safely accounted a fatal obstacle to the like plans.

The idea had long brooded in the First Consul's mind.   The disputes which arose relative to the execution of the treaty of 1802, a few months after it was signed, drew from him the frank declaration to our envoy in Paris, Lord Whitworth, that if war should again break out, he would raise his army to 480,000

men, and make a descent on England.[1] War was
declared in March, 1803, and instant preparations were
made for the invasion. By the summer of 1804,
25,000 men were got ready to sail from the Texel for
the east coast; as many more were to be despatched
from Brest to Ireland, on a guarantee by the Irish
refugees of a rising to at least an equal extent; and
120,000 infantry, with 30,000 cavalry and artillery,
were massed on the heights of Boulogne, where a
fleet of 2,000 armed vessels was prepared for their
transport. The arming of the transports was afterwards described by Napoleon as a feint, to render the
enemy careless as to the position of the French fleet,
which was the real force by which he intended to
protect his passage; but the anxiety he evinced to get
the heaviest guns and howitzers possible on board the
transports, shows clearly that his original idea was
certainly to make the attempt without first driving the
English from the Channel.[2] Reflection, however, convinced him of the danger of any such scheme, and the

---

[1] Letter of Lord Whitworth to Lord Hawkesbury, 21st February,
1803.

[2] See objections of Admiral Decrès to the possibility of a flotilla
passing the Channel without disorder. (THIERS, vol. v. p. 174.)
Napoleon's prevision of the effect of horizontal-shell firing against
ships was very remarkable; and had it been carried out by his
admirals, the issue of Trafalgar might have been reversed. See
NAPOLEON's *Correspondence*, 2nd July and 6th September, 1804.

invasion was accordingly deferred till the following season; while a profounder design for obtaining the command of the narrow seas for the requisite space of time was devised. In the end of the year, the whole of the fleets of Toulon, Rochefort, L'Orient, and Brest received orders to take troops on board, and to sail on an expedition for the capture of the British possessions in the West Indies. Sealed orders were, however, given them, by which the admirals were directed, on their arrival at their ostensible destination (without communicating the plan even to any of their captains, lest if a vessel were captured by the enemy, it should become known), instantly to return and rendez-vous off the coast of Spain, where, after raising the blockade of the Spanish fleet, they should together make for Brest and the Channel, leaving, it was expected, the English and the dreaded Nelson many days behind them in the West Indies.[1] In pursuance of this plan, the Rochefort fleet sailed under Admiral Missiessy on 11th January, 1805. The Toulon fleet, under Villeneuve, after one failure, escaped from Nelson on 30th March, and favoured by an easterly wind, effected a junction with the ships at Cadiz, and speedily

---

[1] *Correspondence*, 12th December, 1804; 4th and 16th January, and 23rd February, 1805. Treaty between France and Spain: DUMAS, *Précis*, vol. ix. p. 215.

made the West Indies. The English commander, on
4th April, learned, with bitter anxiety, its departure;
but for a few days was uncertain of its course, and was
then prevented by strong head gales from passing the
Straits of Gibraltar till the beginning of May.[1] The
Brest fleet was, however, less fortunate, and was unable
to escape its blockaders. New instructions were therefore sent to Villeneuve, desiring him without delay to
return to Ferrol, and after being reinforced by the
Spanish fleet, to proceed on to Brest, raise the blockade
of that port, and then hasten to Boulogne.[2]

A statement of the total English naval strength
was considered on the 25th May. Napoleon estimated
it at 72 sail of the line fit for service,—of which he
supposed 12 in the Indian seas and at Jamaica, 20 in
pursuit of Admiral Villeneuve, 22 off Brest, 10 off
Ferrol, 6 at Gibraltar, 3 at Torbay, and 3 at
Yarmouth. While he computed his own at 21 at
Brest, 15 at Cadiz, 12 at Ferrol, 1 at L'Orient, 5
with Admiral Missiessy (West Indies), 20 with Admiral Villeneuve,—in all 74, of which he considered
he might reunite 65 if favoured by some happy
chances. On 26th May, with a more detailed estimate before him, he came to the conclusion that

---

[1] NELSON's *Despatches*, vol. vi. pp. 407, 410.

[2] See *Correspondence*, 23rd and 30th April, 4th, 8th, and 25th
May, 1805.

the English could not bring more than 40 together.
Then came a time of intense anxiety. The only
comfort was, that the English were believed to be
in a state of equal alarm and incertitude.[1] The fleets
were due off Ferrol on 1st August: and a squadron
was meanwhile despatched to cruise off Ireland, and
further confuse the enemy,[2] while attempts were also
made to draw the English ships towards the defence
of the Thames by menacing an attack from the Texel.[3]
Fresh instructions were despatched on 16th and 26th
July, to await Villeneuve at Ferrol or Cadiz, in which
the utmost urgency was expressed. On the 18th,
Ganteaume was reproached with tardiness in issuing
from Brest. If he should find himself with 21 vessels
against the English 16, he was ordered instantly to
attack, and by every consideration of honour, patrio-
tism, and duty, he was pressed to make for Boulogne
with all speed. On 4th August Napoleon himself
reached Boulogne and reviewed 100,000 troops on
the sands. At length, on 8th and 11th August,
news was received of the returning fleet being off
Ferrol, and having there had, on 20th July, an
encounter with the enemy, in which two Spanish
ships were lost; but the English fleet was sup-

---

[1] *Correspondence*, 31st May and 9th June, 1805.
[2] *Correspondence*, 9th June, 1805.   [3] 27th June, 1805.

posed to have been dispersed. But on 13th August fresh orders of haste were despatched to Villeneuve, who lingered at Ferrol, his fleet of 18 French and 10 Spanish ships blockaded by—it was supposed— 13 to 18, or at most 23 English.[1] The Rochefort fleet failed, however, to join Villeneuve, and the Brest fleet remained motionless. Napoleon despatched couriers and telegraphic messages on 20th August in hottest impatience. The moments were slipping by fruitless. Villeneuve had in fact put to sea on 14th August. Once more, on 22nd August, Ganteaume was invoked " by his talents, his firmness, and his character, in circumstances so important. Set sail and come here. We shall have avenged six ages of insults and shame. Never have my soldiers on sea and land exposed their lives for so great an object." Villeneuve was implored, by a despatch sent to meet him at Brest, to hasten on to the Channel. "England is ours. We are all ready, everything is on board. Appear for twenty-four hours, and all is won." But Villeneuve and Ganteaume never did appear. The former retreated to Cadiz, the latter never sailed.[2] On 23rd August Napoleon writes calmly, that if the fleets appear, he will still make the expedition ; if by

---

[1] Its real numbers were 15 liners. JAMES's *Naval History*, vol. iv. p. 4.

[2] JAMES's *Naval History*, vol. iv. p. 17.

contrary winds or cowardice they were delayed, he would adjourn it to another year, and meanwhile would speedily be found in the heart of Germany with 300,000 men. He could not put his own spirit into his admirals, but he kept his word as regards himself, and the battle of Austerlitz on 2nd December was some recompence for the extinction of his hopes at Trafalgar on 20th October.

Such were the schemes which presented themselves to the mind of this great and sanguine genius. We see from this narrative that success, in his matured opinion, demanded for its elements—

1st. An invading army of not less than 120,000 infantry, 15,000 cavalry, and 15,000 artillery.

2nd. That such an army should be landed in one body, not in separate or successive detachments.

And in order to accomplish these indispensable conditions of *military* success, the following *naval* arrangements were necessary :—

1st. That sufficient transport should be provided to carry over the whole in one tide.

2nd. That his fleet should hold the mastery of the Channel for that time, so that no interruption could be offered by the English fleet.

3rd. That in order to secure such mastery, the enemy should be deceived by the pretence that the fleet was not to be employed, but merely the transports armed, and should also be drawn away by elaborate manœuvres, extending over several preceding months.

At once, therefore, by this transfer of our attention from the vague generalities of parliamentary eloquence to the actual conditions of serious war, we are saved from the necessity of considering one form of the question. When we find that Napoleon considered a descent of not less than 150,000 men, with due proportion of horses, to be the sole scheme promising success,—looking upon a diversion in Ireland as only practicable if to 25,000 French troops there should be guaranteed him a rising of an equal number of armed native insurgents,—we may upon his authority dismiss the idea of a number of isolated descents of ten, twenty, or thirty thousand men, as so contrary to the principles of war, that there is no need for considering how they should be met. What an enemy always chiefly desires, is the breaking up of the total opposing force into fragments, each of which may be successively crushed. It was this fatal error on the part of the Austrians which gave Napoleon his victories in the brilliant Italian campaigns over forces in all far superior in strength. When, therefore, Lord Palmerston tells us that such will be the tactics adopted by the French in attacking us, he offers a suggestion which we may be quite certain the French will not adopt, and which, therefore, we 'need not waste time in considering. The idea of an isolated descent of a small body, not as part of a combined invasion of England, but for the purpose only of attacking a town or dockyard, sacrificing itself to effect a limited amount of destruction, is a separate problem which we shall further on endeavour to solve. But for the present our concern is limited to the serious invasion of England with a view to its permanent occupation, or, at least, to the striking a fatal blow at its very heart.

Keeping, then, this great and suggestive example before our eyes, let us see how we stand now in relative power, compared to that of our neighbour, and in comparison with the relative strength of both in 1804-5. And for the full examination of this question, the following will be convenient, and I believe exhaustive divisions, under which it may be examined :—

1st. What is now the relative strength of the land forces of the two powers, as compared with what it was in 1804-5 ?

2nd. What is now the relative strength of the navies of the two powers, as compared at the same periods ?

3rd. What are the modifications of modern science, and how do they affect both parties ?

The two former of these questions will be considered in this chapter, the third in Chapter V.   We shall then be in a position to estimate, in Chapter VI., the systems and armaments proper for defence at the present day.

In reference to the first point, it will be certainly fair to recollect that we are now at peace, and were then at war. Giving our neighbours all possible credit for treachery, there is yet a large difference between the state of preparation possible on their part, and necessary on ours, in the two periods. With all the aid of modern appliances, no power has yet succeeded in setting a large army on foot, ready for offensive movements, without an obvious preparation of several months. The French did not precede us in the occupation of the Crimea; and, long as war had been brewing, and though it was declared on the 28th of March, and detachments were instantly poured into Turkey, it was the middle of May before they were ready to be moved forward into the presence of the enemy. In 1859, Napoleon III. spoke on New-year's Day the words which thrilled Europe with foreboding of war; but though the Austrians violated Piedmontese soil on the 23rd of April, it was the 10th of May before the French Emperor reached, with the vanguard of his army, the friendly port of the ally they came to succour. So, in considering the case of a landing to be made in force on a hostile shore, we may certainly consider that not less than several months of obvious warlike preparation would be indispensable for so vast an enterprise. In consequence, we may so far take into account the present state of peace, when comparing our position with that we occupied in 1804, as to reckon troops on a peace footing, but capable of within that time being made fit for service, as fairly computable against those whom, when each morning we looked over the sea for the enemy's flotilla, we kept in a state of instant preparation. So we may count our militia, although at present only drilled for a month in the year, as properly equal to the militia of 1804, which was steadily under arms from the time the war broke out. In an opposite direction there must be some difference allowed to exist between our present volunteers and those of 1804. In that year we had 420,000 volunteers enrolled. But of these Lord Castlereagh stated in the House of Commons, on the 9th of December, 1803, 120,000 had no muskets, and were not even fully armed with pikes. We cannot, therefore, consider them as exceeding 290,000 under arms, and they were admittedly in a very inferior state of discipline. But at present, though the numbers of our volunteers fall far short of these figures, they are all armed with rifle and bayonet, and Colonel M'Murdo three years ago [1] said that 48,000 would require little more drill to

---

[1] Ev. Volunteer Commission, 1862, answ. 4593.

enable them to take their place in a line of battle.
Moreover, he stated on the same occasion his conviction, from the aptitude for drill now displayed,
that a space of only 20 days would suffice to enable
a new recruit to take his place in a trained regiment,
while throughout the country there existed a vast
reserve of drilled men who had retired, but would
return on emergency. At present the actual total
of volunteers is 160,000, of whom 121,000 are effec-
tives.   Finally, it is necessary to explain that in
the regular army of 1804-5 there were included
20,747 men raised only for "limited service," that
is, raised under special Acts (afterwards superseded
by broader militia statutes) to serve for a limited
number of years, and within the United Kingdom alone.   These were, consequently, in fact,
militia; and I therefore transfer them to that head.
Subject to these explanations, the following table will
now exhibit at a glance our relative strength at a date
when we had been nearly two years at war, and
menaced with an invasion for which the utmost
resources of the French empire and the profoundest
combinations of her imperial ruler had been called
into play, and of which the issue was within a few
months of determination, compared with the present
period of peace, and of absence of any hostile preparation :—

Strength of Land Forces in 1805 and 1865.[1]

	1805.	1865.	Increase.
Regular troops at home and in colonies (excluding India)	117,969	141,518	23,549
Militia	110,556	128,969	18,413
Total paid troops (excluding India)	228,525	270,487	41,962

Thus the number of paid British troops available for defence at home and in our colonies is, in 1865, nearly 42,000 more than when Napoleon was menacing our shores, and war was raging all over the world. What the exact numbers are at home just

---

[1] The numbers for 1805 are taken from a return by the Adjutant-general to the House of Commons in that year, No. 14. Those for 1865 from the reduced estimates for the current year, 1865-6.

There were in 1805, 13,890 men of foreign and colonial corps, and in 1865, 7,546 of colonial corps, included in the above totals.

The militia strength in 1865 is that stated in the estimates for this year. The number actually under arms and trained in the year 1864 was 103,021.—Parliamentary papers, 1865, No. 181.

There are at present about 15,000 yeomanry, and an equal number of pensioners, besides local defence battalions and army reserve men, not included in the above figures. In the colonies there are above 150,000 militia and volunteers enrolled.

The number of British troops in India was, in 1864, 52,775 infantry; 13,901 artillery; and 6,005 cavalry: in all, 72,681. There were also 114,833 native troops; 154,435 native police, and 19,792 levies and contingents.—Parliamentary papers, 1865, No. 67.

Thus the paid troops of the British empire always under arms reach a total of 848,824. Including militia and volunteers (but not police), we have a military force of 817,793.

now it is impossible to state with minute accuracy, for there are no returns of the distribution of our forces in the colonies later than 1860-1. But it may be convenient to show what it was in that year, as compared with the year 1805.

Distribution of Land Forces at Home and in the Colonies.[1]

•	1805.	1860-1.
Ceylon	6,724	2,313
Mauritius	.....	2,042
West Indies, &c.	16,242	4,225
Bermuda	} 478 {	1,102
Bahamas		424
North America	4,194	4,329
Australia	490	1,250
New Zealand	.....	3,626
Falkland Isles	.....	35
St. Helena	.....	676
West Africa	344	1,001
Cape of Good Hope	.....	4,840
Corfu	.....	4,256
Malta	6,490	7,112
Gibraltar	4,586	5,913
Total in Colonies (excluding India)	39,543	43,144
Regular Troops in United Kingdom.	78,426	100,218
Total Regular Troops at Home and Abroad	117,969	143,362

We have at present, however, a larger force in the colonies than in 1860. Probably our troops in North

---

[1] The strength and distribution of the regular army for 1805 are taken from the return of that year before referred to. Those for 1860-1 show the present normal colonial distribution, and are taken from the appendix to the report of the committee on colonial military expenditure in 1861.

America and the West Indian stations may be estimated at 22,000 men, and those actually in New
Zealand at 10,000. On the other hand we have
now abandoned Corfu, and five regiments are under
orders to return from New Zealand. Making these
alterations in the colonial force of 1860, and taking
the estimated total of the present year, we shall not
be greatly in error in stating the number of regular
troops in the colonies at about 58,000, leaving at home
85,518. These figures are confirmed to a certain
extent by the estimates of the current year, which
state the infantry of the line (and guards) at home
as amounting to 47,452; in the colonies, to 39,111.
There are further 6,360 infantry of the Indian depôts
at home, while 12,144 cavalry, 20,812 artillery, 4,692
engineers, 1,822 military train, besides the auxiliary
services, are to be apportioned between the home and
colonial stations. Thus then we have—

Strength of Regular Army and Militia at Home and in Colonies.

	1805	1865	Increase.
Regular troops at home	78,426	83,518	5,074
Militia at home	110,556	128,969	18,413
Total forces at home	188,982	212,487	23,505
Regular troops in colonies	39,543	58,000	18,457
Total regular and militia force at home and in colonies (excluding India)	228,525	270,487	41,964

These results are, it must be admitted, sufficiently startling. They show that we are now, according to official returns, maintaining a force of 5,000 regulars in this kingdom, and of 18,000 regulars in our colonies (exclusive in both cases of India), beyond what we considered, and found, sufficient for our security when the French eagles were hovering in the air overhead, poising themselves for their swoop. In another view they show that, were we still to retain the same force of regulars and militia together that we had in 1805 in these islands, we might nevertheless despatch to-morrow an expedition of 23,000 men, without recruiting a man beyond our present strength, and which would be over and above the war establishments which we at present have in Canada and New Zealand. Thus, even if on account of the increase in our colonial posses-sions, we leave the augmented force in the colonies out of view, it is obvious that we are, and have been for some years, without adverting to it, maintaining a most powerful permanent war establishment. For even if we take the militia only at its strength as actually trained last year, we must remember that we have now 121,000 volunteers, whom we are entitled to count as equal to them, and that these would bring up our total strength to 100,000 more men than stated in the table.

The sole numerical difference in favour of 1805, is

to be found in the strength of the volunteers. I have already adverted to the composition and efficiency of this branch of the service in 1805; and we may perhaps reasonably count that the 160,000 volunteers we have now, are not much less in value than the 400,000, in part pikemen, of our fathers. But the difference is, in truth, little material; for beyond a doubt it would instantly disappear were real danger of attack to arrive. And it is chiefly interesting as showing that in the opinion of the country such danger does not exist, although we are content to let our chiefs keep on foot a regular army so much exceeding our requirements at home, even if war were declared.

In the materials of war our present superiority is not less decisive, though less easily shown by figures. But it may be conceived by remembering that we now have rifles in room of muskets, Armstrong 100lb. guns in place of 48-pounders,[1] 20,812 artillerymen instead of 15,156,[2] and 4,692 engineers instead of 903. That our arsenals are filled with all manner of supplies needful for the service of our weapons, is admitted on all sides.[3] The effect of such new engines in war will

---

[1] 1,190 Armstrong guns, of which 405 were 100-pounders, had been issued for service on 1st March, 1862. 745 were in store.—(Report of Ordnance Committee, 1862. Appendix, p. 218.

[2] Parliamentary papers, 1859; Sess. 2, No. 88.

[3] Returns of our guns in store were made to the Defence Commission of 1860, but not printed.—(Report, p. xxi.) See also speech of Sir G. Lewis, 9th March, 1863.

come properly under our view in another place; all that is necessary here is to recall the fact that in them we have at least kept pace with the times, and outstripped our possible enemies.

Nor let it be said that we must now keep a large force on foot, because our neighbours maintain a larger army. We have seen that Napoleon himself fixed the number at 480,000 men ; but by August, 1805, this was surpassed, and Sir A. Alison gives the detailed strength, amounting in all to 590,000 regulars, besides 100,000 coast-guards.[1] In 1865, the number is 400,000. But of that number, 13,000 are now in Rome, 30,000 in Mexico, and 80,000 in Algiers, leaving only 276,000 for France and her other colonies.[2] It is true that there is a reserve of 214,000 men, who may on emergency be recalled to the service, and that there are National Guards. But there are veterans also in England ready on a like emergency, as well as volunteers ; and it is therefore futile to set what one country might do against what the other is actually doing.

The year 1804-5, which we have thus considered, is unquestionably the crucial test of any question of invasion or of home defence, and it was so treated by

---

[1] Vol. vi. p. 644.
[2] Report on the Budget in the Corps Législatif, 1865.

the Duke of Wellington in his famous letter of 1847. But it may confirm the results drawn from it, if we glance at the experience of subsequent years, and review the forces we sent from home to wage a bloody war against an army of 300,000 French soldiers in Spain, while still reserving enough to meet any attack on our shores.   These facts must, however, be obtained from sources less simple than the blue-books which have hitherto furnished our data; for in the official military returns, all troops not on colonial are classed as being on home service, and hence there is no clue, except in historical works, to ascertain how many were sent to Spain, and how many retained in Great Britain.

The year 1808 saw our first attempts to carry the war into the Peninsula, the first victory of Wellington at Vimiera (21st August, 1808), the advance of Sir John Moore into Spain, and his retreat before Napoleon in person,—a retreat crowned by the glorious battle of Corunna, fought on 16th January, 1809.   In 1808, to enable us to make these exertions, we had an army at home and in the colonies (excluding India) of 235,442 regulars.[1]   Of these, about 72,000 were in the colonies. Our total of embodied militia was 79,126.   Consequently we had then an army of regulars and militia,

---

[1] Parliamentary papers, 1859; Sess. 2, No. 88.

of only 242,000 men for home duty and military expeditions, or only 30,000 more than in this present year. Yet out of this force we despatched 48,341 men to Spain and Portugal between 12th July and 31st December ;[1] we had 10,000 men operating in Sicily ; and the Duke of York, Commander-in-Chief, declared his ability to send four more battalions of infantry, four regiments of cavalry, and two brigades of Guards, or about 8,000 men more, to Spain.[2] On the whole, therefore, it appears that in that year of bloody European war, with Wellington in command of our armies, and Napoleon facing us across the Channel, and with the combined powers of Europe in alliance with him, we considered, and proved ourselves able to defend our shores, and to supply the constant drain of a continental war, by retaining a force at home less by 46,000 men than that which we now keep at home for our safety. Next year, out of a force of regulars only 5,000 men greater, we had 35,000 in Spain, 41,000 at Walcheren, and 10,000 in Sicily—in all, 86,000 men—leaving at home only 90,000. Now-a-days, with Lord Palmerston instead of Wellington, we are told that 90,000 regulars and 128,000 militia, and

---

[1] NAPIER's *Peninsular War*, vol. i. appendix, p. 497.

[2] These were actually embarked, but were landed on news arriving of Sir J. Moore s retreat. Our force at Vimiera was 19,000.— See *Napier*, p. 500, and speech of Mr. Canning, 24th February, 1809.

121,000 effective volunteers ready, are requisite as a standing force in peace, for " defence, not defiance." Surely either there is here some enormous self-deception, or our spirit is less than that of our forefathers in a ratio even greater than the difference between the military genius of Lord Palmerston and the Duke of Wellington.

Nor was this a solitary exertion at the very commencement of the war. Our force only slowly increased, by not more than 5,000 men a year down to the date of the supreme struggle in 1813-14, when it rose to a total of about 270,000 regulars, of which 70,000 were still in the colonies. Thus in 1812, it consisted of only 250,000 regulars, and of 88,000 militia.[1] Yet 1812 was the year of Badajos and Salamanca, and the expulsion of the French from Madrid.

If, finally, we would desire to confirm these figures by the teaching of the most cautious and enlarged experience,—an experience gained in camps, and not at the desk of the War Office,—we have only to turn to the opinions of the great Duke himself. On 9th January, 1847, in the ripe prudence of very advanced years, and struck by the aid given to invasion by the new application of steam to naval propulsion,—an influence which subsequent reflection and actual trial

---

[1] Parliamentary papers, 1859; Sess. 2, No. 88.

have proved to have been then overrated,—the aged
leader penned his celebrated letter of warning addressed
to Sir John Burgoyne. In this letter, after painting
in strong terms our danger, with the force then
existing in the British Islands, he goes on to say :—
" The measure upon which I have earnestly en-
treated different administrations to decide, which is
constitutional, and has been invariably adopted in
time of peace for the last eighty years, is to raise,
embody, organize, and discipline the militia of the
same numbers for each of the three kingdoms united
as during the late war. This would give a mass of
organized force amounting to about 150,000 men,
which we might immediately set to work to discipline.
This alone would enable us to establish the strength
of the army. This, with an augmentation of the force
of the regular army, which would not cost 400,000*l*.,
would put the country on its legs in respect to personal
force, and I would engage for its defence, old as I am.

" I shall be deemed foolhardy in engaging for the
defence of the empire with an army composed of such
a force of militia. It may be so. I confess it, I
should infinitely prefer, and should feel greater confidence in an army of regular troops. But I know
I shall not have these. I may have the others ; and
if an addition is made to the regular army of a force
which will cost 400,000*l*. a year, there would be a

sufficient disciplined force in the field to enable him who should command to defend the country."

Now, on 1st January, 1847, there were in the United Kingdom 67,000 men, including artillery and engineers, and also including two regiments on their passage home, but not yet arrived.[1] The Duke desired an increase to this of regulars, costing 400,000*l*. At the present rate of computation this would only give 4,000 men ; but in the Peninsular war men were reckoned to cost only 40*l*. a-head, and we may therefore grant that the Duke wanted 10,000 additional, or a total of 77,000 regulars. To these he desired to add militia sufficient to bring the combined total up to 150,000 men, or about 73,000 militia, which, as he correctly observes, was about the average strength of the militia during the French war.[2] And although he speaks of this militia being *embodied*, it is plain he does not mean this in its technical sense—of being called out for permanent service ; for in that case they would be quite equal to the regulars, and would inspire him with equal confidence, while he also speaks of them as being the force " invariably adopted in time

---

[1] Parliamentary papers, 1849, No. 56, and for artillery and engineers, 1859, Sess. 2, No. 58.

[2] Parliamentary papers, 1859, Sess. 2, No. 88. This fact shows the error Mr. Gleig has fallen into in his Life of the Duke (last edition), where he supposes that the Duke desired the militia alone to be 150,000 strong, or double its average strength during the war !

of peace for the last eighty years," and it was only in time of war that they were embodied. He meant, therefore, that they should be exactly as we now have them —enrolled and trained for a few weeks every year.

Having thus ascertained the Duke's meaning, let us compare what we have now on foot with what he declared would be efficient :—

	Regulars	Militia actually Trained.	Volunteers ready for Service.	Volunteers in Reserve.	Total.
Total home force when the Duke wrote	67,000	None.	None.	None.	67,000
Total home force which he desired to have	77,000	73,000	None.	None.	150,000
Total home force now maintained	83,500	103,021	121,000	40,000	347,521

The total now being more than *five* times what existed when he wrote, and greatly more than double what he asked for as sufficient; the regular troops and militia actually trained within the kingdom being 35,000 men above the strength he thought sufficient.

It would be idle to comment upon the result of the figures and authorities thus adduced. If Napoleon, with two years of preparation, and in the prime of his career, while we had as yet only average generals to oppose to him, considered that 150,000 men must be landed to avail against the 188,000 we then maintained in arms at home; and if our own Duke, desiring to leave a legacy of safety to his country, besought it to keep a disciplined force of 150,000 men ready to be called on for service within its shores, what shall we think of our present position with 347,000 disciplined troops maintained to be absolutely necessary on the theory of defence alone?

No doubt we ought to consider that the whole of this force is not available for foreign service. But at least the 84,000 regulars are, for their places could be instantly supplied by the 103,000 militia trained last year. Thus, one of the military journals last year estimated that if war was declared in favour of Denmark, we could the next week despatch an army of 48,000 regulars to the Baltic, even before the militia were called out. And we must remember that the moment a popular war breaks out, recruiting in the militia, and volunteering from the militia into the line, proceeds at a very rapid rate.

We may now pass to a brief review of the second branch of the subject,—a review of the strength of our navy during the period of a real threat of invasion, compared with what it is now.

Here we cannot use with equal advantage and conclusiveness the figures given in official statements; for when applied to the ships of 1804 and of 1863, the numbers mean a very different thing. The ship of the line of 1804 averaged only 2,000 tons; many of our frigates now exceed that size. Our ships of the line range from 3,000 to 4,000 tons; and some of the new iron-clads, in technical description only corvettes, are above 6,000 tons. On the other hand, the weight of broadside has not proportionately increased. In the beginning of the century, after 24 lb. and 32 lb. carronades were substituted for the long 9-pounders, the broadside (single) of a 100-gun ship was about 1,160 lbs. After the introduction of 68-pounders in 1839, the weight of broadside of a 120 gun ship was 2,136 lbs ?[1] The *Warrior*, however, armed with twenty-eight 68-pounders, and twelve Armstrong 100-pounders, throws a broadside of no more than 1,612 lbs. The numbers, however, whatever their worth, are these. In 1804, Lord Castlereagh stated our actual strength to be 469 vessels of war, and 800 vessels of the coast flotilla. These last being small, and hastily fitted up from fishing boats, &c., we may assume that in a similar emergency they would be forthcoming to at least an equal extent, and so leave them out of count. In the present year, our navy consists of 540 vessels, of which 471 are steam, and only 69 sailing vessels.

The only true comparative test is, however, to take the number of men voted, remembering only that

---

[1] Report of Committee on Ordnance, 1849, p. 896, Appendix.

by the use of steam, and of fewer, though heavier
guns, we now require fewer men, on board each
ship, and that therefore the same number gives now
a preponderance of force.[1]   In 1804, there were
100,000 seamen and marines voted;   in 1811,
130,000; while this year there are 69,000 voted,
with 16,000 of the new Naval Reserve, and 8,000
coast volunteers, who may be accounted a naval
militia, bringing up our strength to within 7,000
of the same as when we were in a death-struggle
with France and Spain.[2]   In the comparative strength
we are able to send to sea, it will be remembered
that in 1804-5 our fleets were generally below the
numbers of the enemy they engaged; that Napoleon
computed his own total at 86, and the British at only
72; that Nelson, with every exertion, could only
gather 37 ships to meet 38 of the combined fleets at

---

[1] The crew of a 100-gun ship was 900 men; of the *Warrior* and
other largest iron-clads it is 704.   The crew of the *Royal Sovereign*,
turret-ship, is only 200 men.

[2] The figures for England are from a return to the House of
Commons, 1865, No. 51 ; for France, from the official state for 1862,
transmitted by our Ambassador (Parliamentary papers, 1862, No. 177.)
I have not been able to obtain later official figures for vessels or
men in France, but it is well known that there has been no material
increase in either, and in particular, no new iron-clads have been since
commenced. In the numbers for both countries, mortar vessels or floating batteries are not included in the number of armour-plated vessels.

Trafalgar. At the present day the account stands thus, including vessels afloat and building :—

	Armour-plated.	Liners. Screw.	Frigates. Screw.	Frigates. Paddle.	Corvettes. Screw.	Corvettes. Paddle.	Blockships. Screw.	Other Steam-Ships.	Total Steam.	Total Sailing.
England	30	58	38	6	27	—	8	304	471	69
France	16	37	29	18	7	9	—	244	360	122

The number of men voted for the French marine in 1862-3 (including an extra vote of 15,885 men on account of the Mexican and Cochin-China expeditions) was, according to the same authority, 46,381 on shore and afloat, against our 69,000 for this year.

Modern scientific applications have, however, so far modified the capabilities of ships as engines of war, that we must here notice their bearing on the practical computation of the numbers available on both sides. We have seen that Napoleon urged upon his admirals the use of horizontal shell-firing; but the idea apparently was in advance of the age, for fifty years of war and peace passed away before it was put to real proof. At Sinope, however, the Russians adopted it against the Turkish fleet with tremendous effect, though using only shells with ordinary time fuses (far inferior to the percussion shells now employed); and in our attacks on Sebastopol it was

proved that even British crews could not be brought
to face a second time the havoc wrought by one or
two of these missiles.   These results were only confirmed at Hampton Roads, when the Merrimac, with
one or two rounds of shell, converted the Cumberland
and Congress into helpless, burning charnel-houses.
Meantime, however, it had long been known by
experiments in this country, though with guilty
supineness they were concealed by Government from
1850 to 1858, that iron plates, even of half-an-inch
in thickness, are impervious to cast iron spherical
shell, causing it to shatter to pieces on striking,
without the powder having time to explode.   And at
Kinburn, the French Emperor proved that iron-clad
batteries could without injury sustain a fire which
would be utterly destructive to wooden vessels.   He
pursued the conclusions thus arrived at, and finally,
in 1858, ordered the construction of four iron-plated
frigates, *La Gloire*, *L'Invincible*, *La Normandie*, and
La Couronne.   The first three are on wood frames,
the latter is iron throughout.   They are about 255
feet in length, 55 feet beam, and 25 feet load
draught, carrying 34 rifled 50-pounders (throwing
a bolt of 100 lbs.) on a single protected deck,
with two more on an upper deck unprotected.
Their engines are of 900 horse power, and the
crew 570 men.   All these are at sea, and have

been found successful; but the ports being only about six feet above the water when at load draught, they are placed at a certain disadvantage in bad weather. Subsequently two others, the *Solferino* and *Magenta*, were ordered, which have now been completed. They are armed with a "spur," projecting from the bow, carry their guns in two tiers in the centre of the ship, and the lower ports are eight feet from the water-line. Their length is 288 feet; breadth, 56½ feet; draught, 26 feet; and horse-power, 1,000. In the Atlantic they have made seven knots under sail alone; the *Solferino* has steamed 14 knots an hour, the *Gloire*, 13·5. In November, 1860, ten more were ordered, some of which are now ready, and others nearly ready for sea. They are of the *Gloire* type, and all of wood frames, except the *Héroine*, which is of iron: but the thickness of the plates has been increased from the 3½ to 4 inches of the *Gloire*, to 4½ to 6 inches.[1] All the other iron-plated vessels under construction in France at the present moment are merely floating batteries for harbour defence.

Our own armour fleet, though more tardily commenced, now stands as in the table on next page :—

---

[1] See article in *Revue Contemporaine*, May, 1862, by M. Boinvilliers, one of the commissioners on the navy of France. Also articles in the *Revue des deux Mondes*, June, 1862, and January 1, 1864, by M. Xavier Raymond. The last contains very interesting details of the trials of the first built iron-clads at sea, in comparison with crack vessels of the old wooden navy.

Names.	Guns.	Tons.	Horse Power.	Load Draught.		Length.		Breadth.	
Afloat— *Iron Hulls.*				Ft.	In.	Ft.	In.	Ft.	In.
Minotaur	26	6,621	1,350	25	8	400	0	59	3½
Achilles	20	6,079	1,250	26	3½	380	0	58	3½
Black Prince	41	6,109	1,250	26	9	380	2	58	4
Warrior	40	6,109	1,250	26	3½	380	2	58	4
Hector	24	4,089	800	24	8	280	2	56	5
Valiant	34	4,063	800	24	8	280	0	56	3
Defence	18	3,720	600	24	11	280	0	54	2
Resistance	18	3,710	600	24	10	280	0	54	1
Wood Hulls.									
Caledonia	35	4,125	1,000	25	10½	273	0	59	2
Ocean	35	4,047	1,000	25	10½	273	1	58	5
Prince Consort	35	4,045	1,000	25	10½	273	1	58	5
Royal Alfred	35	4,045	800	25	10½	273	0	58	5
Royal Oak	35	4,056	800	25	10½	273	0	58	6
Building— *Iron Hulls.*									
Agincourt	26	6,621	1,350	25	8	400	0	—	
Northumberland	26	6,621	1,350	25	8	400	0	59	3½
Mr. Reed's *Afloat—* *Iron Hull.*									
Bellerophon	12	4,246	1,000	26	0	300	0	56	0
Wood Hulls.									
Lord Clyde	24	4,067	1,000	26	0	280	0	58	0
Lord Warden	24	4,067	1,000	26	0	280	0	58	0
Zealous	16	3,716	800	25	3	252	0	58	7
Pallas	6	2,372	600	24	0	225	0	50	0
Research	4	1,253	200	14	0	195	0	38	6
Enterprise	4	993	160	14	4½	180	0	36	0
Building (Wood).									
Favourite	8	2,186	400	20	5	225	0	46	9
Corvette (unnamed) at Pembroke	8	2,969	600	—		—		—	
Viper	4	737	160	10	6	160	0	32	0
Vixen	4	754	160	10	9	160	0	32	5
Turret— *Afloat.*									
Royal Sovereign (old vessel converted)	5	3,963	800	22	11	240	7	62	0½
Scorpion } Wyvern }	4	1,890	350	—		225	0	42	6
Building. Prince Albert (*Iron*)	4	2,529	500	20	0	240	0	48	0

Some of the vessels above classed as afloat, are not completed, but it has been stated that all comprised in this table will be finished this year, except the Prince Albert and the Pembroke corvette.

Two points will strike the reader in looking over the preceding table.   The first is the very much greater size and power of many of our vessels beyond that of any of the French—not for all purposes an advantage—but of which the objection is more than balanced by the number of experiments we have in hand in the construction of small vessels on various plans.   The second is the predominance of iron over wood in the construction, the former beyond doubt a better material, and one in which this country has an unquestionable advantage over any other.   As all the iron-hulled ships in the table (except Mr. Reed's) have been built in private yards, the new fleet may be said to represent what the country can effect over and above the Admiralty establishments, a producing power, it need hardly be observed, of incalculable value in the emergencies of war.

It is, however, impossible not to advert, in connection with the vessels now under construction, to the conduct of the Admiralty in awarding so marked a preference to the system of Mr. Reed, and displaying so marked a disfavour to the turret principles of Captain Cowper Coles.   Mr. Reed has brought to his office no prestige of success, for prior to his appointment as Chief Constructor of the Navy, in 1862, he had never built a ship.   On the other hand the turret system has been within the last two years proved in actual war with most remarkable success by both Denmark and America, and in consequence several of the European powers have largely adopted it. Its working was experimentally tried in this country so far back as the summer of 1861, and was found to possess several eminent advantages. And last year the Royal Sovereign, during a trial cruise in the channel, displayed qualities which satisfied her commander that the turret system was for fighting and manœuvring superior to any other, and that his vessel could sink any other of our iron-clad fleet. Yet, in spite of this concurrence of testimony in favour of the sole system which has enabled guns of the greatest weight to be worked on board ships of war, the Admiralty has not yet ordered one sea-going vessel to be built on this plan. The Scorpion and Wyvern were purchased from Mr. Laird, having been built by him for the Confederates, and are now not to be rigged for sea. It appears, also, that the only new turret vessel ordered by the Admiralty (the Prince Albert) has not yet been even launched, though in the same time three or four of Mr. Reed's vessels have been completed, and besides those now in construction several have been ordered to be commenced. This instance of personal favouritism and official jealousy, displayed at so tremendous a peril to the country, is only one instance of the necessity,

on which I have insisted, of the public acquainting
itself sufficiently with the details of the national
business to be able to enforce at once economy and
honourable and judicious management.

But whatever exception may be taken to the
errors and faults of the Admiralty administration, it
is certain that the lavish outlay which the nation
has during the last five years enabled it to make
has now furnished a fleet of iron-clads which, as a
whole, is far more powerful than any which could
be directed against us. As compared with France,
our strength in this main department may be fairly
reckoned as double. Nor while France remains so
little disposed to extend her naval power as she has
shown herself for the last two or three years, is there
excuse for more than a very moderate expenditure
on our part, if only it is wisely laid out.

Thus, then, there is evidence that at sea our
supremacy is maintained as it was before. And so,
in comparing our armaments during war with those
of this time of peace, and in counting up our strength
in order to measure our safety, we find that the
enormous increase of our force on shore is not justified
by any new deficiency at sea, but is rather supported
by an aggregate naval preponderance exceeding what
we have before found enough to rely on for security.

CHAPTER V.

MODERN CONDITIONS OF NATIONAL DEFENCE.

IN the last chapter we passed in review our strength by sea and land at present, in comparison firstly, with what it was in seasons of imminent attack by the most powerful combinations, and secondly, with the existing amount of force which could be directed against us. We ascertained by this conclusive test, that our armaments are far beyond our actual need in time of peace, if there are no circumstances in modern war to render them comparatively less powerful than they were sixty or even twenty years ago. But those who have persuaded the country into this expenditure tell us that there are such circumstances, and that in presence of them we must for our safety keep up larger forces and build greater fortifications than formerly were proved sufficient. It is necessary, therefore, to examine in what such circumstances consist. They fall under three heads; the first regards motive power at sea, by the introduction of steam propulsion; the second, the improvement of weapons for use by sea and land; the third, mobility on land by the use and extension of railways.

In this inquiry we have no longer experience to resort to as a guide, nor is it possible to cite authorities whose names carry unanswerable conviction.   The questions to be solved are in their nature new, and can only be decided by reasoning on principle and by the application of known facts and rules to cases that have not yet occurred in practice.   It follows necessarily that there is considerable difference of opinion upon them amongst professional men.   Yet in these circumstances the public must ultimately determine, and it can only do so by considering the arguments addressed to it by its rival instructors.   As one of the public, therefore, I have endeavoured to obtain the fullest information of what is advanced on both sides, and if in laying before the reader in the following pages the views which have appeared to me the soundest, and supported by the greatest weight of naval and military authority, I do not cite references to published opinions on every point, I trust it will be understood that I have not presumed to offer any suggestion save such as I have found sanctioned by the judgment of those best qualified by education and experience to form an opinion.

The introduction of steam as a propelling power of ships has been regarded by some persons as wholly revolutionizing all previous systems of defence. The Duke of Wellington adopted this idea; but Lord Palmerston above all others has maintained that the new system has " bridged the Channel "—a notion which Sir Robert Peel vigorously repudiated on its being first mooted, but which, in 1860, his lordship, with a curious lapse of memory, declared Sir Robert Peel to have originated and maintained.[1] The Report of the Defence Commission of 1860 adopted, though with less positiveness, the Premier's idea. It suggested that not merely might a body of troops be transported across the Channel by aid of steam with an ease and certainty before impossible, but that blockades are now become impracticable; that the facility with which foreign fleets could combine their movements would render absolutely indispensable the maintenance on our part of a fleet greatly larger than was formerly requisite; and that the supremacy of British fleets and vessels would be less than formerly, because of the diminution of the value of superior seamanship. Endorsed by such authority (for although these opinions are generally rather those of landsmen than of sailors, the Commission numbered

---

[1] Cobden. *The Three Panics*, p. 111. See also the debate on the Fortifications Bill, 7th July, 1863.

two naval officers, Admiral Elliott and Captain Key, among its members), such suggestions call for careful examination.

It must, of course, be admitted that steam propulsion renders greatly easier the sea transport of an army, if we are to consider only the elements as warring against its progress. By this wonderful application of nátural laws man has in fact vanquished nature, and every day brings proof of the completeness of his victory. But the cases in which as yet the new propelling power has been applied in war have not been such as to afford any proof of its relative value; for they have occurred when there were no enemies but those of nature to contend with. Our expeditions to the Crimea and the Baltic, those of the French to Italy, of the Americans to the Virginian peninsula and other points of the Confederate coast, have taken place in seas where no enemy dared to show, and the landings have been effected either in friendly ports or on shores which the enemy did not profess to defend. No conclusion, therefore, can be drawn from such expeditions as to what might be the result if the transports were either to be encountered in mid-passage by a hostile fleet, or if the landing of the troops were to be seriously disputed by a nation standing on the defence. We must not therefore assume as proved, either by experience or reason, that steam, which has bridged the Channel to tourists, has also bridged it to armed invaders; and we must, in default of experiments, examine how its use would affect the various operations necessary to make such an attempt successful.

The first inquiry, then, is necessarily not that of the landing on our shores, nor even that of security of passage, but whether the fleet of transports would now have more facility in putting to sea than it had in former days. In so far as being now less dependent than formerly on a fair wind and smooth water, the facility will be increased. But then it is to be kept in view that we should still pursue the same tactics as formerly, and seek either to destroy the transports before they put to sea, or at any rate to blockade them in the enemy's ports. And though the question has been greatly debated among naval officers, there seems to be a preponderance of opinion among them that steam will give the principal advantage not to the blockaded, but to the blockading force. The opposite opinion is founded upon the idea that the blockading ships would speedily exhaust their coal, while the blockaded would at all times be ready to sally forth with full supplies on board, and that, in the event of a dark and stormy night, the blockading ships might be passed without discovery. It must, however, be remembered that the consumption of coal by steamers when stationary is very trifling, and the vessels would keep their stations off the port by sailing rather than by steaming; indeed, the fires would be banked up, and kept barely alight. Their supplies would therefore last a long time; and by having coal-tenders always in attendance on the fleet, advantage might be taken of every interval of calm weather for keeping the coal-boxes constantly filled. As to the possibility of escape in storm and darkness, that is obviously dependent on the number of the blockading fleet; for it is unquestionable, that if it were sufficiently numerous, no enemy would dare attempt to break their line, and certainly could not effect it in force without being discovered. But, at least, it is abundantly clear that such a possibility, if it exists, is not one of which a fleet of transports, conveying a large army, could avail themselves; and we may therefore dismiss it from our thoughts in any question as to the invasion of England. The experience of "running the blockade" of Charleston, Wilmington, and other ports by single merchantmen, or of the escape of the *Alabama* and others from neutral harbours, which blockading vessels could not approach except under the penalty of twenty-four hours' detention, cannot be considered as at all illustrating the power of a fleet of transports to escape a blockading squadron.

On the other hand, it has been argued, that as

the real difficulty in maintaining a blockade arises from the risk of a gale blowing the ships off the station,[1] and so enabling the enemy to run out before they can return, the use of steam, which would in general prevent this result, would be far more in favour of the blockaders. Further, while the blockaded are confined to their port, steam would enable the enemy's ships to take up many positions in which they could not have ventured to lie, had they been exposed to the risks of currents, tides, or changes of the wind, with only their sails to rely on. It is also important to observe, that steam, aided by telegraphy, will henceforth make impossible such ruses as we have seen were put in practice by Napoleon to decoy the English fleets from their stations. Our first operation in war (even if it be not executed in peace) will be to lay down a submarine electric cable from Alderney to Plymouth, and probably between the Scilly Islands and Gibraltar. The Toulon fleet cannot then pass the Straits, nor the Cherbourg fleet put to sea, without instant notice being given at once to our stations at Malta, Gibraltar, and at home, and the sailing of a fleet to intercept them will be almost

---

[1] The fleet of Admiral Cornwallis, blockading Brest, was thus dispersed on 25th December, 1803, and driven to take refuge at Plymouth, and the blockade was not re-established till 16th January, 1804.

simultaneous with their own departure. Calms and
head winds will not again detain our future Nelsons
a full month in the pursuit between Toulon and
Gibraltar. But even without telegraphic intelligence,
it will be easy for this country, by its innumerable fast
ocean-going steamers, to keep a close watch upon
every movement of an enemy, to dog as it were his
footsteps, and to send rapid information of the development of all his plans. For it must be kept in view
that the French ships were, as a rule, always faster
sailers than ours; so that it was only the lucky capture
of the French brig *Curieux* that enabled Nelson to send
from the West Indies intelligence of the return of the
French fleet in time to allow them to be intercepted
off Ferrol. But steam has reversed our position in
this respect, while its introduction has made mercantile
ships even more useful (from their speed, light draught,
and large stowage for coal) as *watching* vessels than
men-of-war are, so that they are now able to attend,
with assured safety, the movements of an enemy's
armed ships at any required distance. Therefore the
introduction of steam will not merely free our navy
from the anxious and harassing duty of furnishing
convoys to mercantile vessels, but will allow us to
select, from our enormous mercantile marine, vessels
fit to perform those important services, which formerly
could only be entrusted, with far less advantage, to
fighting ships.

As regards, then, the blockading of an enemy's forts, and the watching of his movements, steam, in truth, gives us advantages greater than it confers on him. And, indeed, it would be strange if this potent auxiliary should not be found to give most advantage to that party which can make most use of it. When none but sailing ships ploughed the sea, we had many rivals in that element, in peace as well as in war. The French, the Dutch, the Danes, the Russians, the North Americans, all fairly competed with us. But with steam we have swept them from every sea. The American lines of steamers have long ceased to run against our own. A line from the Elbe, and one or two from Havre, to America, a few short lines in the Mediterranean, are all that the European continent can show to match the fleets which day after day we send from the Clyde, the Mersey, the Thames, and from Southampton, to traverse every part of the globe. Strange, indeed, would it be if the possession of coal and iron, of the mechanical skill and seamanlike daring, which are every year making our pre-eminence in the use of steam for peaceful purposes more marked, and apparently more secure, should all at once turn to our ruin when war breaks out, and make our hands fall palsied by the very possession in a higher degree of the advantages which, we are told, are to bring about our destruction when wielded by the hands of others.

Intimately connected with this branch of the question is the suggestion, that the introduction of steam in navigation will diminish the relative superiority arising from our better seamanship. Such a suggestion is, however, founded on some forgetfulness of the objects towards which seamanship is only a means, and takes no account of the qualities from which our superiority arose. The truth is, that steam will enable either us or our enemies to do at once what it formerly needed much skill and time to effect. Our superior skill made our movements quicker, our superior daring made them more effectual. But their object was, in almost every case, very simple. It was to chase and close with the enemy, if on terms which made victory possible; to escape, if his force was overwhelming; to maintain our station if the object was to watch. All these objects steam will facilitate. Nelson, in pursuing the French fleet to the West Indies, declared his hope that by better seamanship he might gain fourteen days upon him.[1] Steam would have enabled him to fix the hour of his arrival, and so to lay his plans with certainty. But when he encountered the hostile fleet, his instructions to his captains excluded manœuvring. He tells them—

---

[1] NELSON *Despatches*, vol. vi. p. 443.

" The business of an English commander-in-chief being first to bring an enemy's fleet to battle on the most advantageous terms to himself (I mean, that of laying his ships close on board the enemy as expeditiously as possible); and secondly, to continue them there without separating till the business is decided; I am sensible beyond this object it is not necessary I should say a word. If the two fleets are both willing to fight, but little manœuvring is necessary; the less the better—a day is soon lost at that business."[1]

And again, while cruising before the battle of Trafalgar—

" Thinking it almost impossible to bring a fleet of forty sail of the line into a line of battle in variable winds, thick weather, and other circumstances which must occur, without such a loss of time that the opportunity would probably be lost of bringing the enemy to battle in such a manner as to make the business decisive, I have therefore made up my mind to keep the fleet in that position of sailing (with the exception of the first and second in command), that the order of sailing is to be the order of battle; placing the fleet in two lines of sixteen ships each, with an advance squadron of eight of the fastest sailing two-decked

---

[1] CLARKE and M'ARTHUR's *Life of Nelson*, vol. ii. p. 427.

ships, which will always make, if wanted, a line of twenty-four sail on whatever line the commander-in-chief may direct."[1]

There can, therefore, it would seem, be little doubt that our great admiral would have rejoiced not more in the new power which would have saved him these precious weeks spent in battling with head-winds in the Straits of Gibraltar, than in the facilities it would have given him for closing when he came up with his enemy. To the different tactics which new material means render necessary, genius will always speedily adapt itself. But that which has given the British sailor his real superiority over every other lies in his moral qualities, rather than in any accident of their application. His energy, daring, and coolness are what have made him, as they have made the British soldier, superior to his enemies; and whatever the vessel he sails in, the guns he fires, or the tactics he is required to adopt, these will always display their supremacy.

From these considerations, I believe it may safely be laid down, that the new agency is of such a nature that a very slight predominance in its possession will henceforth insure an easy victory. For steam is so infinitely more serviceable than sails, that henceforth

---

[1] NELSON Despatches, vol. vii. p. 89.

sails will be only the auxiliary, and without steam they will be practically of no real avail. But steam depends on coal; and a fleet can go but a short cruise in war unless it reaches stations where it can fill up with coal. That power, therefore, which has just superiority enough to enable it to destroy its enemy's coal depôts in foreign stations, and prevent their replenishment, will annihilate its adversary's navy. Thus, on the outbreak of war, we should—if merely so far stronger than the French as to be able to destroy their coal depôts in Newfoundland, the West Indies, the Isle of France, and the East Indian seas— practically close the ocean to their cruisers; for a fleet or a ship which is well supplied with coal, can always, by waiting its time, hold at its mercy an enemy whose fuel is exhausted. So, also, a slight superiority would insure the capture of all the coal-ships by which fresh supplies might be sent out. We ourselves, on the other hand, could suffer in this way only if taken by surprise at the commencement of a war, and then only a slight and temporary inconvenience; for our naval superiority would soon sufficiently clear the seas to enable the coal-steamers from Newcastle or Wales to deliver their cargoes with punctuality even in the remotest stations of our navy.

Let us, however, proceeding now to the consideration of the influence of improvements in modern weapons, accept even the supposition that some singularly lucky chance has neutralized all the advantages of steam power in blockading and watching, and has enabled the invading army to put to sea and to reach the mid-channel, or even our own shores. We are to suppose that our blockading fleets have been defeated, or enticed away,—that a smooth sea favours the enterprise,—that the transports, towed by steamers, have far advanced on the short passage,—that the men-of-war laden with troops are approaching the land, while the frigates keep watch, like careful sheep-dogs, to hold at bay any stray attack from a chance British cruiser. These, surely, are circumstances as favourable to the attempt as the most despondent alarmist can suggest, and we admit a most miraculous concatenation of chances in supposing the possibility of their concurrence. But still there must be limits to possibilities. We may grant that the British fleet is sent to the bottom; but we cannot grant that every British gunboat, every British revenue-cutter, every British block-ship, floating battery, or vessel of whatsoever character or class, mounting so much as a single Armstrong gun, has also disappeared from the Channel; or, even if this also should be granted, we cannot admit that a long day will pass without so much as a field-piece being brought up to within range of the place of debarkation. But if so much as one piece can be brought to bear, at sea or on shore, within a mile range of the hostile fleet, the invasion of England can scarcely by any existing means be accomplished. For we have seen that the system of horizontal shell-firing has abolished the use of wooden vessels in time of war. But it has done more. The effect is so terrible that a small vessel is thus made practically a match for a large one, since but one or two such discharges taking effect must end the combat on either side. The result has thus realized the anticipations of the first officer who practically developed the new system, General Paixhans, who declared that his purpose was " de mettre toute navire, même une faible navire, tout batterie, même une batterie de peu de pièces, en état de detruire tout vaisseau, même le colosse à trois ponts qui porte cent vingt bouches à feu."[1] But it is obvious, that while the effect of shells is proved to be such when directed against men-of-war, intended expressly to encounter all forms of danger, it must be tenfold enhanced when directed against helpless craft crowded on deck and below with troops. In such a position, but one shell hitting would insure the most murderous slaughter, and produce inextricable confusion. Now, is it pos-

---

[1] PAIXHANS, *Constitution Militaire de la France*, p. 267.

sible to imagine that the fleet of transports shall be able to cross the Channel and to land, without being met by so much as a single fast gunboat, which, too small herself to be easily hit, shall somewhere find an opening in the cordon of frigates sufficient to enable her Armstrong, at two miles' range, to plant in the huge hulks a dozen of such fatal missiles? Or, can we suppose that an invader will be so reckless as to send forth a great army in a fleet exposed to be thus disordered and annihilated by the attack of the tiniest antagonist?

It is quite clear that this is beyond the range of probability, and that henceforth, therefore, no invasion will be dreamt of, save such as can be effected by transport in iron-plated vessels. Now this result introduces some new conditions into the attempt. In the first place, no such iron-plated vessels yet exist as would suffice for it. It is a high average if we compute each iron-clad man-of-war as capable of carrying 1000 men under cover, besides its crew; and it is a low average if we compute each vessel of such capacity as costing 300,000*l*. To bring over an army of 150,000 men, then, by such means, will require a fleet of 150 iron-clads, built at a cost of 45,000,000*l*. This is an outlay not yet contemplated by any European power; but till it has been made, we may rest in absolute security. But even this is not all. Vessels of such size are inevitably of such a draught of water that there are few harbours in which they could embark troops, and few points of the coast in which they could lie near enough to effect a rapid landing. Boulogne will cease to be a point from which we can be menaced, for its harbour is too shallow to admit such vessels. Cherbourg will be the nearest port from which danger can come ; and the added distance will add greatly to the chances in our favour. But still greater difficulties will attend the landing. The ships must anchor far from the shore, and disembark their men by the slow process of boats. These boats must of course be of wood or of thin iron, and will be exposed to the same dangers of being cut off, shelled, or sunk, by our own light craft as attend the larger transports. As they near the shore, a new danger will await them. Even if a point is found where there are no guns of position commanding the beach, it will be strange if our artillery, regular or volunteers, cannot in the course of the morning bring a field-piece to bear upon the boats and the shingle on which their successive freights are attempting to form. Now the powers of the new artillery in this respect also offer singular advantages to the defenders. Formerly a landing could always be protected by the fire of the ships, because their heavy guns had a range sufficient to prevent the approach of light guns on shore sufficiently close to bring boats and landing-place within their shorter range. But rifling has given to the smallest ordnance a range almost, if not quite, as great as the largest has; consequently, field-pieces on shore will now command the beach and the shallow water between it and the ships, while they are themselves in safety from the fire of the ships. The introduction of rifled small-arms has also a similar tendency in favour of the defenders. With the old Brown Bess no effective fire could be maintained beyond 200 yards; and as there is seldom any shelter within that distance of a beach, the ships could keep all infantry attacks at bay until the newly landed troops had formed. But now that rifles are sighted up to 1,100 yards, and are effective against masses at a half farther, it will almost always be easy for riflemen to get secure cover from the guns at sea while still within deadly range of the heavily freighted boats and of the confused masses on the shore. The superiority which is thus conferred on the defence by the introduction of the new weapons, is, I believe, admitted on all hands.

It remains now that we glance at the effect which the use of railways for the land transport of troops may be expected to have on the chances of a general invasion. To a certain extent, like every other improvement, it doubtless favours both parties. It

would enable our opponents to conduct all the
arrangements for the ultimate concentration of their
force at a distance from the coast, and to defer to
the day or two prior to the embarkation the actual
assembling of the men. But it may be doubted
whether this advantage is not compensated by the
indirect results of the railway system. There is now,
in consequence of the facilities for travelling, such
rapid and incessant communication between this
country and all the principal inland and seaport
towns of France, that no very extensive movement,
either of troops or ships, could take place without our
Government being instantly advised of it. Suppose,
for example, that at a period of profound peace the
French navy, to the requisite extent, were all collected
in Brest and Cherbourg. Our consuls, commercial
houses, newspaper correspondents, and travellers,
could not fail to apprise us that a fleet was being got
ready, manned, and victualled,—an operation not to
be effected in a few days, even though not a soldier
had yet been moved. Now, notice of a sinister movement is all that is required for its defeat. We are not
to suppose our naval department to be guilty of such
supineness as to allow our shores to be denuded of
vessels, without having very positively ascertained the
position and readiness of preparation of every fleet
which might attack us. It is constantly to be kept in

sight, that the first and universally admitted axiom of
the policy of this country is, that her fleet is to be
always superior in strength to the fleets of our neighbours; and if this axiom is observed, it does not seem
possible for an apparent friend suddenly to equip, and
fill with troops, a number of iron-plated vessels, even
if he had them, without our having such notice of the
movements as would be sufficient for our warning. As
to what might take place, either when war is openly
threatened, or after it has broken out, we need have
little concern. Our duty then will be to put out of the
question a descent at any moment; and it can matter
nothing to us whether the troops, whose arrival we
are prepared for, have been brought up by rail the
morning before, or have bivouacked for months in the
neighbourhood of the port of embarkation.

Very much more material to us, however, are the
facilities which are given by railways for moving
troops within our own limits. In the case of an
anticipated invasion, we are in the position that,
though we know whence the blow is to come, we
cannot predict with certainty the spot on which it is to
light. Supposing the enemy once to succeed in
getting to sea, he may either direct his course to the
western or eastern part of the south coast, and a
previous concentration of our forces on any one point
might be rendered nugatory by his sudden appearance

elsewhere. This is a contingency which formerly obliged us to keep on foot a far larger number of troops than would have been actually necessary to make a landing at a given point impossible. But now, railways on land outstrip even steamers at sea, and the telegraph communicates instantaneous intelligence of the most distant occurrences. We shall, consequently, now be able to keep the bulk of our army in hand at a few central points of our railway system, knowing that, on the first appearance of a hostile fleet, we can launch them to the spot with the certainty of their arriving more rapidly than men can be landed from the ships. The immense carrying powers of our railways have been well tested by the Brighton volunteer reviews, when, in addition to accommodating without stint all the private excursion traffic of the principal holiday in the year, the Brighton Company has carried 16,000 troops from London to the coast between five and eleven o'clock in the morning. This was by only one line of railway; but there are no points on the south coast, from the mouth of the Thames to that of the Exe, to which there are not at least two converging lines of rail; and therefore, as the private traffic would on such an occasion be wholly suspended, it is a very moderate estimate to say that the railways would enable us to pour down, between dawn and dark, 50,000 men on any menaced point; while, unlike the processes either of marching or of landing from ships, the stream would be kept up with unabating flow all through the night. Nor would it be possible for an enemy, whose movements must thus so greatly lag behind the intelligence of the telegraphic wire and the transmission of troops by railway, to gain anything by a mere feint. We shall be able to defer the expediting of our main body till we have positive intelligence of the reality of the attempt; and the force we might think it advisable to send could be moved in an hour by our inner lines to the point which it would cost him three hours to make by sea.

In this matter also, then, it appears that, by the wise ordering of Providence, the advance in our knowledge of His laws regulating physical matter, tends marvellously to the security of those who chiefly desire the peace which His moral laws enjoin as the highest earthly good. As wars become less bloody and frequent in proportion to the scientific appliances introduced to increase the momentary destruction they spread, so the adaptation of the discovery of natural laws to the purposes of war tends to make war more costly and dangerous to those who invoke it, and less hazardous to those who stand on the defence. Therefore, far from exposing us to fresh danger, and calling on us to maintain increased armaments to meet it, as short-sighted or interested statesmen have urged upon us, the new discoveries and appliances of war really tend to make smaller armaments sufficient. For above all to us, who are the great pioneers of peaceful progress, the great employers of all newly found aids to our natural powers, does the advantage accrue which the enhancement of natural powers gives even to the feeble, when they only desire to preserve their freedom and their rights. We, to whom all nations come for the very ships of war they need—we, who furnish coal and iron even to those who seek to manufacture for themselves—we, whose engineers and skilled mechanics are bribed into the service of foreign powers—have now an assurance, far firmer than when by sheer pluck and coolness we held the world at bay, that henceforth we shall enjoy a security so impregnable, and be able to carry to another people, fighting for a just cause, a reinforcement so overwhelming, that none will dare to beard us at home, or to neglect the warning whisper which may reach over the seas of the approval or disapproval of a free and powerful nation.

CHAPTER VI.

MILITARY SYSTEM AND EXPENDITURE.

HAVING now pointed out the useless increase in our annual naval and military expenditure, into which we have allowed the chiefs of the Whig party to beguile us during their term of power, and the conditions under which modern science has now added so largely to our actual and relative strength; it remains to consider what amount, disposition, and organization of force we really should require to insure our safety and honour without futile waste of public resources. For those who advocate economy hurt their cause if they confine themselves merely to criticism, without indicating clearly the policy they would substitute for that which they attack. No doubt, whoever ventures to make a definite suggestion exposes himself in turn to criticism. But that criticism need not be very much feared which is itself barren of suggestion; while that which is fairly and reasonably directed against a definite system, and not only points out defects, but suggests

the method of amendment, aids materially in evolving
at last a scheme which, resting on sure principles, will
command the approval and confidence of the public.

It is necessary with this view, first to examine the
defensive system which has been recommended by
the commission of 1860, and for which a sum of
4,500,000l. has been already voted, leaving it still in
all points incomplete. It must, however, be premised
that this system is not of the character of a national
defence. The commissioners were appointed primarily to inquire into the condition and efficiency of the
fortifications in progress or proposed, and only secondarily to consider the defence of the kingdom. And in
their report they presupposed the failure of the fleet to
prevent the landing of a force adequate for the purpose
of subjugating the island by defeating its defending
armies. They took, therefore, for granted that the
main point for their consideration was the defence of
our chief arsenals and naval ports, Woolwich, Chatham,
Dover, Portsmouth, Plymouth, Pembroke, and Cork,
from an attack by sea after our fleet was beaten or
dispersed, or from an attack by land by a large army
operating already in the heart of the island. If we
are satisfied, from the considerations submitted in the
preceding chapter, of the groundlessness of this imagi-
nary danger, it may therefore be thought needless to
show the futility of the defensive works proposed.

But in order that the case may be more fully judged, let us examine in a little more detail the perils which are said to menace us, and against which provision has thus been made at so immense a cost.

Taking first the land defences, the general system of the commissioners may be described as the construction of a series of separate forts round each point to be defended, at such a distance from it as should keep an enemy beyond the ranges of which rifled ordnance is now capable, which may be taken at nearly five miles. These forts consequently embrace an enormous circuit, forming, according to the configuration of the ground, a semicircle, or three sides of a square, of ten to twenty miles in length. The forts themselves are, however, to be small, but powerfully defended towards the land side, and armed with the heaviest possible artillery. They are to be at an average of nearly a mile apart, and not connected by any intervening lines, the whole defence of the ground between being entrusted to the guns.

The leading objection to this system is one which is scarcely technical, but which has not yet been fully discussed. It consists in the very large force necessary to maintain an *enceinte* so extensive. There is, indeed, a tendency at present to speak of fortifications as if they possessed an intrinsic strength, and especially as if the modern system of detached works was sufficient of itself to supply the place of an army.   But the truth is that no works whatsoever can do more than support an army, and that they can only support an army which is duly proportioned to the extent of line to be defended.   A single fort, under-garrisoned, must fall at the first assault, and a system of forts is in no better position.   A daring and disciplined enemy cannot be prevented from pushing through the line, if at any point he encounters a force greatly inferior to his own.   The instance of the lines of Torres Vedras, so often referred to in needless proof of the value of fortifications, confirms these limitations of the principle. The main line was only twenty-four miles long; it presented a front in many places physically inaccessible, and it was held by an army of 120,000 men, of whom 70,000 were regular troops, Portuguese and English.   It is obvious that this position, so held, presents no points of resemblance to a line nearly equally long, every foot of which is practicable to an enemy, and held by only five, ten, or fifteen thousand men.   Of what such lines, so held, can *not* do, we had examples in the manner in which Soult was driven from position to position in the Pyrenees, and still more recently in the Federal assault on Petersburg. That town defied its assailants so long as its circuit of works, some twenty miles in length, was defended by above 60,000 men.   When by an attack on its prolongation, a portion of this force was drawn away, the Federal army made an assault on the centre, without any preliminary siege operations, broke through the circuit, turned, and captured the forts, despite all their crossing fire, and despite the desperate valour with which the Confederate troops they supported strove to hold the ground. Yet even when thus overpowered there is reason to believe that the Confederate force defending the Petersburg works had not been reduced below 20,000 or 25,000 men, all veterans.

The Royal Commissioners, however, deem it sufficient to assign for the defence of Portsmouth thus encircled with a cordon of forts a mile apart from each other, extending on the land side over a line of twelve miles of nearly level ground, no more than 15,000 men in time of war. To the whole of the five ports they proposed fortifying they assigned a total of 69,000 men in such case. And it would seem from the speeches of the Commander-in-Chief that it is thought sufficient if only a portion of these are seasoned troops, the fortifications being vaunted as capable of defence by volunteers and militia, and thus as " setting the regular army at liberty." During time of peace it does not appear to be contemplated that any increase in the present garrisons shall take place, and thus these enormous entrenched camps on the principal points of the coast will be left to be tenanted by only some 2,000 or 3,000 men apiece.

Very serious objections may be stated to such a system both in regard to time of peace and time of war. As regards the former, it ought to be remembered that one of the reasons pressed for such works is the danger of our being surprised. We have been told that without any warning 20,000 men may be collected on the opposite coasts, transported across the Channel in the night, and thrown on our shores before daylight. It is obvious that if any such danger exists the proposed fortifications with their 2,000 men could offer no resistance, but would be at once seized and held by an enemy's force of ten or twelve times that strength. And as, when so held, they would really be of importance, and afford a *tête du pont* for further operations, it seems that in constructing them, and then leaving them to defend themselves, we are offering the strongest possible temptation to an invader. And as soon as they are finished this will probably become so apparent, that we shall be obliged largely to increase our standing army to supply them with adequate garrisons. For of course neither volunteers nor disembodied militia can occupy them in time of peace.

But even in time of war it may be seriously doubted whether they will be of value worth their cost. They must then be fully garrisoned, and will probably be found to absorb more than the calculated 69,000 men. But these men must also be regulars, or, what is their equivalent, embodied militia, since volunteers will not undertake permanent duty. And very high authorities have expressed the strongest doubts whether it is a wise course to deduct 70,000 men from our main force in the field, for the purpose of shutting them up in small detachments in a number of widely separated places of strength. They argue that if an invader effects a landing, such a body of troops would far more effectually prevent his being able to advance on any of our dockyards or arsenals, if held in hand in readiness to crush him before he has secured his footing, instead of being distributed among our seaports, whence they could not be withdrawn till the irregular troops were collected to take their place.

Objections of a different character have been stated by naval men to the sea defences of our ports which the Royal Commission proposed. Their system in this respect was similar to that which they proposed on shore. They recommended the erection of separate forts in the channels of the principal harbours, to be armed with guns of the greatest calibre and range, with the view of making the passage impracticable to an enemy's vessels. But in the case of Portsmouth this plan had the fatal defect that the depth of water

and width of the channel are so great, that after the
forts are erected there will still remain an open
entrance of nearly two miles in width; while after this
is passed the enemy will reach an anchorage whence
his vessels can shell the dockyard, while themselves at
a distance of above 2,000 yards from the nearest fort.
Now, though modern guns can throw shot or shell to
an immense distance with accuracy enough to destroy a
building, or fire a town or wooden ship, yet their practice
against iron-clads in motion at even a thousand yards has
never yet proved very serious. And although at Charleston the *Monitors* were unable to pass Fort Sumter, it
was chiefly because of their want of steam-power
(their speed being only seven knots) and their entire
dependence on their screws, which got fouled with
floating cordage; and thus they form no precedent
of the failure of iron-clads of twice the speed and four
times the size, able to sail as well as steam. And
against that instance of repulse there must be set the
success of the assailants at New Orleans and at
Wilmington. In the case of New Orleans a fleet of
only wooden vessels ran the gauntlet of most powerful
batteries, guarding the river at short range; at Wilmington a fleet of iron-clads silenced Fort Fisher, a
large and strong earthwork, mounting very heavy
guns.

The chief objection, however, to these sea forts

is not their uselessness, but the false principles of
defence they encourage. They prevent us from
depending for naval security on our fleet. Suggested
on the idea that they would be useful if the fleet were
sent away, they would, if relied on, lead us to deem
the maintenance of our naval supremacy a thing of
not vital moment. For if besides the forts we are to
maintain squadrons sufficient for the defence of all and
each of our ports against any possible attempt of the
enemy, then clearly the forts are superfluous and a
mere waste of money. If they are to be useful they
must come in the place of a certain number of vessels
that we are to do without, and so supply an inferiority
in our naval strength. But why should such inferiority
exist ? If we do not spend money in building forts,
which being fixed can only be of service on one spot,
and can do nothing against our foe unless he chooses
to lie within short range of their guns, we might have
vessels which could move to any position menaced,
or which, adding to our strength at sea, would enable
us to destroy the enemy's fleet in his own harbours,
or upon the ocean. And in fact we have already
evidence of the negligence which reliance on fixed
fortifications induces. Their advocates in and out of
Government have always allowed that by themselves
forts would be insufficient, and that their use would
be to support the vessels specially constructed for

harbour defence. Yet though five years have elapsed
since the system was adopted by Government, there
is not yet one vessel built or even commenced for the
purpose of harbour defence in aid of the costly forts.
There exists of such a class only the *Royal Sovereign*
and the two Confederate rams, which are accepted by
the Admiralty as mere experiments, and relegated to
the class of harbour batteries not as part of a defensive
system, but only because their purchase was compelled
by political reasons.

Since then, the preponderance of argument based
on principle and experience is adverse to the defensive
system adopted by Government, and at the same time
it has been proved that our expenditure in the military
department is unwarranted either by older authority
or modern science, it only remains to suggest the
elements in which our true strength consists and the
organization which at least cost would render them
most effectual.

Far from the Channel having been abolished as a
line of defence, the considerations which have been
offered show that it is more than ever valuable. In
all its extent there is now only one port from which
danger can come, or on which watch need be kept.
Even with steam that port is farther from us, in point
of time, than Calais was from Dover, and close to

its entrance we have a station at Alderney, from which we can have instantaneous intelligence, by day or night, of all that goes on. And the sea is more than ever ours. The French beat us in the construction of wooden ships, we now beat them in the use of iron. Our merchant service supplies us with sailors in larger proportion than ever; our new guns, destructive at sea, are more than ever destructive on shore, when directed against ships or boats with troops; and nothing can live now at sea under their fire, unless what is constructed of iron of enormous weight and at enormous expense.

To employ these advantages so as to ensure our safety, ought not to be difficult. We must of course keep up our regular fleet for foreign service, for blockading an enemy's ports in case of war, for destroying his coal depôts abroad, and cutting off his merchantmen, besides also so disposing our numerical superiority at sea—a superiority, it must be kept in view, which we have always maintained, which we at this moment possess, and which it is to be assumed we shall retain in due proportions—as to secure to us always a sufficient Channel fleet. But over and above this fleet of large vessels, we ought to establish a fleet of gunboats, for, as it were, patrolling our shores. They ought to be armour-plated, of the lightest possible draught, and carry one, or at the most two, of the heaviest guns. For such service the turret system is, in the opinion of all unbiassed authorities, the most suitable. The effect of the presence of these tiny but formidable vessels would be to convince the enemy of the utter hopelessness of making use of wooden transports or of boats for landing from iron-clad ships. He would know that even if he could evade or disperse the blockading Channel fleet, he must still reckon on falling in with at least one (whose fire would speedily draw her consorts) of these active and deadly antagonists, which could stand for hours the pounding of his heaviest guns (as the *Monitor* did from the *Merrimac*, and the *Rolf Krake* from the Prussian batteries), while all the time hurling death and fire among his transports and boats. Then along the shore, wherever there is a beach practicable for a landing, low batteries, at a couple of miles' distance, mounting one or two of the heaviest guns on traversing platforms, or within the Coles cupola or turret, would not only so sweep the intervening beach as to render it impossible for any living thing to obtain a footing there, but would also, by their fire seawards, burn, destroy, and sink all such wooden vessels or boats as might come within their range. Whether such batteries could themselves be silenced or destroyed by the concentrated fire of iron-plated ships, is a question that for this purpose we need

not discuss. Enough that they could be silenced
only by iron-clads, and that, till silenced, they would
forbid the approach of wooden transports. In either
case time would be consumed, disorder introduced,
and all attempts prohibited which were not preceded
by the warning of a combat between our shore batteries
and the enemy's fleet.

By such simple naval and engineering precautions
and dispositions the problem of the amount of land
force which it is proper to retain for defence in peace
becomes greatly simplified. Seeing as we have done
that an invasion of the realm will not be contemplated
unless an army of 150,000 men can be at once landed,
and that the collection of means for transporting, in
iron-clad vessels, such a body of troops must visibly
occupy many months, during which we can raise our
force to any point judged expedient, we need not care
to provide in peace for what can only occur months
after a state of war has commenced, and then is
capable of being easily repelled. But contemplating
the possibility of an attempt to throw on our shores
twenty or thirty thousand men, ere war has yet been
declared, on which Lord Palmerston has so often
insisted, what are the forces necessary for our security ? It has been observed that our coasting-vessels
and batteries will, at least, give us a few hours' notice
before the landing is commenced, and it is admitted

that it cannot be completed in less than a full day.[1] Now, leaving out of count any standing camps, we have every garrison in the United Kingdom within a distance of twelve hours from any point on the south coast; and we have volunteers ready in two hours' notice to relieve and to follow these garrisons. Can more then be needful than that we should be able to collect from these garrisons twenty-five or thirty thousand men if such alarm is given? Can we conceive an enemy daring to take a chance opportunity of throwing such a body of troops on a hostile coast, certain to have their sea communications cut off next day, certain to meet by dawn a body of regular forces equal in number to their own, certain to be confronted the day after by 50,000 disciplined volunteers, and the succeeding day by 100,000 drilled militia, with 100,000 more volunteers at their back?

It is obvious that no temporary success could, in the eyes of sane men, justify an attempt so sure to be immediately followed by disaster; provided only that we do not tempt them with the spectacle of empty places of strength on the coast which they can seize

---

[1] General SHAW KENNEDY, *The Defences of Great Britain.* See also evidence of Captain Coles (who superintended the landing in the Crimea) before the Defence Commission. The Federals threw on shore 4,000 men in an hour at Fort Fisher, employing 200 boats; but the landing was unopposed, and the second 4,000 occupied much more time.

on landing, and in which they can then defy us till reinforcements have an opportunity of reaching them.

And such a force would not only secure us at home, it would, if properly organized, be amply sufficient to enable us to hold our place and credit in any emergency abroad.   Prior to the increase in our army, we were able when the Russian war broke out to send at once 10,000 men to the East, and to follow them up with as many more as soon as the militia regiments were embodied.   When then we are told that our " want of preparation " exposed us to suffering and loss, we must remember what that want of preparation was.   It was not want of numbers, but want of sense and system.   Fast as we sent out men they died, not by the sword of the enemy, but of pestilence, famine, and exposure, because we placed them under officers unfit for their work, and under a system which could not provide us with better.   Our army perished because its leaders lay in their yachts, or sat keeping accounts and writing returns in their tents, while the men were dying of hunger and cold, and all the time masses of food and clothing were rotting in Balaklava harbour; because, in short, the system of the Horse Guards was to "take care of Dowb," and the consequent practice was to let the commissaries serve out green coffee to the men.   Our " want of preparation" did not then find us without an army fit for foreign service, it only killed the army by the faults of organization. If we remedy these, we have no need to desire a larger force than before that war we possessed.

Nor can any exception be taken to our counting militia and volunteers, as, for all purposes of defence, worthy of full confidence. The question would not be of a campaign but of a battle, and young troops have always been found, when properly handled and in sufficient strength, and with the support of a proportion of veterans, to fight as well in battle as the seasoned regiments by their side. This stands on the testimony of the Duke of Wellington himself, who having commanded newly-raised militia at Waterloo, declared in the House of Lords that they had behaved as well as any troops could do.[1] And, as we have seen, he was quite willing to peril the defence of England on a far smaller militia force than we now possess. No doubt in the operations of a long campaign their inexperience would be against them, and no doubt, if overmatched, their steadiness could not be depended on. But with English militia and volunteers of a strength eight times as great as the enemy before them, standing also by the side of troops of the line, and fighting on English soil, it is impossible that there should be a moment's uncertainty of the result.

---

[1] In his last speech, on the Militia Bill, 15th June, 1852.

It is, indeed, always urged, in answer to any suggestion of computing or employing the volunteers as an element of our practical defence, that their purpose was not to supersede, but only to supplement our regular troops. But this is really inaccurate. If we did not have them, the country would insist on either a larger body of regulars, or on calling out more militia. Unless, then, they come in place of other forces, they are obviously useless; an estimate of their value which nobody will admit. But if they are useful, we are certainly entitled to count up how much they can do, and to hold that what a volunteer can do and means to do, we need not keep a regular soldier to do also.

In fact, we should greatly add to the spirit of the volunteer movement if we were occasionally to give to volunteers real duties to perform (such as are further on suggested), and allow them to feel that they are of real service to their country, and really depended on by their country. But then it would be necessary to see that not merely the men, but the officers are " efficient." And it is not enough considered that the officers, on whom most depends, are at present, as a body, the least efficient. It would be most advisable to require them, as a condition of holding commissions, to pass an examination such as officers of regular troops undergo. For, in fact, it is even more important in

the case of half-disciplined than of fully-disciplined
troops that the officers should thoroughly know their
duties.   There would be no difficulty in enforcing the
condition, for, if it caused resignations, there are
plenty of men in the ranks who would be able to
fill the vacancies.   And all who have served in the
volunteer ranks are aware that the greatest of all
hindrances to the progress of the force, in numbers
as well as efficiency, lies in the disgust occasioned
to the men by being placed under the command of
ignorant or negligent regimental officers.

It is clear, then, that having reserves so capable of
immediate service, we cannot need a regular strength
sufficient both for garrisons and for the field.   And
the fact is that we have such a strength at present.
Our fortresses and barracks are filled, and we are
obliged to draft off our superfluity of battalions to
the great camps at Aldershott, Shorncliffe, Colchester,
and the Curragh.   It has, indeed, been urged that these
camps are necessary places of instruction for officers.
They may be of service in this respect to a few generals
of division, but it is a costly method of instruction when
it requires the maintenance of a superfluous army of
25,000 men, equivalent to an expenditure of 2,500,000l.
a year.   For the purpose of instruction to any officers
of inferior rank the camps are wholly useless ; and it
seems to be agreed that they are so detested by the

men, that their existence is one of the most powerful
obstacles to our retaining the services of the 10-years'
soldiers. But though they were abolished, there would
be no necessity for discontinuing the instruction of
general officers. The authorities in command of the
army have only to take a lesson from the leaders of
the volunteers. There could be no difficulty in making
arrangements to •bring together the garrisons from
adjacent towns, to any strength required, for field
days, as often as wished during the year. The
volunteers in these towns would be proud and
pleased to furnish detachments for performing garrison duties during the absence of the regulars.
Some of the well-drilled regiments of volunteers in
the neighbourhood of the place of assembly would
be glad of the distinction of joining and swelling their
force. And the practice of transit by railway at short
notice would be of infinite value to the regulars themselves. Such a substitute for camp instruction would
therefore not merely be effectual, but would indirectly
produce some material advantages.

But though this surplus strength of the army has till
lately been defended chiefly on the pretext that it was
needed for our defence at home, a different reason
has within the last two years been advanced by the
authorities, and tacitly acquiesced in by the House of
Commons. This is, that such strength is necessary to

furnish reliefs to our colonies and India.   The rule is
that a regiment shall have five years at home for every
ten abroad.   Hence, having now 44 battalions of
infantry at home, 46 in the colonies, and 56 in India,
it is argued that we cannot diminish the number of
our home force without imposing a longer period
of service on regiments abroad.

The first point to be noted in connection with this
argument is, that it makes our colonies to be more
expensive to us than we have hitherto considered
them.   We must now compute them to cost us not
merely the sums charged for the troops within them,
but the sum necessary to maintain reliefs for these
troops.   Thus though India pays for all troops within
its limits, it imposes on us a burden of keeping 36,000
men as relief for the 72,000 for which it actually pays,
or, in other words, lays a tax on the British tax-
payer of 3,500,000*l.* a year.   So Canada and New
Zealand are retained by us, not merely at a charge of
10,000 men, or a million a year each colony, but of
15,000 men, or a million and a half a year each.   Are
any one of them worth to us a tax of this amount ?

But, in the next place, is the assertion true that
such force is really needed by our colonies, or, if
needed, that it must be thus relieved ?   If we insist on
governing colonies, we must of course defend them.
But if we give them, as we have given to both Canada

and New Zealand, representative institutions and self-government, may we not fairly ask them to take on themselves the burden of self-defence? There is no reason to assert that this would be to deliver them up to their enemies. Against barbarous assailants they are strong enough for defence, though perhaps not for aggression. Against civilized neighbours they have the same security as the smaller states of Europe, the security of public justice, and of a due measurement of their own strength or weakness. If not, by our attempted protection, made to suffer for our quarrels, or induced to depend on our support in errors of their own, there is really no ground to suppose that they would encounter greater difficulties than their own good sense, and knowledge of the limits of their own strength, would easily surmount.

Nor would there be any abandonment of them on our part if they should be unjustly assailed by a more powerful neighbour. The principles which, in Chapter II., I ventured to urge as calling on us to give practical aid to nations defending their independence against foreign attack, would plead still more powerfully in behalf of those of our own blood and language. But what for their sakes and ours is desirable is that they should not be so closely bound to us as to be the object of attack merely to wound us, and that we should not be so bound to them as to

13

be obliged to support them with men and money in any unjust quarrel which they may provoke.

With India the case is different. But when we amalgamated the forces of the Company with those of Great Britain, it was certainly never explained to us that the effect of the measure would be to cost us three millions and a half a year; and if that had been explained, it is very certain that the country would have refused assent to a change, itself of most doubtful expediency, and carried out against the remonstrances of our most distinguished and experienced Indian officers. But we can at any moment reverse that policy, and by merely making the Indian army again a separate establishment, we should remove any pretence for maintaining 35,000 men at home for its relief.

It is obvious from such considerations that we have drifted into many sources of military expenditure, only because we did not understand the real effect of the measures that were proposed. It is clear that, instead of 80,000 men being necessary for home defence, we should find an effective force of 30,000 men, with 20,000 more for depôts and non-effectives, most ample for all purposes of safety in time of peace, backed as they are by nearly 300,000 troops of reserve, some of whom could in a few hours, and all in a few days, be brought into the field. It is also clear that

such a nucleus of regular forces, if thoroughly organized, and with all the collateral services in complete
efficiency, would be ample for all our need at the commencement of a foreign war, if unhappily it should
be our fortune to engage in one. And lastly, it is
clear that far from our present immense superfluity
being needed for the purpose of maintaining reliefs for
India and our colonies, there is in these departments
opportunity for further reduction to an extent that can
hardly be foreseen. And it is thus evident that by
giving up all control of the national armaments to
Government, and by allowing a Government professing
principles of economy to obtain any votes it likes to ask
for on the most untenable and inaccurate pretensions,
we have laid on ourselves a needless burden of many
millions a year, and have postponed a reduction of
taxation which would have added tenfold to the wealth
of the country and to the comfort of its inhabitants.

PRINCIPLES OF REFORM.

LEGAL.

L E G A L,

CHAPTER I.

SIMPLIFICATION OF LAW.

THAT men should be called on to obey a law which they cannot know is a singular anomaly. That they should be punished by civil loss or criminal penalty for transgression of rules which it was impossible for them to discover, is a proposition which, in its announcement, startles us with its injustice. It is the worst reproach levelled against a despotism, that men are liable to be punished in the name of law for offences which were unknown to be prohibited; it is assumed as a token of unquestioned barbarism when in any State the regulations which govern social life are uncertain and arbitrary. Yet such is the position of the British people in this latter half of the nineteenth century. By a fiction of the Constitution every man is supposed to be present in Parliament, and to give his assent when laws are made, and his knowledge of them is assumed in a legal maxim, daily enforced, *ignorantia juris neminem excusat*. But what is the law thus accepted and sanctioned? The statutory part of it is to be found in forty-four quarto volumes, extending over nine feet of bookshelf, and every session adds at least an inch more. The expository part of it, and all that supplies the blanks of positive statute, is to be found in 1,200 volumes of folio, quarto, or octavo reports, extending over some two hundred feet of bookshelf, to which each year adds some twenty new volumes, or about fifteen lineal inches of solid learning. One would be apt to say that only a lifetime devoted to this sole pursuit could master a system of rules extending to such enormous bulk, did we not know, as matter of fact, that many lives *are* devoted to this sole study, and that they fail to bestow any certainty of knowledge in it.

On this point let us call the evidence of lawyers themselves. The present Lord Chancellor, the chief lawyer in England, personally a man of rare mental vigour and grasp, tells us that, from the number and undefined authority of the precedents, "the result is that it is impossible to predicate with any degree of satisfaction or certainty beforehand what will be the issue of a cause;" and that even "your Statute Book is a mass of enactments and statutes which are, in a great degree, discordant and irreconcilable. Hence the utter impossibility, sometimes, of arriving at a consistent interpretation."[1] Sir S. Romilly says: "Of what importance is it that by a legal fiction the law is supposed to have had pre-existence, since being unknown till it was promulgated by some decision, it was not possible that men could have conformed to it as the rule of their conduct, and it can hardly be said to have been previously known even to the judges themselves."[2] These are the expressions of men who had long themselves been practising barristers of the highest rank and reputation. And Mr. Austin, the greatest among our few scientific jurists, declared that our system of law "is known imperfectly to the mass of lawyers, and even to the most experienced of the legal profession;" and that necessarily their opinions, by which the unlearned are to be guided, are often "worded with a discreet and studied ambiguity, which, whilst it saves the credit of the uncertain and perplexed adviser, thickens the doubts of the party who is seeking instruction and guidance."[3] Nor let it be said that these ignominious confessions are only applicable to the legal system of the southern half of this

---

[1] Speech of the Lord Chancellor on the revision of the law, House of Lords, 12th June, 1863.

[2] *Edinburgh Review*, vol. xxix. p. 217.

[3] *Lectures on Jurisprudence.*

island. If the Scottish Statute Book is less voluminous, it is by no means more clear or certain; if the
reported decisions are less numerous, they by no
means leave fewer points of doubt unascertained. For
to both countries, over and above the admissions of their
lawyers, there is equally applicable this indisputable
test of the uncertainty of the law, that not merely is
there an enormous mass of litigation, indicating
ignorance of the law on the part of the general public,
but the mass of litigation is supported by the diametrically opposed opinions of the eminent lawyers whom
the parties have consulted; while a large proportion
of it actually discloses a difference of opinion on the
bench itself, and probably is signalized by conflicting
decisions on the part of the courts which in succession
must authoritatively expound the law.

We thus acknowledge ourselves to be in a state of
barbarism as regards our law. And this state is more
than disgraceful; it is most hurtful and cruel. It
involves to the nation the absolute loss of all that
time which is taken up in trying to find out what the
law directs, or what remedy it gives. It involves the
increase of the body of lawyers, by which a large
portion of the energy and intellectual strength of the
nation is turned from productive pursuits to the barren
office of keeping their fellows from blundering. It
involves the commission of a great deal of wrongdoing,

by leaving it doubtful whether certain acts are legal
or prohibited, and by making it doubtful whether the
perpetrators of injustice may not elude the legal
penalty. But to individuals it causes yet more injury.
It encourages evil-doers; it rewards chicane; it ter-
rifies honesty. On every man, honest or dishonest,
litigious or placable, it lays the tax of the time
absorbed in trying to regulate his conduct by obscure
provisions. It seduces the best intentioned into fatal
errors; it blights the close of many an honourable
life; it casts forth from their home many a widow and
orphan. For there is no inward monitor to interpret
a doubtful civil regulation, and therefore the purest
intention and the most anxious desire to do what the
law commands, are of no avail to preserve from the
heavy penalties attaching to its breach. Ruin may
light on the most honest trader for some unsuspected
legal flaw in a bargain; on the most scrupulous
trustee for his ignorance of some subtle fiction implying legal breach of trust; on the matron, for some
new legal exposition given to a phrase in her
marriage-settlement; on the child unborn, for some
misapprehension of legal obligation on the part of his
unsuspecting parents. No one can count his dearest
interests safe, where the law that affects them is
incapable of being beforehand ascertained with reasonable assurance of accuracy.

Is then this blot of barbarism in the midst of our high civilization inevitable? Is it, as some would have us believe, itself the necessary result of our high civilization, because the product of that infinite variety and change which social progress is perpetually introducing in our social relations? These are questions which, for three hundred years, have been agitated among the more advanced lawyers of this country. They were raised by Ellesmere and Bacon, and revived by Bentham, Romilly, and Brougham. In the long interval the prosecution of the inquiry lay in virtual abeyance, smothered by the excitement of politics, the strife of parties, the clang of arms, and the prudent inertia of the profession which is immediately concerned in the solution. In our own more happy day the discussion has been re-opened, some slight progress has even been made in the way of attempted improvement, and two sessions ago, the Lord Chancellor invoked public consideration of a scheme which, though not very clearly defined, seemed at least more comprehensive in scope, and more philosophical in principle, than had hitherto been practically contemplated. But as, without public compulsion, no measure of reform, whether political, social, or legal, can be carried against the resistance of the classes who live upon the abuse, some service may be rendered towards an object so important, by an endeavour to make clear to those who have not studied the technicalities of law, the nature of the difficulties to be encountered, the measure of success to be aimed at, and the nature of the means now proposed to be employed for the remedy. A brief statement of the measures which have already been in some degree commenced, with a view to facilitate or inaugurate the steps of the reformer, will find a fit place in the discussion.

It must be admitted at the outset, that absolute perfection is as impossible to be attained in law-making, as it is in every other human science. Even if perfect wisdom and prescience were to inspire the lawgiver's intention, the expression of it must be exposed to the ambiguity and incompleteness of human language, and to the variable and inaccurate interpretation of human intellect. For it must, at all events, sometimes happen that the legislator cannot help using words or phrases to express his meaning which, to another man's mind, admit of a different sense. And even although they should be sufficiently clear, supposing them to be applicable at all, yet cases must very frequently arise in which it is open to doubt whether they are applicable or not. Definitions will do a great deal to remedy this uncertainty, but even they must sometimes fail. Between two definitions, intended to distinguish between two classes of subjects, there

inevitably lies a neutral or debateable ground. It is
thus that in natural science different genera or species,
however clear may in the main be their distinction,
are yet linked together by individuals, that long
perplex the philosopher with doubt to which class
they should properly belong. Different minds will
attach a different degree of weight to the indications
assimilating the special case to one or other of the
classes, and until men have debated, criticized, and
refuted each other, the question must remain undeter-
mined. So it is that one judge will hold a statute
applicable to a certain collocation of circumstances,
while another will maintain that it was never meant,
and cannot, without a strain put upon its terms, be
made to include such a case in its purview. Thus,
for example, every one will see that the subjects of
theft and of embezzlement, of property and of a power,
of a binding guarantee and of a mere statement of
opinion, must frequently so approximate, that there
must be reasonable difficulty in deciding whether a
given fact falls within one or the other of the definitions to which legislation has attached certain rules
of conduct.

And as a judgment once pronounced by a court
on any disputed point becomes a precedent, and, as
such, a guide to all who find themselves in the like
circumstances thereafter, there is obviously introduced

by every judgment a fresh element of uncertainty in the
law, similar to that which would have arisen had the
rule been established by statute.   For, even supposing
what might be, though it is certainly not now the
case, that every judicial decision bore authoritatively
on its face the circumstances in which it was pronounced, and included in them no more than was
absolutely essential, so as to exclude all question
whether one circumstance or other was material or
not ; yet, unless the identical circumstances shall recur,
which is scarcely in the limits of possibility, there
must in every new case be encountered the question
whether its peculiar circumstances invoke or exclude
the application of the rule.   Suppose, for instance,
that the Legislature enacts that a will signed by the
testator shall be valid, and supposing a court has
decided that it is still valid though the signature is
partly written over the last line, it will still be open
to be debated whether the precedent will apply to a
case where the last line on which the signature is
superinduced, is written in a closer hand than the
rest of the will.   Here the special peculiarities of
the case call not merely for a decision whether the
document, as regards its last line, is really, in the
sense of the statute, the will of the testator; but
further, whether the general rule established by
precedent, is not subject to exception when circum-

stances occur which were not found in the precedent. From the disputes, of which such an instance may serve to illustrate the nature, it is obvious that no law can ever hope to be wholly free.

But then it is important to observe the extent to which uncertainties of this character would be injurious. The great proportion of them would, at least, be avoidable by ordinary prudence, intelligence, and honesty. It will always be possible for the subtlety of lawyers to "drive a coach and six" through any legislation, and to refine interminably upon the hair-splitting of precedents. But if the law were only in its main provisions tolerably clear, moderately brief, and reasonably simple, it would be possible for plain men to keep out of its entanglements. A man of good intentions need never raise any question as to the doubtful line between stealing and swindling, and neither would a man of average capacity fall into any error respecting his duties and obligations in the eye of the law, if only a broad path were laid down, by keeping in the middle of which he could be sure of finding safety. Thus every lawyer knows that the rules respecting the execution of wills have given rise to a thousand questions. What is signature, what is formal and proper attestation, what a correct form of authenticating an alteration, have been the subject of numerous decisions, arising out of the endless forms in which ignorant perversity or roguery have exhibited themselves. But every lawyer also knows that he can instruct a client in all the imperative provisions of statute or practice on this subject in a couple of short sentences, so plain and precise that the most ordinary intelligence, if fairly applied, could not fall into a blunder. Now, it is for the honest and the sensible that we must legislate, and we are not to be deterred from amending our laws, so as to make them a sufficient guide to such as these, by the objection that we shall still leave loopholes for knavery, and a possibility of straying to those who purposely or recklessly choose to walk on the verge of the legal pathway.

Mr. Austin, in the two volumes of lectures, posthumously published by his widow, and which, though unhappily fragmentary, and without the benefit of the distinguished author's revision, are a storehouse of deep learning and clear thought, devoted a large space to the consideration of codification and its kindred questions. He was a man anxious to a fault to avoid inaccuracy in statement or extravagance of expectation; he avowed the difficulty of the task, and urged "the mischief done to the cause of codification by over-stating the degree of simplicity which might be given to the law;" but he thus, in the notes intended to be enlarged upon *vivâ voce* in his lectures, defined the limit of simplicity and clearness which he contemplated as of practicable attainment.

" I am far from thinking that the law can ever be so condensed and simplified that any considerable portion of the community may know the whole or much of it.

" But I think that it may be so condensed and simplified that lawyers may know it : and that at a moderate expense the rest of the community may learn from lawyers beforehand the legal effect of transactions in which they are about to engage.

" Not to mention (as I shall show when I come to the *rationale* of the distinction between law of things and law of persons) that the law may be so arranged that each of the different classes of persons may know something of the part of it with which they are particularly concerned."[1]

While, therefore, we must admit it to be inherent in every system of human law—if not indeed in every system of law expressed by human language—that there shall still be matters left unprovided for or left doubtful, even to the minds of trained lawyers ; and while the whole code must necessarily be so voluminous that none but lawyers can know it fully ; yet,

---

[1] *Lectures on Jurisprudence*, vol. ii. p. 364.

on the other hand, this limited proposition is laid down by the advocates of simplification, that the law might be so framed as to be infinitely less bulky than it is at present, infinitely more plain and precise, so that lawyers should, in the majority of cases, be able to advise their clients with tolerable confidence, and that the general public should be able to proceed in the beaten way of their ordinary avocations without risk, and only need to resort to lawyers when unusual circumstances arise to carry them beyond their depth.

And, indeed, when we turn to the consideration of the means by which this result may be brought about, we find that to a certain extent the evil is so gross and palpable that it is admitted on all hands to be capable of some amelioration by merely mechanical remedy. For, within the forty-four volumes, or nine feet lineal, of solid statute, and the twelve hundred volumes or two hundred feet lineal of solid judicial exposition or interpretation, there is confessedly an immense proportion which is wholly void of force at the present day. Many of the statutes are expressly repealed, many of the decisions are expressly overruled, many more in both classes are virtually set aside by later laws, or are no longer applicable to any existing state of circumstances. Confessedly all these might be expunged. The process as regards the statutes has

14

been commenced by the Acts passed in 1860 and 1863, for the express repeal of a mass of "expired, exhausted, or obsolete" statutes. A new edition of the statutes at large, were it now to be published, without further emendation than the omission by the printer of those which have been authoritatively declared to be no longer binding, would occupy a very considerably smaller space on the library shelves. And it is obvious that any lawyer of average intelligence might easily perform a similar operation of excision in our volumes of reports. And though, as I have said, this is a merely mechanical or typographical reform, for it affects only those parts of the collection which are beyond any possible doubt effete and invalid, yet the mere reduction of gross bulk would be a sensible gratification to the eye, a relief to the pocket, and a saving of the time spent in turning from volume to volume for the grains of wheat scattered throughout the chaff, and in running the finger and the attention over a multitude of useless entries in a variety of separate indexes before lighting on the one which is sought.

By a further mechanical or typographical modification, a further advantage would be gained. This would consist in the grouping together, without other alteration, all the enactments, and all the decisions, bearing upon each particular subject. Thus the necessity of turning to an index at all would be obviated, and the law would be more easily apprehended from being brought consecutively under the eye. There would follow the further important, though indirect advantage, that its contradictions and obscurities would thus become so palpable that they would be forced on public attention, and every popular reformer would find without labour a fund of materials for indignant declamation. Not that we can anticipate any practical benefit from easy popular declamation, but we can look for no benefit at all until the public has been so roused to the neglect of its legislators, as to exact from them harder work and more careful attention. But on the other hand, this operation would involve a slight increase of the previously reduced bulk, for while the subjects remained in their present unscientific confusion, it would be necessary to repeat sometimes the same enactment or the same decision under more than one title.

So then when these mechanical improvements are effected, which nobody pretends to deny might be effected with very little trouble or difficulty, we should have advanced to a stage in which we might find our body of law greatly reduced (perhaps we may roundly estimate it as at least a half), made much easier of apprehension by the lawyer, made in so far more certain that he could be sure that nothing had been left unconsidered by him through failure to discover it, or through error in regarding it as not operative. But we should still find that it was scarcely more capable of popular comprehension, that it contained all its present contradictions and obscurities, and that every partial amendment by the Legislature, or new decision of the courts, opened half-a-dozen fresh difficulties for the one which it set at rest.

For the character of this effective residue of operative statute and binding decision is this. The root of all our law is to be found in the common law of the realm, which is said to exist by force of immemorial custom or consent. But it is known to us only through two sources. The one is the meagre statements of one or two old "text-books," which are now received as of equal authority with judicial decision. The other is through the exposition of the judges, when cases have arisen to call for their determination. The legal theory is that the whole of the common law lies "in the breast of the judges," and as, in point of fact, it lies in their arbitrary opinion, there is no reason to call, as some have done, the theory a fiction. But unfortunately it is uttered by the oracles, not in the shape of broad rules, simply expressed, but in the shape of bit by bit announcements, made to meet the exigency of special cases as they chance to occur. Moreover, as this "Common Law" does not even exist in the breast of the judges as a formed and definite code, but is really created by them, according to the best of their capacity, when emergency calls for it, the successive enunciations are inevitably unsystematic, founded on no general view of principles; made, as Mr. Austin observes, "generally in the hurry of business, and not with the mature deliberation which legislation requires;" not necessarily conclusive, for one judge is entitled to set aside as bad the law which another of equal rank has declared; and open further to the objection which is thus stated by Sir S. Romilly:—

" Not only is the judge, who at the very moment when he is making law, is bound to profess that it is his province only to declare it; not only is he thus confined to technical doctrines and to abstract reasoning,—he is further compelled to take the narrowest view possible of every subject on which he legislates. The law he makes is necessarily restricted to the particular case which gives occasion for its promulgation. Often when he is providing for that particular case, or, according to the fiction of our Constitution, is declaring how the ancient and long-forgotten law has provided for it, he represents to himself other cases which probably may arise, though there is no record of their ever yet having occurred, which will as urgently call for a remedy as that which it is his duty to decide. It would be a prudent part to provide, by one comprehensive rule, as well for these possible events as for the actual case that is in dispute, and while terminating the existing legislation, to obviate and prevent all future contests. This, however, is to the judicial legislator strictly forbidden, and if, in illustrating the grounds of his judgment, he adverts to other and analogous cases, and presumes to anticipate how they should be decided, he is considered as exceeding his province, and the opinions thus delivered are treated by succeeding judges as extra-judicial, and entitled to no authority." [1]

While to the uncertainty arising from the right of one judge to reject, as in his opinion absurd or erroneous, what another has laid down, Lord Westbury adds a suggestion of the evil consequence of even following a prior decision :—

" In the present system there is another evil necessarily inherent also, and it is this—in the language of Lord Bacon—' that the unlearned age governs the more learned,' because you take your rule as it is laid down in an early and undeveloped stage of society, and you are compelled to abide by that rule, if, for instance, it has regulated the dispo-

---

sition of property, until the legislature intervene to rescue the law from the necessity of following that which is often unreasonable and absurd."

Thus, then, the basis of our law (alike in Scotland as in England, for the Justinian Code, or the Feudal Law in the north, is only applied as an authority which may or may not be followed, just as the works of Bracton or Littleton are in the south) is, by the statement of those who best know it, incontestably arbitrary, uncertain, piecemeal, improvident, narrow, and technical, and often besides antiquated and irrational. And it is only the gaps in this struc-ture which Parliamentary legislation fills up. Small amendments indeed it may here and there patch in, but if they are inconsistent with the rest of the edifice they introduce the more confusion. And by consequence, as Mr. Austin shows, "the Statute law is not of itself complete, but is merely a partial and irregular supplement to that judiciary law which is the mass and bulk of the system."[1] It has the sole merit of being as certain as its phraseology allows it to be; a judge cannot disregard, he can only misunderstand it. It sometimes introduces a general principle, but it more frequently adds only a variety of minute alterations, equally unsystematic

---

[1] *Lectures on Jurisprudence*, vol. ii. p. 369.

with the original rule. And the verbosity, inaccuracy, and obscurity of its language is proverbial. Some statutes are founded on the supposition that the enunciation of a doctrine is all that is required, and that the whole manner of its application to the concerns of life may be left to be elucidated by the Courts who will have to decide on the disputes to which it will give rise. Others assume that every imaginable quibble or fraud must be foreseen and particularly provided against. Nearly all are in construction at once loose and incomplete. Grammar is set at naught; an interpretation clause gives an appearance of definition, but it is neutralized by the common addition, "unless the meaning now given shall be inconsistent with the context," and the conscious obscurity of the draftsman seeks for help in the futile clause,—"this Statute shall be liberally interpreted." Such is the character of most bills even when laid before Parliament, but the unchecked fertility of imagination of that august body adds new difficulties in the shape of clauses "added in committee," which may invert the whole design of the bill, or add an exception contradictory to some clause which is left standing. Lord Westbury himself gravely tells the House of Peers :—

"You have no persons to assist you who are trained or educated in the great work of legislative composition. But legislative composition is one of the most difficult things that can be conceived. When you address yourselves to a new Statute, after having considered the general principle of the proposed measure, the bill is subjected to the process of committee, and there it constantly happens that things are grafted upon a statute, under misconception, at variance altogether from the original conception of the framer. Your new acts are patches on an old garment. You provide for the emergency, but you pay not the least regard to the question whether the piece you put into the old garment suits it or not. Such being the mode of your legislation, it would be utterly impossible that your Statute Book should be other than it is—a mass of enactments and of statutes which are in a great degree discordant and irreconcilable. Hence the utter impossibility frequently of arriving at a correct interpretation."

So Lord Langdale, speaking in the same assembly in 1836 :—

" Without a proper guide, the Parliament proceeds from year to year blundering in legislation, accumulating one statute upon another, without system and without order ; and the statutes themselves are often framed in such a manner as almost to defy interpretation, daily provoking observations in the courts of justice upon the carelessness and want of skill of the legislature."[1]

This, then, being the character of our law and of the records which contain it, it is clear that very much will remain to be done after every obsolete provision or judgment is expunged, and the remaining mass arranged under distinct titles. It has indeed sometimes been said, that what else is necessary is provided by the numerous compilations of learned writers, in which the law as it stands is abridged, systematized, and explained. But any one who desires to avail himself of this suggestion will, in the first place, have to purchase and peruse a library or a set of volumes, according as he desires to acquaint himself with the whole law or with only a single point, considerably more bulky than the statutes or reports in which the original law is embodied.

Nor will he after all attain certainty. He will find authors, entitled to equal respect, maintaining opposite views. He will find the highest among them subject to be overruled by the Courts. Lord St. Leonards has, as most of us know, published for the use of laymen an admirable handy-book on the branch of which he is confessedly the greatest living master, the law of real property. But the law laid down by the

---

[1] Speech, 13th June, 1836.

ex-Chancellor has already been, in at least one particular,[1] declared unsound by the decision of a Court, from which a few years ago an appeal would have lain to himself. And the authors themselves will, in a very large number of instances, decline to deduce any certain rule from the precedents they cite. More than half the bulk of our ordinary "text books" is made up of argument, distinction, and doubt; so that when the layman or the lawyer resorts to them for information, the only information he gains is, either that there is no positive rule bearing upon his case, or that, from the conflict of authorities, it is impossible to say which of them might prevail when the judgment of a Court is invoked.

Neither, therefore, will mere mechanical abbreviation, excision, or consolidation, nor will unauthoritative compilation, form any adequate remedy for the evils of uncertain or incomprehensible legislation and decision. For any improvement in our position beyond the slight one we derive from excision and collocation, the intelligence of our legislators must be appealed to. It is authoritative compilation that is wanted to resolve doubts, and to exclude uncertainty, and this the legislature alone can give. Draftsmen may prepare, Chancellors may introduce systematic amendments in

---

[1] *Lofft* v. *Denis*, 1 Ell. & Ell. 474.

our Law, permitting the repeal of incongruous and disputed points ; but unless the legislature shall brace itself to the task of considering these amendments, with the full intention of converting them into law, their preparation and introduction are unavailing. For the further task is purely one of legislation. It is not the taking on trust that only consolidation is intended, without a real amendment of the law. There cannot be useful consolidation without including amendments. The law has not only to be re-stated, but to be reconciled. Where contradictory rules exist, the one must be abolished, the other enacted. Where incongruous provisions exist, they must be reduced to symmetry. And that the consolidated statute may be capable of being understood, there must inevitably be often incorporated in it some portion of that Common Law which has never before been stated in the form of statute. All this demands mental exertion in our legislators, for it involves responsibility. But without it we can make no real progress.

And now, having thus seen what needs to be done, we may, before proceeding to consider the methods proper for effecting it, usefully cast a brief glance over what the Legislature has actually done in this direction. And first of all, it is to be remarked, that it has always in modern times refused absolutely to entertain any other statement of its duty save such as was limited solely to the consolidation of Statute Law. We must at least go back to the reign of Edward VI. to find any proposal, accepted by Parliament, for "digesting the common and Statute Law under titles and heads." No approach has since been hinted at in Parliament towards dealing with that great reservoir of the Common Law which is contained in our Reports. But as regards the comparatively small portion of our law which has been introduced by enactment, Parliament has frequently confessed its duty. In 1650, a committee was appointed "to revise all former statutes and ordinances, and consider as well which are fit to be continued, altered, or repealed, and how the same may be reduced into a compendious way and exact method." A second committee was appointed in 1666, and the matter was again adverted to in 1796 and 1803. In 1816, the Houses of Parliament, after conferences with each other, agreed to the following resolution :—

" That from the present state of the Statute Law of this realm, it is highly expedient that effectual measures should be taken to arrange the matters contained in the Statutes of the United Kingdom of Great Britain and Ireland, and in the Statutes passed in the separate Parliaments of England, Scotland, and Ireland respectively, under distinct and proper heads."

A second resolution affirmed the propriety of appointing a "person learned in the law," with twenty clerks under him, to do the work. Nothing was, however, done. In 1833, a Royal Commission was issued to consider the expediency of consolidating the Criminal Law, including the Common with the Statutory Law, and of consolidating the remaining part of the Statutory Law. It reported strongly in favour of both measures, but the Legislature took no action, except in the enactment of several measures relating to the Criminal Law in 1838, and of an Act for Relief from Penalties for Religious Opinions in 1847. The Commission prepared a Digest of the Law on Crime and Punishments, which was laid before the House of Lords by Lord Brougham in 1849; but the Judges having strenuously objected to the including the Common Law in the enactment, it was not seriously discussed. In 1853, the Lord Chancellor (Cranworth) re-opened the question by obtaining the nomination of a commissioner and four other gentlemen to attempt the consolidation of the general Statute Law, and the following year this "Board" was superseded by another Royal Commission for the same purpose, but to which power was given "to combine with that process, if they should think it advisable, the incorporation of any parts of the Common or unwritten Law, in such

manner as should seem to them desirable, and also
to devise and suggest such rules, if any, as might
in their judgment tend to insure simplicity or uniformity, or any other improvement, in the form and
style of future statutes."

This Commission made annual reports down to
1859, since which time no Parliamentary trace of
its vitality has appeared, except in the production of
a series of bills consolidating the statutes on the
Criminal Law, which were passed in 1861, and of
the statutes for repealing sleeping or obsolete enactments, one of which was passed in 1861, and another
in 1863.   It has, however, also prepared a large
number of other "Consolidation Bills," which are
not yet introduced.   That these will be of some
value need not be doubted.   But that they will not
be of the value which they might have been appears
from the timid rule which the Commission laid down,
that they are to include mere re-statements of the
existing law, as already expressed in the Statute
Book without even including such important enactments (e. g., the Statute of Uses or of Frauds) as had
been the subject of much judicial interpretation, and
not including more of the Common Law than was
necessary for intelligibility.   Nor did the Commission
even resolve to proceed on any predefined system, but
only to select certain convenient groups of subjects,

and consolidate the enactments upon them. Against this idea the present Lord Chancellor, then Attorney-General, vigorously protested. He contended that—

"Before the process of consolidation is commenced, the whole body of the law ought to be reviewed and arranged analytically, the parts of it which consist of statutes should next be placed under their proper heads, and the process of consolidation should then be applied to those parts of the Statute Law which fall together under this arrangement. The whole operation would thus be performed with regularity and system, and should be laid before Parliament not in detached portions, but as a complete work. He thought that if it was shown that it was a mere consolidation, and that it was carefully executed on fixed principles, the bulk of the work would not be an obstacle to passing the whole through Parliament at once."[1]

But Lord Cranworth and the Commission overruled these suggestions, and insisted on proceeding with what Mr. Austin calls "bit-by-bit codification," and of which he says:—

"It seems to me that codification carried on in this manner (and which, I know not why, has gotten to itself the honourable name of practical) is far

---

[1] *Minutes of Proceedings of Commissions*, 1854-55.

more rash than any conceivable scheme of all-comprehensive codification, and is much more likely to
engender the confusion which, it is commonly supposed, all-comprehensive codification must produce.
Unless projectors are insane, every process of codification is wrought out on a pre-conceived and previously stated plan of the whole system to be
wrought upon."[1]

The learned peer who, as Attorney-General, advo-
cated the adoption of Mr. Austin's eminently rational
and sound views, has, however, subsequently proposed (adopting the ideas of Bacon's " Proposition
for the Compiling and Amendment of the Laws of
England") to attack the Reports and the Common
Law as well as the Statute Book. We have already
seen that both may be dealt with to a certain extent
in a mechanical way, and this necessarily forms one
branch of the work. And in regard to the Reports
the Lord Chancellor's proposal goes indeed little
further. He suggests besides the excision of useless
or erroneous cases, only the abridgment of the
earlier cases, reducing, he anticipates, the bulk to
one-tenth of its present extent, and reducing, if not
removing, contradictions and uncertainties. But then
he proposes to extract from the Reports the leading

---

[1] *Lectures,* vol. iii. pp. 879, 880.

rules of the Common Law, and to append these to the several heads of the Statute Law after it has been digested. The result of the whole, he tells us, " would be this :—A body of reports in which nothing should be found except what is authoritative, the earlier portion containing only the maxims or resolutions established, the later ones admitting more of circumstance and detail ; and a body of statutes, made homogeneous by the admission of well-ascertained fundamental rules of the Common Law, and containing also, in the briefest possible space, the chronological rules laid down by Parliament, all collected under distinct heads." This measure of reform is all that has as yet been practically proposed in England. And at present, it must be admitted, forcible reasons may be urged against going further. The Lord Chancellor, while confessing his preference for a Code, declared that the law of England is still too barbarous to admit of useful codification. Mr. Austin insisted on the advantage of professing no more at first, in order that unnecessary alarm might not be given to the legal profession.

Yet, though even this much would be a great gain, and though it seems so difficult that two years have passed since the Chancellor made his proposal, without, apparently, any further steps being taken to carry it into effect, it is important to remind the public that this is not all at which it should be contented to aim. The law would by these means be simplified and purified, but it would still be for the use of lawyers only, and that stage ought not to be contemplated as final. Taking the Lord Chancellor's estimate of a reduction to one-tenth of the present bulk, we should still have four quartos of Statute Law, and one hundred and twenty volumes of Reports. We should have removed a very great proportion of the addition since Bacon's time, but we should still have a bulk double that which excited his regret and his desire to amend. This bulk would still be so great as would prevent any considerable number of the public from attempting to master the rules which even more particularly concern them. But it cannot be thought that a wholesome state of things is arrived at until such mastery shall be in the power of any one of moderate or average intelligence.

Let it not be urged against this idea that it involves an unsettling of the law by the introduction of new rules in the place of old. Nothing of the sort is a necessary element of systematizing our existing law. The law so systematized and reduced in bulk may indeed be barbarous, and may be very capable of being improved. This is only to say that it is subject to progression, even after it shall be clearly and orderly expressed, a proposition which no one will dispute.

But however stupid and irrational a rule may be, it is at least capable of being expressed with distinctness, and in a single statement, instead of being nowhere expressed at all, and left to be gathered from a number of cases which in part illustrate or turn upon it. And it may also be placed in such position in the whole system of the law—bad as that law may be—as shall show its relative scope and application. But this is all that codification really signifies. It means no more than the reduction of the existing law, be it bad or good, to order and system, the expression of its rules in plain words, and the removal of dubiety in cases where it now exists, by selecting and fixing beforehand the rule which is to govern them.

Nor need we tremble at the thought of thus fixing the law. The opponents of codification tell us that no human ingenuity or skill can embrace in language the unforeseen cases of the future, and that the only safety is to leave them to the flexibility of the unwritten law. But what is this but to tell us that to be subject to no law at all is better than to be subject to an imperfect law? No one pretends that a Code can be made so perfect as never to need interpretation by a judge, or alteration by the legislature. But it surely is on the whole better that a definite rule should exist, which may on occasion be so interpreted or altered, than to refuse to express any rule at all, in the hope that when one is wanted the judge may happily light upon the best that can be found. The cases, however, in which legislative alteration would be required, would be far fewer than those in which it is now required, and must be made, because of the bad rules which creep into our jurisprudence through the decisions of isolated judges. For a single case, perhaps hastily decided, turning possibly in a great degree on special circumstances, may at present become the basis of a whole system in our jurisprudence. The system is then built up like an inverted cone, upon one original point, and perhaps comes to involve so many interests that no judge can dare to disturb it, after we have found that its foundation was originally laid in error. But a Code, commencing with broad and well considered principles, could scarcely err in them. Its defects would only lie in expression or in details, and a correction in these could be made by the legislature when required, without disturbing the rest. Composed deliberately, by the united labour of many heads, submitted to the wisdom of Parliament and to the consideration of all who might be interested in its provisions, it would indeed be obviously far less likely to include serious error than the decision of one judge, which now so often forms the sole basis of an important rule. And therefore it would really require far less revision, although such revision would be infinitely safer than the present haphazard and reckless style of judicial legislation.

Nor, on the other hand, would such a work open up so much opportunity for litigation as our present system. It may be observed that there are in our courts far fewer disputes caused or supported by obscurity in a passage of a text-book, than by obscurity in the application of a decision. The reason is this :—A tolerably well-written law-book is tolerably clear and precise in its language, and as far as possible it states only general rules. Hence, though its authority may be disputed, its meaning seldom is ; and there is not very often any question as to whether it applies to the case in question or not. But a decision, however clear and precise the language in which it is expressed may be, is in its nature generally obscure, for the language does not express a general rule, and, as it applies only to the particular circumstances, there is inevitable doubt whether it would apply where the circumstances are ever so little different. Now a Code, being as we may suppose constructed with more method and perspicuity, and from its authoritative origin being able to lay down its general and particular rules with more symmetry, would in this respect be superior in clearness to the best written treatise which we yet possess.

Those indeed who tell us that the text-books or

treatises of lawyers are sufficient for the use and
guidance of the public, do in fact concede the practicability of a Code of our existing law. For what is a
Code but a collection of treatises, containing, more or
less systematically, the general rules, and the particular exceptions, established in each branch of the
law ? The books, as at present written, do not
indeed, as we have seen, supply the place of a Code,
for having no authority in themselves, the law, as they
state it, may be overruled, and they are necessarily
filled with matter of mere argument and dubiety. But
converted into a Code they would be free from these
defects. They would fix the law by stating it, and
thus fixing it they would be " unmixed with baser
matter." Let us suppose, for example, that the late
Professor Bell had been invited to convert his *Principles
of the Law of Scotland* into a Code. While he could
have added nothing to the clearness and precision of
the leading rules which he had laid down, and of the
minor rules and exceptional rules by which they are
carried out or modified, he would have been able to
sweep away all matter of mere doubt and conflict,
and to adopt positively those half-established rules
which in his opinion were the most correct. He would
also, at the same time, have been able to give a little
more breadth to his leading principles, and more
sharpness and distinctness to the details. The result

would have been a manual of the Law of Scotland in which scarcely an ambiguity could be found, containing all that was necessary to guide men through the ordinary concerns of life; containing further, all the principles by which the most abstruse questions arising out of the most complicated transactions could be decided by the lawyer. And yet this Code would have occupied no more space than that of an octavo volume of extremely moderate thickness. It is a misfortune for English law that it has not been explained in any work so methodical, complete, and concise, but it is capable of explanation in the same way, and Englishmen will be able easily to recognise the nature of the illustration.

And in truth it would not be difficult to show that the very opponents of a Code are themselves codifiers, only that their Codes are partial instead of complete; and their hard labour is Sisyphean, because they refuse to employ it systematically. For if one of our ancient text-books, Coke, for instance, on real property law, or Hale on criminal law, anywhere lays down a definition or a rule, which future ages accept, that is then, so far as it reaches, a fragment of a genuine Code. The law ceases to be unwritten when it has once been accepted in the form of written expression. The rule is thenceforward fixed and unchangeable. No lawyer now-a-days would dream of adding to, or taking from (except of course by interpretation of Parliament), a single word in the established definition of "hereditament" or of "murder," or in the "rule in Shelley's case." Now so soon as a general rule is thus fixed, whether by enunciation of one great lawyer, or by agreement of the judges, or by the court of ultimate appeal, or by statute, it is thenceforth in exactly the same condition as if it were verbatim inserted in a Code. The sole difference is in position : at present it forms but one fixed rock peering above a boundless ocean of uncertainty; in a Code it would be a cornerstone in a stately and symmetrical building. But the sagacity which has been able to make a definite rule in one class of subjects is surely not incompetent to make definite rules in other classes. And when these definite rules are propounded by authority of the Legislature, instead of being left to struggle for existence through all the perverse ingenuity of lawyers, and the (sometimes) stolid bigotry of judges, we shall have neither more nor less than a Code.

But not only are bits of a Code thus in daily use and in perpetual process of irregular construction ; it is in truth the hourly business of our courts to frame them. When a case is brought before the courts, it is the office of the counsel on both sides to bring it if possible under some rule that has already been established. For this purpose they go over all the statutes

and all the cases that have any bearing on the
question; they extract from them the general rule
which they have affirmed or constructed, and they
point out that the matter at present in dispute is
regulated by that rule.   The counsel on the opposite
side either deduce a different rule from the same cases,
or build up another rule from other cases, and show
that the peculiar circumstances of the present case
exclude it from their adversaries' rule, and bring it
under that which they maintain.   The judge settles
the point by declaring what are the really essential
circumstances of the case, and what is the true rule
deduced from all the precedents by which it is to be
governed.   Now this process, which is repeated half-
a-dozen times a day in every court in the kingdom, is
nothing more nor less than the construction of a
portion of a Code by the judge, aided by the suggestions
of possible codes from the bar.   It is the construction
of a syllogism, of which the major premise is a fragment of a code.   This premise is generally expressed
in a few words, it seldom exceeds a couple of short
sentences.   It may of course be right or wrong, but it
is the only logical way in which a judge can make
any use of the precedents by which he is avowedly
governed.   And since this is the inevitable method of
deciding every cause which falls under old precedents,
it is impossible to see how greater risk of error could

be run if the premises were constructed before the
case is considered at all; that is to say, if the rule
which the precedents have established were ascertained
and extracted from them and declared to be their true
meaning, by the concourse of many heads instead of
by the judgment of one, and if it were found written
down in a certain section of a general Code, instead of
being left to be expiscated by the *ex post facto* acute-
ness of the judge, without time for reflection or
advising with others.

And the reason why, though we are thus constantly
having forensic and judicial bits of Codes constructed,
our law is still so rude and heterogeneous is this—that
we waste deliberately all the energy thus applied,
because though a rule must be manufactured for the
decision of every case, yet no sooner is the case decided
we tear the rule to pieces, by refusing to regard the
judge's deduction of it from the precedents to be
conclusive, and only casting his own decision into the
pot along with the rest, and requiring every succeeding judge to go through precisely the same labour,
with full liberty to arrive at a wholly different conclusion. For, as we have seen Sir Samuel Romilly
observes, a judge is by our theories to decide no more
than the bare facts before him, and every suggestion
he may make of the propriety or true nature of the
rule which he thinks the precedents establish is not

binding on his successors, but may be treated by them as *obiter dicta*, propositions which they may receive with respect or with thinly covered contempt, but which they are in no way bound to follow if they can imagine a different method of explanation.

There is indeed a phrase of some celebrity originating with Paley, and criticized in succession by the authors so often cited, Romilly, Austin, and the present Lord Chancellor, which, at first sight, seems to suggest a different method of judicial decision. This phrase is "the competition of opposite analogies." Paley, in his Moral Philosophy, tells us that whenever a case is not precisely the same in all its facts with a precedent, but "resembles those formerly adjudged only indirectly and in part, and in certain views and circumstances, and seems to bear an equal affinity to other adjudged cases," then it is by the suggestion of these competing analogies that the contention of the bar is carried on; and "it is in the comparison, adjustment, and reconciliation of them with one another, and in the discerning of such distinctions, and the framing of such a determination as may save the various rules alleged in the cause, or, if that be impossible, as may give up the weaker analogy to the stronger, that the sagacity and wisdom of the Court are seen and exercised." Now though it is certain that when a case is very nearly alike to a precedent, a judge will lazily decide it as if it were identical, saying, perhaps, that it "cannot be distinguished," without taking the trouble to extract a general rule from the precedent; and though judges and counsel of inferior mental calibre may often argue and decide cases which are more remote from the precedents in the same loose way, yet this is certainly not the most common method in which, in 'the Superior Courts, questions are discussed; and neither by the leading commentators, judges, nor members of the bar is any method commonly adopted in cases of delicacy, save that construction of a syllogism which we have already analyzed.

But, in truth, the example which Paley gives to illustrate his theory shows distinctly the limited class of cases on which his mind was then resting. He instances the contention respecting literary copyright, and tells us that the question being new, the argument on the one side was that this was a species of property most nearly resembling the work of the hands, and therefore entitled to the same protection with the fruit of manual labour, while the other side asserted that it rather resembled the product of the inventive faculties —such as a new machine—the idea of which, unless protected by express patent, was public property. He was, therefore, speaking and thinking of a case in which the judges were in fact called on to legislate, there being no prior rule at all to guide them, and in which case they therefore took into account the analogy of our legislation in matters more or less similar. But though this still sometimes happens, it certainly does not compose the bulk of judicial employment. And even if it did, it would only indicate that still, whatever may be the available materials, a part of a Code must be constructed, promulgated, and acted upon, whenever a judicial decision is pronounced, whether founded on precedent or analogy.

The conclusion which must be drawn, then, is this: That at this moment we suffer under every one of the evils and inconveniences which can be alleged against a Code, without benefiting by any of its advantages. For that our whole judicial business is conducted through the medium of shreds and fragments of a Code, scraped together to meet the exigency of each case, framed by the ability and discretion of one man, or at most of three or four men, in the hurry of despatching their daily business, without opportunity for looking before or after, and which, after having served their immediate purpose, are commonly torn up and scattered to the winds, or which, if preserved, fulfil exactly the same purposes which they would have fulfilled had they been previously meditated and digested into a formal and complete Code. While the fact that they were not previously meditated and digested leaves the law a mass of uncertainty and incongruity, and adds every year to its confusion. The sole advantage alleged in favour of the present system, that, if a precedent has proceeded upon a misapprehension of the law (*i.e.*, upon error in the major premise or statement of the rule), it carries the error no farther, is sometimes unfounded in point of fact, and at any rate is inconclusive. For a bad rule is at present sometimes perpetuated avowedly, only because it has once been enunciated. And if it were in a Code, it could remain there only by virtue of the negligence of the Legislature. For it certainly were as easy, and more consonant with our Constitution, that, upon an erroneous rule being detected in a Code, it should be deleted, and a better one substituted by authority of Parliament, than that it should be left to the discretion of a judge to say whether he will follow or not a given precedent, or accept or not the reasoning on which his predecessor based his decision.

Therefore I cannot agree with the Lord Chancellor in his opinion that a Code would be yet premature. None can indeed agree with him more heartily than I do, that much of the law in both England and Scotland is still barbarous and disgraceful. It contains hundreds of instances of the palpable absurdities which arise at this day from the conservation of rules

adapted to the state of society of the middle ages.
But there is no reason why these should not be swept
away as we advance, and why a Code must be delayed
until every remnant of folly is expunged from our
legislation.   On the contrary, the mere effort to make
a Code embodying such absurdities, would make them
so glaring and palpable to all that they must be rooted
out.   Public opinion endures them because it does not
recognise their existence; it accepts tacitly the fact
that law cannot be understood by any one save a
professed lawyer, and it consequently adverts to none
of the details of the heterogeneous mass.   But once
reduce the mass to a brief and plain statement, and
the thinking part of the public will turn their minds
to it as to any other question of policy; and when
this has been done, the factions of lawyers will be
compelled speedily to yield before the common sense
of the community.

The public, indeed, must not only be the ultimate
arbiter of the fitness of every measure of legal reform,
but it must be the original motive force.   If it is
content with our present legal system, there is no
more to be said.   But if it is ill-satisfied with a state
of things in which the law that governs us is filled
with gross absurdities that hamper every social relation,
and is at the same time so utterly beyond the comprehension of the community, that no effort in the way of

reform is made, merely because the public cannot find
out what the evil is of whose effects it is so painfully
conscious, then the first, most urgent, and most persistent demand must be for law simplification. There
is nothing in the nature of law which should make the
expression of it so obscure as to be beyond the understanding of ordinary intelligence. Lawyers indeed
must construct the expressions. But they can do
this plainly enough if they will. Now the will is that
which the public must supply them with. For so
great is the resistance offered by the dead weight of
the profession, that no single individual, however high
placed, can make way unaided against it. There are
above a hundred barristers in the House of Commons,
and the law Peers form a strong phalanx in the House
of Lords. All but a few of these have natural sympathies in the direction of mere conservation of existing
rules. They have spent a lifetime in acquiring or admi-
nistering them, and the knowledge which is beyond
a layman's power places the lawyer on a pedestal
above his fellows. These circumstances, more or less
unconsciously, add force to the natural aversion to
change which is so largely developed among Englishmen in prosperity. Nothing but help from without
will overcome the resistance of this inertia. By the
people the question must be forced on the Government.
Our rulers and legislators must be made to feel that

the tenure of their posts depends on their earnestly
labouring in the cause. Without this motive to exertion, they will continue to shirk the question; they will
refer it from committee to committee, seeking only to
throw the work off their own shoulders; they will recoil
aghast from the magnitude of the task, and demand,
half in indignation and half in entreaty, whether it
can be reasonably expected that the House shall ever
get through such a multitude of clauses. All this is
the stereotyped reception of any honest work of legal
reform. But the country may well answer, that to do
this work of purifying our law is what they are made
legislators for. And it will be done, if the country
really insists. Therefore, laying aside for the present
all other demands for Law Reform, let the country
unite in demanding that the law shall be first of all
so expressed that it can be known. The root of all
law amendments is law simplification.

CHAPTER II.

LEGAL REPORTING.

An important question, intimately connected with the simplifying of the records of our law, whether we codify it or not, has of late occupied much of the attention of the legal profession. This is the system of reporting the current decisions of our Courts. There are in the three kingdoms some fifty different series of reports annually published. In England alone there are sixteen series of regular or authorized reports of the separate Courts. There are five more of very nearly equal authority and much greater punctuality, embracing the whole of the courts, viz., the reports of the *Law Journal*, of the *Law Times*, of the *Jurist*, of the *Weekly Reporter*, and of the *New Reports*. Besides these there are the daily reports in all the London newspapers. It is admitted on all hands that this multiplicity is an enormous evil. Excluding those of the daily papers, there are six barristers engaged in reporting, almost officially, every case. It is impossible that they shall all report with equal accuracy, or equal

16—2

comprehension. They are besides, in many cases, paid by length, which is a premium on prolixity. Hence enormous redundancy of detail, both for the sake of pay, and lest any rival reporter should seem to be more complete. Hence a variety in the statement of the facts, compelling the lawyer who hereafter uses the precedent to examine all the six statements, lest any point be omitted in one. Hence the reporting of a number of useless cases, only fit, as Bacon says, "to season the wits of students in a contrary sense of law," and to favour legal fraud and oppression. And hence the evergrowing mass of judicial law which no brain at the present time can master, and which it is sometimes argued would immediately overwhelm any code with its sheer bulk and weight.

We need, however, spend no time in the discussion of this last proposition, since it is evidently futile to argue with those who tell us that the abrogation of twelve hundred volumes in favour of two or three is useless, because every year will add some dozen either to the twelve hundred or to the two or three. So far as affected by a code, the annual increase would indeed be in some measure checked by its introduction, if it answered the expectations of its advocates by diminishing the ignorance of law, and the consequent amount of litigation to be annually reported. But in any case we may accept as a fact, that under the present system of reporting, there must be an annual addition to the records of our law, of a huge undigested mass of decisions—a great and pregnant evil,—and we may properly consider what are the steps which may be taken for its future abatement.

Three different schemes have at different periods been announced for this purpose. The first, indeed, is scarcely a scheme ; it consists only in leaving matters alone, in the hope that some of the competitors will at last see that it is their interest to supply brief compendiums of the facts and law in place of the present voluminous records of every detail and every argument. But to expect competition to cure an evil which it has directly engendered is a rather Utopian idea. If none but scientific lawyers wanted the reports, doubtless scientific reports would be furnished. But as all classes of lawyers want the reports, and the scientific lawyers form a very small proportion of the body ; as, moreover, some occasionally want the reports, not to establish law on a correct foundation, but to confuse an adversary and snatch a decision from a judge, there is really no hope that the demand for multitudinous detail will cease, or that a demand for brief precision will spring up. And experience confirms this view, for though several of the existing series have at different periods professed to abstract only the parts strictly essential in each decision, yet they have always been compelled to abandon the design, and to return to the voluminous system which the profession prefers.

The next plan is one that has at various times been agitated, and even put in practice, and in a modified shape has lately been revived by Mr. Daniel, and obtained the approbation of the English bar to its being tried.   It is, in brief, that the number of competitors shall be choked off by the resolution of the higher branch of the profession to admit as authoritative only one regular series, and to use the emoluments thus derived from monopoly for the purpose of offering such salaries as shall secure the best reporters, and allow them to be placed under the efficient control of a " Council of Reporting," and of the respective judges.   It is argued that in this way regularity and completeness might be enforced, and useless matter excluded.   The plan is undoubtedly plausible, and for a few years might be effectual.   But in Scotland, at least, it has been found by experience to be incapable of being long maintained.   There once existed in that country the *Faculty Collection ;* reports prepared under appointment of the bar in the way Mr. Daniel desires. But the issue became by degrees irregular and imperfect; another series sprang up, conducted on commercial principles; it flourished, and ultimately extirpated its rival.   It is impossible, indeed, to prevent this com-

petition. The cases which the authorized reporter
excludes, as in his opinion trivial or useless, will be
reported by an outsider, and as the authorized reporter,
being human, will sometimes be wrong or obscure, it
will be impossible to exclude the outsider who corrects,
supplies, or explains. The thin end of the wedge
must thus inevitably speedily enter, and as the outsider
will be the cheaper, he will ultimately prevail, as he
does now. Nor is it possible that a strict superin-
tendence shall be long exercised by the " Council of
Reporting." The council will be the personal friends
of the reporters; they will make allowance for occasional
neglect occasioned by the pressure of private business,
which they can well appreciate, and every instance of
neglect will be a prize to competition. So this scheme
also must stand condemned by the test of reason as
well as that of experience.

A third proposal has been that the State should
undertake the duty of recording judicial decisions. As
it has not, I believe, been proposed that it should do
this otherwise than through the agency of members
of the bar, this suggestion falls under the same objections which would be fatal to Mr. Daniel's plan.
Imperfections would occur, competition would enter,
and we should speedily lapse again into the ruts in
which we are now grinding along.

The Lord Chancellor hinted once at a modification

of this plan, by the institution of a Department of Justice, which should be charged with "an annual revision of the reported cases, with power to determine what is to be regarded as entitled to authority, and what ought not to be quoted hereafter for the purpose of determining the law." The object of this scheme is excellent, and the idea philosophical, but its practical development is surrounded with difficulties, and until the Lord Chancellor farther indicates the manner in which he proposes to deal with them, it would be premature to criticize it.

I ventured, during the recent discussions, to bring to the notice of the profession some considerations pointing to a plan of a wholly different character from any of these. As it is at least founded upon observation of the erroneous principle which lies at the root of not merely the present, but of every other system which has been proposed, I will here offer a brief outline of that which I believe to be the only true principle on which satisfactory reporting can rest.

It must be confessed that it is at least a singular anomaly, that when we desire to preserve, for the purpose of a precedent, the judgment of an eminent lawyer of the bench, we commit to another lawyer, of very inferior standing and experience, and presumably of inferior knowledge and powers, the duty of dis- covering and stating what was really meant by the

decision. For though we obviate, as far as possible,
danger of error in the reporter, by encouraging him, at
whatever cost of iteration and prolixity, to take down
the words of the judge's speech verbatim, yet we do
not thereby secure that we have got the exact motive
and extent of the judgment, and, above all, we do not
secure that we have not got something more which
vitiates the report. For very few judges are themselves
so accurate that they will introduce in their speeches
(which are generally extempore) the precise facts, and
no more, on which their judgment turns ; and even if
they do, they may often omit some matter arising
merely out of the shape in which the case has come
before them, but which is really important as forming
a limit to its applicability as a precedent when the
same point shall arise in a different form or at another
stage. And even if they succeed in expressing all
this exactly as it exists in their own minds, yet still
the reporter, being a different mind, cannot possibly
be sure of it ; he, therefore, out of caution (and to
supply the professional craving for circumstance and
exception), gives his own detail of the facts, adding
some which the judge has not alluded to, and passing
over some at whose existence he has hinted as material
elements of his decision. Then, when a third mind
comes to apply this decision, it is filled with still more
uncertainty respecting what are the real facts on which

the decision turned; the opposing sides throw more darkness on the question; and finally, the judge must frequently declare that he cannot tell on what reason, out of several that are possible, the decision really went, and consequently what rule it established. Thus both diffuseness and uncertainty are the product of our system of setting one man to think, and another man to tell us what the first thought. And, of course, both evils are enhanced when we allow several men of equal non-authority to act as priests and diviners of the original oracle.

It may be gathered from this suggestion of the source of the evil, what is the nature of the remedy proposed. It is, in a word, to make each judge his own reporter. It is to call upon him to state briefly in writing, before he pronounces judgment, 1st, the facts, so far as he considers them material; 2nd, the form of the suit and the stage it has reached; 3rd, the precedents cited on each side; and 4th, his decision. If the labour of this shall be so great as to prevent him from getting through so much judicial work, the judicial staff must, of course, be increased. The cost would be well repaid by the advantages of the arrangement. But a little reflection will show that the object would be attained with very little, if any, increase of labour to the occupant of the bench.

For a case, when reduced to the facts which are alone essential, can almost always be stated very briefly. The cases stated on appeal from the inferior to the superior courts, are generally very short, yet they contain all the useful facts. The note of objections to a judge's charge is very short, yet it sufficiently raises the point of law in dispute. So there is no doubt that the great majority of cases could have their pith and marrow expressed in a very moderate number of sentences. And it is almost a necessary rule, that the more important the case the more succinctly it may be put in words. It is only the minute questions of detail, of evidence, or of narrow exception, that need copious explanation. Now, the judge does actually enter in his note-book, as each case is argued before him, the several statements of fact which he thinks material. Before he decides, he mentally, perhaps actually, arranges these, strikes out what he finally disregards, makes a brief note of the cases cited, and of the rules which the counsel on each side deduce from them, and probably concludes his notes with a concise record of the rule which he himself deduces, and the tenor of his judgment. A very little more method given to this necessary duty would make these notes the best possible report; the most concise yet exhaustive record of the facts, the arguments, the precedents, and the judgment. And, obviously, to this task very little, if any, more time would be requisite than that which is now given to the hearing and consideration of the cause, because the process is no other than that which the judge ought to do, and generally must do, at present, while the cause is being argued, or when he takes his notes and the papers home for consideration.

I have supposed the case of only a single judge. But in a court composed of several judges, the system would be very slightly modified. Each would take down his own notes as now; if they found they agreed in opinion, they would select that which best expressed it ; if they differed, each would, as now, issue his own opinion, and if he thought some fact material which the others did not, he would state it as now. But the evil of long loose speeches would be abated by the introduction of this logical method and regular system of arrangement.

No court or judge would thus give judgment till a correct report had actually been prepared, of which the judgment would form the conclusion. Many of course would be useless as precedents, and unfit for preservation. But it would not be safe to leave to each the selection of what he thinks proper to be kept, for human nature is weak even on the judgment-seat, and a case might be slurred, on pretence that it was unimportant. Therefore every judgment thus given, final or interlocutory, should be thus noted, and the note sent to the printer by the registrar of the court, on the evening of the day on which it is pronounced. Copies of the proofs should next day be sent to all the judges of equal standing. These might meet once a week, and by a majority determine what cases should be preserved. This would not imply much labour, for the question at this stage would be only what cases were important, not whether they were rightly decided or not. Those preserved would be at once printed, and thus delay in the issue would be impossible.

So much as regards the practicability of this plan, and its leading advantage—its unquestionable accuracy. Two other collateral advantages, among several which it presents, may be further briefly touched upon.

It would, in the first place, greatly promote correctness of judicial legislation. There are, at present, occasionally such things as judgments confused, illogical, and moved by a trivial circumstance which is really irrelevant. All these defects are so easily fallen into, and so easily veiled by an extempore speech, that they must be expected under the present system to occur not infrequently, to the great detriment of legal science, and of the public weal. They would, under the proposed system, be at least greatly less prevalent.

No better guard against loose thinking is to be found than to require the thinker to put briefly his thoughts into writing. The error in his reasoning, which never occurred to him before, stares him plainly in the face when it is set down on paper. The bias produced by sympathy stands confessed when it is necessary to state the simple facts, and to say on which of them the opinion rests. And the judge will besides be rendered more careful, when he knows that in the record which his brethren and the profession will criticise, there will be no excuse for him on the ground of error in the reporter, and no hope of escape from censure by hiding inaccurate thought in a multiplicity of irrelevant statements.

In the second place, the new system would settle at once all question of authority. That report, in which the judge himself states the facts, arguments, and precedents which influenced his judgment, must necessarily be the sole authentic report. Consequently there could be no competition, for there would be nothing which a competitor could usefully add. The judge might be right or wrong, but a rival reporter could not correct him. He might not have considered important a fact which really was so, but there would be no use in the reporter telling us a fact which we know formed no part of the motive for the judgment. No other reports, in fact, could ever be cited, because they would be utterly irrelevant; none others could be in demand by the profession, and consequently none would be offered. Thus, definitely and for ever, we should reduce our reports to a single series for each court appearing weekly, containing the briefest possible statement of the facts, arguments, and precedents which moved the judgment, and not a word more.

This scheme, which owes its simplicity as well as its other advantages to the fact of its being based on sound principle, would not interfere with any question of codifying or consolidating the law, or of revising, at the end of a year, the decisions, with a view to expunge such as contained bad or doubtful law, as the Lord Chancellor suggests. It would adapt itself so readily to existing arrangements, that it might be put in force next term, by the mere consent of the judges, or next year by a parliamentary enactment. It would facilitate any future consolidation, lend itself easily to the process of annual revision, and by degrees raise the scientific study of law. Making the judges more logical and careful, it would beget corresponding improvement at the bar, to the expediting of public business, and the repression of litigation. And therefore I conceive that if its adoption should render necessary some slight addition to the strength of the judicial staff, the expense would be manifold repaid to the country.

CHAPTER III.

THE ASSIMILATION OF LAW.

No scheme for the practical improvement of the law
seems at first sight to be more easy, reasonable, and
safe than that of the assimilation of those different
systems which prevail in England and Scotland.   The
grievance caused by their divergence appears on the
surface to be very serious.   Where there is an intercourse so incessant, where the relations of life are so
intimate and interlaced as between the subjects of the
two parts of this island, where the social habits and
the political constitution are all but identical, there
would seem to be a perpetual source of inconvenience,
and a frequent cause of injustice in the fact that the
codes of law are in many respects so different that
knowledge of the one is not even a help to knowledge
of the other.   And the circumstances which render the
discrepancy so peculiarly objectionable seem also to
render it capable of easy and beneficial removal.   No
à priori argument can be suggested why Englishmen

and Scotchmen should not conform to the same legal arrangements and rules. Alike as they are in many points, it would seem a simple matter to establish entire similarity in the legal and judicial systems of the two countries. And the benefit to follow from extending over the whole realm the rules which guide civil conduct and by which civil relations are construed, would seem to more than balance the supposed slight and temporary inconveniences which might attend the introduction on both sides of such novelty as would suffice to reduce the two systems into uniformity. Accordingly, there is no branch of legal reform which is so frequently discussed, and so strenuously urged as that of which the object is to bring about in some way or other an approximation tending ultimately with more or less speed to a complete assimilation of the law of England and Scotland.

But there are some considerations which in the argument are commonly lost sight of by the advocates for unlimited assimilation. On their own theory they must be root and branch reformers, for they insist that every instance of legal diversity is an evil, and the symmetry of system they sigh for would be marred by leaving any instance of divergence subsisting. They therefore take little or no account of any distinction in the character of the cases in which they would introduce uniformity. They do not acknowledge that while in some the law may be merely formal, and therefore admit of alteration without inconvenience to the public at large, since it is only the legal profession that is expected to be conversant with forms; there are others in which the law is really expressive of deep-seated habits among the people. On the other hand, the opponents of assimilation have equally refused to look at the question as a whole. They have been content to trust to the dead weight of difficulty which resists every change, or at most to point out specific objections to each specific measure as it is proposed. Hence on neither side has there been such a fair and candid discussion of the question of assimilation as can alone enable us to discover the principles on which it should proceed, and the consequent limits under which it must be regulated. And the result is that its supporters make little real progress in effecting even those useful approximations which sound principle would recommend, while its opponents are sometimes compelled to submit to see measures of assimilation carried which are not intrinsically bad, but which, from inattention to the principles which should sanction their admission, are productive of serious evil in operation.

Yet it surely ought to be remembered that the mere fact that a dissimilarity of law exists between two peoples is not of itself sufficient to demonstrate that either system should be substituted for the other. Once, indeed, we thought that such a rule applied to political institutions, and believing that our own were superior to those of every other Old World community, we had no scruple in applying them, or recommending them to every other nation. But we have learned by a varied and painful experience that political institutions must grow, and that they cannot be made. We have found that our own efforts to implant them among races subject to our sway but not born of our blood, have everywhere proved a failure ; and we have observed that even the attempts of foreign nations to adopt them by voluntary act have not been attended with any material success. Thus, it is now confessed by all that a political constitution is a thing which must slowly take shape according to the ideas, feelings, and wants of the people by whom it is adopted, and that every effort to alter or hasten its growth results in disaster only. But we do not yet apply this experience to the question of the transplanting of alien codes of law. Many among us see nothing objectionable in introducing the ideas of English real property law into India or New Zealand. Although they would confess the gravest doubts of France being suited for a parliamentary system at all resembling our own, they would admit of no difficulty in the way of supplanting the Code Napoleon by the law as laid down by Blackstone. Nearer home, therefore, there appears to them no cause for delay in extending over the whole extent of this island the system of legal rules which has grown up in one part of it, and they denounce as merely a relic of barbarism such diversities as are still suffered to exist.

But it may well be doubted whether the difficulties which prohibit the sudden adoption of a foreign constitution do not press with even greater weight against the forcible assimilation of legal rules. For a constitution is after all a thing which affects in general only a portion of the community. True, it is that portion in which the real life of the nation resides, that active, thinking, eager-minded section, which in a free country forms directly or indirectly the real government, and in a despot-ridden country forms the irrepressible antagonism that ultimately uproots the government. But the mass of the people is more affected by the administration of the law than by the principles of the constitution. The legal rules which concern the transactions of ordinary daily life not only apply to that thinking part of the public, but they touch the unthinking part even more nearly. And since the unthinking part is after all everywhere the majority, and is, because it is unthinking, incapable of being moved by any reasons that may be offered for an inroad on its habits, a change of law which violates these habits is a matter likely to meet an opposition far more profound and irresistible than even a change in the constitution which would abridge or extend political power.

But indeed it is not stating the objection to such interference so high as it ought to be put, when we speak of it merely as an insurmountable practical difficulty. The habits of nations ought not, any more than those of individuals, to be compulsorily changed, even if such change were possible. For nations are but made up of individuals, and national customs are the customs of the men and women in each nation. But individual customs are the result, the expression, and the only effectual method, of self-education ; that education which, growing out of experience, is the only species which really bears seed. It is the tritest of sayings that we cannot make men moral by act of Parliament. It is no less true that we cannot make them moral by either preaching or teaching alone. They must try for themselves, and make their advance by their own stumbling steps. But their customs of thought, and their customs of outward life, are these very stumbling steps of progress. Leaving to them free scope to move in their own way, to learn by their own experience, to adopt the improvements which to their own ideas seem natural and proper, there can be no doubt of a genuine advance. But breaking in upon their methods of life by imposing the ideas of another nation, or forcing them to submit to alien forms of civilization, we fetter their minds till they wither and perish.

Nor let it be said that legal rules are only the creatures of an artificial state of society and therefore may be altered without affecting the habits, the desires, and the prejudices of those whom they control. For let us only think for a moment what it is that is really expressed by law, such as we are now dealing with. There is no standard of absolute right and wrong to which we can refer it. There is no revelation of abstract justice by which we can be guided. Neither our moral nature nor the word of God yield us here direct assistance. We find no witness within ourselves to tell us whether writing ought to be essential to a contract, or what ought to be the period of limitation of actions. The enactments of social and civil polity prescribed for the Hebrews, such as those of polygamy, of the avenger of blood and cities of refuge, of the slavery of captives in war, of the restoration of property in the years of jubilee, were never intended to be binding on us. Left thus without guidance from inspiration, save such as is found in the general command " to do justly and to love mercy," we fall back, of necessity, upon the general convenience and welfare as our standard for details. We frame our laws so as to make imperative those arrangements which we have already found to be in general most adapted to our situation and our desires. When, in the course of practice, we find an evil which the majority agree in denouncing, we amend it. When society so far changes its relations as to make old rules inapplicable, we alter them. But in every case the rule grows out of our wants, and nothing save despotic authority can possibly establish a rule which is contrary to the general opinion of its need. It embodies, for the time being, the mode of action and the habits of thought which prevail among the people whom it nominally directs.

To be convinced of the truth of this, we have only to reflect how we should regard the imposition upon ourselves, in any matter, of a law which should be at variance with public opinion. Let us suppose, for instance, that the legislature were to enact that here, as in France, a man's property should, on his death, be divided equally among his children—that its disposition by will should not be in his own power. In such an enactment there would be nothing contrary to the spirit of our constitution. At this moment it is partly in force in Scotland. In England, as well as Scotland, the controlling power of law over a testator's last will is a familiar principle. On the one hand, the law often subjects an owner to strict obedience to a rule of descent impressed on his property by a prior owner; on the other, it forbids such a rule to be impressed by any one for an endurance of more than one generation. It annuls gifts of real property by will to certain purposes, such as charities, in England; and within a certain interval before death in Scotland. In both countries, it denies to certain heirs an equal participation, unless they bring in for division what had accrued to them by a different or exclusive title. The authority of law is therefore recognized as supreme over the regulation of property which has become, by the death of its owner, for the moment a *res nullius*, and the will of the late holder is sanctioned just so far as public convenience dictates. But the case supposed, of the establishment of the French rule of division, as it would go beyond our present ideas of public convenience, would be held an instance of tyrannical interference with private rights, — an outrage upon freedom which would almost warrant a revolution,—a proof conclusive that Parliament did not represent the nation, and that therefore the very basis of its constitution must be changed. Or, to take now an instance affecting only a certain class in the community, suppose Parliament were, in its plenitude of legislative power, to abolish the custom of days of grace in payment of bills of exchange. There is no question here of abstract justice, and as little of abstract convenience. The custom does not exist in all nations, and it varies in extent in almost every one in which it is found. Yet a forcible alteration of it would be felt as a grievous hardship by our mercantile community —on no other ground than that it *is* a custom, that it suits their arrangements, and is interwoven with their habits of business. Or, again, take the question of the introduction of the decimal system in the coinage ; or the adoption of the scientific French system of weights and measures, in place of our own irregular, confused, and cumbrous scales. There can be no doubt that the step would ultimately be a great national benefit, an ease to every calculator, a protection against fraud and error, a great means of extending our foreign trade. It was actually the case that one of the principal obstacles to our reaping full benefit from the commercial treaty with France, lay for some time in the reciprocal difficulty of translating readily yards into metres, and francs into shillings. Yet this great national improvement is delayed solely because its adoption would be at the cost of some present inconvenience, affecting chiefly the humblest classes in their smallest transactions ; and it is not doubtful that they would resent, with a vigour which might forcibly displace a Government, an attempt to impose such " new-fangled ideas." The actual rioting with which the rectification of the calendar was received little more than a hundred years ago, has not yet passed away from the memories of our statesmen.

It is obvious from such considerations as these, that the doctrine that constitutions are not made, but grow, is only a statement, in regard to political laws, of a truth applicable in a wider sense to all laws. Whatever spontaneously becomes law in any nation, is an expression of what is found to suit the convenience of the people; and whatever is made law contrary to that convenience, is felt to be an imposition of tyranny. But we may go further, and very safely affirm, that what is thus imposed by a foreign power, will, even though maintained as law for years, either work badly, or become altogether effete and disregarded. Of the first we have an example in the application of trial by jury in civil cases in Scotland. Half a century of practice has not yet naturalized this institution either in public estimation or in the legal mind. Clients still press their adviser to avoid, if possible, the necessity of appealing to such a tribunal. Lawyers still feel all abroad when called upon to conduct a case in which the facts must be thus ascertained. Nor is there anything which strikes with more astonishment an English visitor, accustomed to see, in Westminster or Guildhall, half a dozen cases of this sort disposed of in a morning, with contentment equalling the despatch, than to watch the laborious, clumsy, timid, and superfluous process by which a "jury case" is in Edinburgh propounded to the Court. And his amazement is only increased, if, desirous to see the administration of the criminal law, he crosses the passage into the Justiciary Court, and there finds the comparative merits of the two countries exactly reversed, and trials conducted with an ease, expedition, and accuracy, such as surpass all his experience of criminal business south of the Tweed. To what can we attribute such startling reciprocal differences, but to the fact that the genius of the one people entrusts readily the trial of all questions of fact to the judgment of twelve ordinary men ; while that of the other, where private interests are at stake, weighs timidly every risk of defeat, and trembles at any chance of not proving enough, or of proving too much, for a jury unskilled in the sifting of evidence.

But for an instance not merely of the awkward working, but the positive neglect and defiance, of an uncongenial statute, we need not travel out of England ; we shall find it no further from the metropolis than Manchester, and in no less important a matter than the statutory requisites to make a commercial bargain binding. By the Statute of Frauds, passed in the reign of Charles II., all bargains, if for goods above the value of 10*l*., must be in writing. This rule is in full observance in many parts of the kingdom ; and

when, in 1857, its abrogation was proposed, the
measure was stoutly and successfully resisted by the
merchants of London, who declared that maintenance
of the rule was the keystone of commercial security.
But in Manchester, in which probably more bargains
are every day completed than in any other city in the
world, London only excepted, and in many other of
the trading communities in the realm, the rule is set
at nought, and not a scrap of writing intervenes as
evidence of the largest transactions. Of course, if a
dispute arises, if either party finds it for his interest to
draw back, or if a stranger to Manchester, unaware of
its custom, supposes the bargain still open, because
the legal form is unexecuted, the Manchester men
must take the consequence of disregarding the law,
and submit to the penalty of nullity which it imposes.
But that they knowingly and regularly dare such a
result, and prefer to take their chance of its happening
rather than conform to the law, shows well how little
law avails against custom, and how much injury its
letter may work if it is contrary to the habits and
convenience of those whom it affects.

Such positive facts as these bring to us the conviction that the principles of human nature may, within
even a comparatively limited area, oppose themselves
to the forcible assimilation of law. But we may usefully, for our present purpose, pursue the inquiry which

they open up; and before attempting to educe any determinate rule, cast a rapid glance over the law of England alone, in order to ascertain whether, in any department of jurisprudence, it affords countenance to the doctrine of universal uniformity. Not in its theory at least can such support be found. Its common law is avowedly the growth of custom, and it rejects with scorn the imputation that it can ever have been drawn from foreign teaching or example. But while thus affirming the principle that convenience, which is the sole root of custom, is the only proper root of law, it does not restrict its application of the principle to cases in which the custom is identical throughout the nation. A custom may be local, may extend only over a province, a county, a town; but if it has been of sufficiently ancient date or general acceptance, it receives recognition and respect as part of our modern law. Of this innumerable instances might be given. Primogeniture is, for example, regarded as one of the chief corner-stones in the temple of our constitution. It is not merely a social law of property, it is the foundation of the government of the State. Yet this sacred rule is not universal, but is superseded in many places by opposite customs. In the county of Kent, for instance, there prevails a wholly different rule of descent, preserved intact since the days of the Heptarchy, in virtue of which primo-

geniture gives way to the custom of "gavelkind," and
land is divided among all the sons equally. By a
further exception to the general law, the Kentish
owner may aliene his estate at the age of fifteen, and
it does not escheat to the Crown if he is convicted of
felony. Again, many towns have a particular law of
descent of their own, at variance with the general law
of England. In some it is regulated neither by the
rule of primogeniture nor by that of gavelkind, but
by a special custom called Borough English, under
which the youngest son is the father's heir. Sometimes
also the amount of a widow's dower is by custom of
particular boroughs different from what it is by the
general law. So, too, the law of distribution of the
personal estate of an intestate was, till only eight years
ago, different in different parts of the kingdom. There
was one rule prevailing in the ecclesiastical province of
Canterbury (which was held to include India!), and a
different one in the ecclesiastical province of York, and
in the city of London, which is locally within the
province of Canterbury. The metropolis itself has still,
indeed, a perfect code of independent and peculiar
laws. Within the magic circle of "the City," every
shop is endowed with the privilege of legalizing the
sale of stolen goods, which elsewhere is attendant only
on a sale in "market overt." Wives have there the
privilege, which they have in Scotland, but nowhere

else in England, of being permitted to trade, and to bind themselves in their own names, if deserted by their husbands. Creditors have always there had the privilege, which they have in Scotland, but till very lately had not generally in England, of attaching money due to their debtor in the hands of a third party. All these are instances of the existence of customary law. But the legislature itself has not scrupled to confirm and extend a similar divergence of local rules. The different systems of succession to personalty above referred to, were sanctioned by modern statutes dealing with the subject. The registration of title-deeds is unknown in the general law of England, and its introduction has been fiercely resisted by some of the greatest and some of the least of her lawyers. But it is established by statute in the county of Middlesex, in the West Riding of Yorkshire, and in part of Lincolnshire. Such are a few examples of the points upon which the law of England is subject to local discrepancy. To explain them all would require a volume, and many a volume in the lawyer's library is devoted to their exposition.

And yet the measure of discrepancy is not filled full, even when we have thrown in all the cases in which it is formally enunciated in the legal system. There are local customs which have not obtained the dignity of finding a place in law books, or of

having their range of influence expressly defined,
but of which the extent of application must in every
case be left to a jury to determine, though when so
determined they constitute a binding law.   For it is of
the essence of the law of England, that a custom may
arise, whether in a particular trade or business, or in a
particular district, or even in a particular manor, which,
if not absolutely contrary to the genius of the law,
may, by mere general adoption, become imperative
upon all who come within its sphere.   Thus, the
custom of merchants is an acknowledged source from
which mercantile law is to be deduced.   Thus, too,
every county, or sometimes a district much less than
a county, has its own peculiar law respecting the
payments to be made by a tenant, who is entering
on a farm, to his predecessor, on account of unex-
hausted improvement, manures, fallows, or land in
grass.   And so also every manor may have a different
custom of descent prevailing among its tenants, and
a different custom of the dower of their widows or the
guardianship of their children.   Of customs such as
these no reckoning can be made, but they are all
legal when proved ; and, in consequence, the law in
such respects is of an infinitely diversified character.

The existence of such principles in the law of
England, and their development in practical results,
has an immediate bearing on the question whether

it is possible that the law of Scotland should be assimilated to it. Nor is this merely as furnishing that generally childish form of argument, the *argumentum ad hominem*, and permitting the Scottish lawyer to say to his English brother, First be uniform before you speak of assimilation. The discrepancies in question do indeed oppose the serious obstacle of making it in many cases impossible to say what is the law of England which it is desired to impose in Scotland. Is it, in descent of real estate, to be primogeniture or gavelkind ? Is it, as regards the rights of wives, to be the law of the kingdom, or of its metropolis ? Is it, as regards mercantile transactions, to be the law of London or the practice of Manchester ? All these questions must in each case be weighed and decided before English law is imposed on another country ; and that country might well demur to being subjected to rules, the advantage of which is not clearly enough ascertained to justify their being made imperative in all parts of the kingdom from which they are derived. But a far deeper question underlies these surface disputations. It is, whether the English system of jurisprudence, which recognises and sanctions such diversities within even the limits of a single county or a single city, is not really wisely founded on a just though unconscious appreciation of the fact, that even within the borders of England there are still surviving essential ethnological distinctions, which would make an identity of law an intolerable burden to her people. For if this be so, it will need little further argument to prove that between England and Scotland the same causes more strongly prevail, and must in a more powerful degree enforce the same conclusion.

Nor, to establish this proposition, need we draw deeply upon ethnological lore. Enough for our purpose lies in the common facts within our own cognisance, and which can scarcely escape the most superficial observation. For there seems something in the distinctions of race which keeps them, under all conditions, perennially enduring. Sometimes this inherent force amounts to an actual repulsion, as sensible as that which drives apart the corresponding poles of two magnets. Such an antipathy keeps Jews and gipsies a separate stock in every part of the globe in which they are found. In many of the fishing villages which dot our own Eastern coast, it has preserved the blood of the natives through unknown generations from the smallest taint of admixture with that of the neighbouring inhabitants. But even where the inborn peculiarities of the races do not amount to a repulsive power, they constitute a singular difficulty in the way of their intermingling, though within the same nation, so far as to become thoroughly identified. As when we mix liquids of different densities, we can

long trace, when we hold the compound up to the
light, the streaks and waving lines which show that
the combination is still imperfect, so even among our
Anglo-Saxon races, and even in this age of perpetual
locomotion and intercourse, we can easily distinguish
the various stocks from which the population has
sprung. In mere physical form and cast of features
the tourist cannot fail to mark the differences between
inhabitants of the Isle of Wight, of the Southern
English counties, of Norfolk, of Yorkshire, of the
Lothians, and of Aberdeen. Along the line of the
Western coast, from Cornwall to Sutherland, the
different Celtic races offer equally distinctive characteristics. The very difference of tongues almost
suggests some organic difference of conformation, and it
seems to become more ineffaceable as it becomes more
slight. But these peculiarities of race, thus apparent
on the surface, extend to the profoundest depths of
the mental constitution, and show clearly through any
external identity of forms. Our very government
varies through all the degrees between the sturdy
democracy of the manufacturing towns of the North
to the still surviving feudalism of Hants or Wilts,
the patriarchism of Argyle or Sutherland, or the
priestly authority which rules so powerfully in Ireland
and Wales. But the fullest demonstration of this
truth is to be derived from the recollection of the

18—2

different forms of religious faith which exist in local supremacy among us. In those questions which most deeply stir the heart and most highly exercise the intellect, we find community of allegiance, of law, of language, and of education, powerless to bring about community of conviction, powerless to obstruct the adoption of Roman Catholicism, Methodism, Anglicanism, or Presbyterianism, at the instigation of no other apparent reason than that the respective worshippers are Irish, Welsh, English, or Scottish. What conclusion can we draw but that the feathers and straws on the surface truly show the direction of the current beneath; that, from the moulding of the features and the hanging of the tongue, down to the habits which make laws, and the beliefs which make religions, we are still but a federation of the scarce mixed descendants of the Celtic, Scandinavian, Germanic, and Italian tribes, which in our first historic ages colonized our land?

Thus still distinct, city by city, and county by county, in blood, in habits, and in capabilities, as the English people is, we cannot doubt that it is true wisdom which makes their jurisprudence elastic enough to accommodate itself to their local tendencies. Nor are there wanting indications that, if it failed in so doing, it would either be set at nought, or would work radical and irretrievable mischief. We have already seen the manner in which Manchester commerce defies the law of the land, in regard to the fundamental point of the constitution of commercial contracts. In another point of no less importance, but in which the law has fortunately been less imperative, we may trace the opposite genius of Middlesex and Lancashire. Every one knows that in feudal times, all the land in the kingdom was held to belong primarily to the sovereign ; that it was granted out by him in great fiefs to his lords, and by them bestowed in smaller fiefs on their immediate retainers, until in successive gradation it reached the hands of the final sub-vassal, tenant, or actual holder and tiller of the soil. The process of creating such sub-vassals might, with few limitations, be carried on to any extent. And such still continues to be the law in Scotland, where, on every sale of land, the common form is, that the purchaser becomes at first the mere vassal of the vendor, though with power, at pleasure, to eliminate the vendor from the feudal chain, and so hold his land of the vendor's original lord. Nevertheless, the facility with which such a relation may be constituted leads to its adoption, in many cases, in lieu of an absolute sale ; and so, in towns, large estates are thus parcelled out for building purposes by the arrangement of *feus,* under which each owner, though his property is indefeasible, is technically only the vassal of the original owner, and pays

an annual feu-duty or rent-service in acknowledgment
of the right.   But in England this process of subinfeudation, as it is called, was put a stop to by a statute
of Edward II., which enacted that, on every alienation
of land, the new tenant or holder should come in the
place of the alienor as vassal to his original over-lord.
From the consequent impossibility of making a qualified permanent alienation of land, there has arisen in
the greater part of England the custom of granting it
for building purposes on mere long leases, generally of
eighty to a hundred years' endurance ; after which the
possession, with the property in any buildings meanwhile erected, returns to the landlord.   Thus we may
trace the thinness of modern walls, and the slightness
of flooring timbers, by no remote deduction, to the
legislation of the early Plantagenets.   But so contrary
to the genius of the people of Lancashire is the idea
of investing capital on another man's property, that
the system of building-leases is in that county almost
unknown ; and each plot of ground in a town must be
sold absolutely, the owner only endeavouring, under
much legal difficulty, to reserve to himself an annual
income resembling the Scottish feu-duty, by stipulating
for what is called a perpetual rent-charge.   Now, it is
quite clear that here, had legislation only gone so far
as to prohibit such rent-charges (scarcely known in
the rest of the kingdom), at the same time that it

prohibited subinfeudation, the prosperity of Lancashire would have been less than it is, because the great proprietors near the growing towns would often have been unwilling to sell their land in perpetuity, without reserving an income out of it for their descendants, while the people would have refused to build houses or manufactories on ground of which they only held temporary possession under a lease. And thus, had the legal customs of all England been assimilated by positive law, the whole nation would have suffered by the cramping influence of institutions which were not consonant with the character of a portion of the people.

Now, if these things are so in respect of mere counties and towns within a kingdom which has been undergoing the process of fusion for well nigh a thousand years, what doubt can exist of their truth as between two kingdoms which, for four-fifths of that time, have stood in deadly hostility to each other ? If England, which, whatever convulsions have agitated it, has never felt the disruptive throes of discordant nationalities, yet at this day finds it needful to indulge her people in the enjoyment of laws based upon their own various ethnological tendencies ; and if, when the legislature seeks to reduce them to uniformity, it finds itself perpetually baffled by their innate vitality, what reason is there to expect that good could follow from the wholesale assimilation of the law of two opposite ends of the island, in which national character stands most widely discrepant ?   If London and Manchester, as regards mercantile law ; if Kent, Surrey, Middlesex, Lancashire, and Yorkshire, as regards the law of real property, insist on remaining at utter variance, what hope is there that Glasgow and Aberdeen, Ayrshire and Fife, would find advantage in yielding up their native customs in favour of any of those of England—or, on the other hand, what probability is there that England, who cannot agree with herself, would profit by agreeing to accept the law of Scotland in place of her own ?

For that there yet is, as between these two nations, so united, so similar as they are, a certain fundamental difference of character, which must be allowed still to exhibit itself in different national institutions and laws, is a matter which no candid observer can dispute.   That character which, in the one, finds contentment in the beautiful but unchanging phrases of worship which she has retained, with slight modifications, from the days when they were sung by friar and nun in her cathedrals and convents, and which, satisfied with the ritual, cares less for the doctrine which may fall from the preacher's lips, must, in some deep-seated peculiarity, be different from that of the nation which sought the bare hill-sides to escape from the liturgy, and which, in every

generation, is torn by a fresh struggle to secure the free
selection by the congregation of those who are to
preach the Word to them. That nation which has,
till the present day, left her people without other
means of instruction than what their own private
efforts or the charity of richer neighbours could supply,
must needs be vitally different from the one which
for nearly three centuries, has made provision for the
maintenance, by public rates, of a school in every
parish. That nation which still affords, on every
general election, numerous and notorious instances in
her boroughs of influence which renders the forms of
election a farce, or of corruption which renders them a
scandal, must, in the elements of political life, be
somehow materially different from that which, whatever other faults she must confess to, yet, under an
identical constitution, has in her borders no instance
of a pocket borough, and but one constituency in
which bribery has ever been charged. All these are
not questions dependent on climate, on civilization,
or on forms or prejudices of ancient growth: they are
questions whose arbitrament rests in the very hearts
of the people; and the opposite results in the two
countries denote a fundamental and ineradicable
difference of national character.

Into the precise definition of such difference, so
amply discussed a few years back by Mr. Buckle and

his opponents, it is not my purpose here to enter. But let us simply take those prominent and admitted distinctions which have become proverbial. Scotsmen, by friend and foe, are styled more cautious and more thrifty than Englishmen. Let it be matter of praise or of reproach, it is at least a fact which on neither side of the border will be disputed. Does it then stand to reason, that the same laws shall suit two countries so different in the mental qualities which have the most immediate bearing on legal doctrines? Caution and thrift lie at the very root of the Scottish system of the transfer of land, upon which the whole of real property law is grafted—at the very root of the Scottish banking system from which grows the whole practice of commerce. In Scotland we find a system of conveyancing of a complex nature, but so combined with a system of registration of deeds, as to give absolute security to the purchaser or the lender. In England we find a far simpler and more direct procedure, but one in which certainty of title, though generally realized in practice, is theoretically almost unattainable; we find her, too, when amending it by the adoption of a registration of *title* which would secure an owner by means of annulling every other claim, resolute to resist the Scottish registration of *deeds*, which secures an owner by means of making public every other claim. In Scotland we find the system of numerous banks of issue securing credit by a joint-stock proprietary, granting their own promissory notes down to the smallest sum, and attracting business by cash credits and by the offer of interest on the lowest amount of a current account. In England we find private banks of issue practically scarce existing, paper restricted to amounts of 5*l.* and upwards, cash credit not in use, and joint-stock banking establishments giving no interest on current accounts if under 200*l.* How can we expect that such arrangements of spontaneous growth, yet in their development so incongruous, shall find a common reconcilement— that the fixed ideas of the true method of conducting business which are thus expressed shall be readily abandoned by either nation—how, in short, while the one is distinguished for " thrift and caution " above the other, can we expect that they will agree on a common system of law, which shall deal precisely equal measure of profit and of safety to both ?

On these two cardinal points,—one of real property law, the other of mercantile law,—the case may be left to rest. Did space permit us to follow the argument in its application to the subtler, yet not less potent, elements of national character, and into their development in the law of the personal relations, marriage, minority, the rights of women, or the power of parents, the remedy for injuries by action, or the minute details of the law of local self-government, we should find further proof, perhaps in some respects not uninteresting, of the utter impracticability of any material assimilation of the law of the two countries for at least many generations to come. But ere we leave the subject, it is necessary to advert to two points important for our consideration. The first is, the alleged pressure of inconvenience which the advocates of assimilation deplore as caused by dissimilarity of law; the next is, the scope and manner of the remedies by which alone assimilation could be effected.

On the first head, let us call the evidence of no less high authority than the Royal Commissioners, who,— comprising some of the highest authorities in law and trade in the United Kingdom [1]—were appointed in 1853 to consider how far it was desirable and practicable to assimilate the mercantile law of the three kingdoms. They issued a document in which they stated, under ninety-three heads, the points of discrepancy between the laws, and transmitted a copy to every chamber of commerce, committee of merchants, and legal association in the United Kingdom, " adding a request that the recipients would inform them of any

---

[1] The Master of the Rolls in Ireland, Sir C. Cresswell, Mr. J. Marshall (now Lord Curriehill), Mr. (now Baron) Bramwell, Mr. J. Anderson, Q.C., Mr. K. D. Hodgson, Mr. T. Bazley, and Mr. R. Slater.

other point of difference, and point out any practical
inconvenience which they had known to arise from
existing differences." The report thus states the
response made to this appeal :—

"In the answers which we received, there is a
remarkable paucity of statements as to inconveniences
actually experienced ; and in dealing with many
instances of difference, we have recommended assimilation, not because evils have been traced to the
existing state of the law, but because we think it
probable that inconveniences may hereafter arrive."

Could anything more clearly prove that the outcry
for assimilation is the outcry of theorists merely ?
Here is a body of high dignity, empowered to lay
the foundation for dealing practically with the subject,
calling on all sides for statements of inconveniences
arising from discrepancies of the mercantile laws,—
surely of all discrepancies those which are likely to be
most widely felt and most easily removed,—refreshing
the memories of those lawyers and merchants to whom
it applied with a copious statement of what the discrepancies are ; and yet compelled to make answer
that it finds a "remarkable paucity of statements of
inconveniences actually experienced," and forced to
admit that many of its recommendations were not for
the remedy of evils which, in the intercourse between
the two countries since the Union, had ever been felt,

but of evils which they thought possible might hereafter be felt! Nor is even this admission quite com-
mensurate with the whole truth. There is more than
a "paucity of statements as to inconveniences actually
experienced;" there is an almost unanimous statement
that the respondents had never known a case of inconvenience to occur. What further proof can we
have that the allegation of inconvenience is a pretence
or a delusion?

The truth is, that the relations of commerce and
of society are so adjusted, that simplicity and certainty
of local law are our requirements more than identity.
As the home trade of a nation is always many times
greater in extent and value than its foreign trade, so
in each district the local traffic is generally much
greater than that which it carries on with other parts
of the empire; and what most concerns it is, that this
larger portion of its business should be subject to the
rules which have been found by experience to be most
suited to its inhabitants. Nor does this operate injuriously even in its external dealings. These are,
for the most part, transacted through resident agents
or brokers, whose business it is to know not merely the
quality of the goods, but the peculiarities of the rules
which regulate their sale. By such means transactions
are effected with full knowledge on both sides, and
with the result that "no inconvenience is experienced."

And, in like manner, when we come to review the operation of legal rules other than those concerned in mercantile transactions, we find their operation interpreted in exactly a similar way. By far the greater number of transactions affecting land in England or Scotland, or affecting the domestic relations of Englishmen and Scotsmen, take place as between the natives of each country exclusively, and are wholly irrespective of the law of the other. Buying and selling, hiring and letting, marrying, and will-making, and all the other transactions of daily life, are, in ten thousand instances to one, matters that arise between English and English, or between Scot and Scot, rather than between English and Scot. In the rare exceptional cases, the question is probably one of legal difficulty, which would have required the interposition of lawyers, although it had occurred wholly within the limits of either country, and therefore causing little further annoyance in requiring the interposition of lawyers in both. At all events, it is almost certainly a matter in which the parties know that there is a differince in the law, and in which they therefore take pains to ascertain how the law will really affect it.

A moment's consideration of the manner in which the practical affairs of life are conducted, will, therefore, enable us fully to understand the existence of the fact which the Royal Commissioners recorded with so much astonishment. The truth is, that lawyers are, of all men, the very worst qualified to form an opinion on the social and practical effect of an alteration in the law. Their habit, the necessary result of their profession, is to consider exceptional cases. The point in which a law occasions difficulty comes before. them, but they are never consulted on the points on which the law is clear. In drawing up a document, whether it be a Bill in Parliament, a conveyance, or a pleading, their attention is necessarily and properly fixed upon the minute details, through an error in which subtlety might find an opening. Hence comes a frame of mind which, applied to the laws of two countries, sees in their dissimilarity room for a thousand cases of fraud, or deception, or misunderstanding, but which makes no allowance for common sense, and takes no account of the advantages inherent in each system in the locality to which it is adapted. It seems to them the height of folly to leave standing a system which admits the possibility of misconception, in lieu of establishing certain fixed and unwavering rules, to which all shall be bound to defer. But in this they forget their own maxim, *summum jus summa injuria*. They forget that, after all, legal rules are framed to assist, and not to fetter, human intercourse. And above all, they forget that, while it is impossible to predicate of any rule that it is absolute perfection, it must ever be left to the spirit of each age and people to decide for itself upon the rules which, in the majority of its transactions, it finds to present the highest average of comparative advantage.

But when we turn to the means by which it is proposed to reach the consummation of assimilating the law of the two countries, the Scottish lawyer will find copious evidence that, by one at least of the parties, these principles are, if not understood, at least thoroughly conformed to. There is rarely talk of carrying out assimilation by the adoption in England of the law of Scotland. There is not even the admission that the two nations may reciprocally borrow on equal terms. It is true, indeed, that something has actually been done by England in this direction. Two most important reforms in her law carried a few years ago,—the amendment of the law of divorce, and of that of bankruptcy,—were both approximations to the existing law of Scotland. But, far from being designed for that end, the example of Scottish experience was barely cited in their favour. America was the favourite authority cited in support of the divorce reforms, pure reason the chief reliance of the advocates of the bankruptcy reform. In the speech of the present Lord Chancellor, in introducing his bankruptcy reform measure in the House of Commons in 1861, there was no allusion to the working of the like provisions

19

in Scotland, where, for thirty years, they had been in full operation. A select committee has indeed, with the experience of two more years, at length reported decisively in favour of the almost complete adoption of the Scottish bankrupt law. But considering the admitted success of the Scottish system during a trial of a quarter of a century, and the proved failures of the English system for all that time, it may be thought that the vigour of prejudice which resisted assimilation so long is more wonderful than the tardy confession that assimilation in this point would be useful. Further illustration of the same nature may be drawn from the legislative results of the commission to which I have already referred. Appointed expressly to assimilate the mercantile law of the two countries, it reported that on twenty-four points the Scottish law should give way to the English, but that on only sixteen the English should yield to the Scottish. Nor did the favour shown to English rules arise from attention not being drawn to their defects. In an excellent note appended to the report, Mr. Anderson enumerated several points in the English law, of absurdity so notorious, and injustice so egregious, that only prejudice could overlook them ; but the other English lawyers refused to join him in proposing their removal. The disproportion in the remedies applied was still further increased by Parliament. The Act, as finally passed, established the English principle as the imperial rule in thirteen points, while the Scottish was adopted in only five. No one with any real knowledge of the law of the two countries can pretend to say that this is the just proportion in which assimilation should be effected, if it were to consist in the adoption of what is abstractly the* most reasonable and simple in either country.

We can follow up, by help of these foot-tracks, the ideas of the process by which assimilation is to be accomplished. England will give up such of her laws as are immaterial parts of her system, not deeply stamped in the principles of her jurisprudence, and not vigorously followed out by any section of her inhabitants. But she will not yield in the great features of her code; she will not renounce ancient doctrines, however preposterous they may be; nor part with any enactment which is in present use by any fraction of her people. If, then, Scotland is to be as one nation with England, it is she who must give up her law on all these points. Now, it is worth while for Scotsmen to consider what is the nature of the revolution which this would imply in their daily life and transactions; and, to simplify the matter as much as possible, let us restrict ourselves to the supposition that the assimilation applied in this way only to mercantile law. First, then, they would have to introduce the distinction between law and equity. Merchants must learn to resort to one court, and one method of pleading, when they would recover a debt; and to another court, and another form of pleading, when they would adjust the accounts between partners. They must learn the distinction between legal and equitable assets, and recognise the peculiar luck of getting the estate of a deceased debtor administered in Chancery, where they will find funds made available to them which in a court of law would be beyond their reach. On the other hand, they must renounce the principle of *pari passu* ranking of diligence, and be prepared to allow the first creditor who can snatch a judgment to absorb all the debtor's estate as a reward for his promptitude. They must learn next the different value of a debt according to the method in which it has been constituted, and be prepared to see a rival, who has secured an acknowledgment under seal,—*i.e.* with a wafer affixed to the paper,—obtain full payment, in exclusion of a mere book debt for goods delivered. They must admit the principle, that no obligation shall be binding except for value proved; but they will perhaps think it almost an equivalent to find that, if they can prove the delivery of a pen or of a sheet of paper, they will fulfil the requisites of the law. They must discard all notion of a firm constituting a person in law. They must recognise that the partners and the public can only deal with a firm as a number of separate individuals ; and, in consequence, they must anticipate that the genius of the law will forbid a partner from suing the firm, or the firm from suing a partner, for that would be suing himself with others, which in the eye of the law is manifestly absurd. For° the same reason, they must perforce allow that, if two firms happen to have one partner in common, neither can sue the other ; for that, again, would involve the case of a man suing himself. Yet, in all these particulars, if they only can attain the good fortune of having the proceedings conducted according to the rules of equity or of bankruptcy, they will find their position wholly different from what it is in any court of law, and perhaps not very materially different, except in comprehensibility, from what it would have been under the abolished law of Scotland.

There would be no advantage in extending, as might easily be done, the enumeration of such instances. It must be abundantly clear to every mind not warped by insuperable bias, that the adoption of changes in the law, of such a nature, would be to fall centuries back in civilization ; not certainly in the sense that the English are so much now behind the Scottish, but that the Scottish would be behind the English if they were to attempt thus to Anglicize themselves. All these rules are consonant to the genius, interwoven with the habits, understood in the practice, of England; but many generations must pass ere they could, if they ever could, become approved and familiar in Scotland. Be they good or be they bad in themselves,—a matter which it is not here our province to discuss,—it is most obvious that their adoption in Scotland would be attended with the worst evil which can belong to law,—a discordance with the ideas of those whom it is to govern, a consequent uncertainty in its operation, and at least an equal uncertainty of its being long maintained.

But while protesting thus against the doctrine that assimilation of the law is a matter so important as to be pursued at all hazards, and at all cost of local customs and local convenience, I must not allow it to be supposed that I therefore underrate its real advantages.[1] Dissimilarity of law is an undoubted evil, though it is less an evil than enforcement of an

---

[1] Having been charged in some critiques on this paper, when it first appeared, with a disposition to resist every approach to assimilation, I may be permitted to refer for disproof to two pamphlets I have published, in the one of which I urged the adoption in England of the Scottish law of bankruptcy, while, in the other, I ventured to recommend some improvements in the practice of the Courts in Scotland, suggested by English practice.

alien law. But where it can be removed by measures which will not offend the habits and ideas of the people, beyond all question it ought to be removed. And the occasions on which this course may be adopted with safety are of two classes. The one embraces all the cases in which the alteration would merely affect matter of form; the other, the cases in which either country is, from its own experience, dissatisfied with its own rules, and is disposed to try the effect of rules which seem to work better in the sister realm. As examples of the former class, may be instanced the English principle, that it is sealing and not signing which constitutes a deed; that a debt cannot be assigned in law; or that a mortgage transfers the property, leaving only a right of redemption in the mortgager. On the side of Scotland, among principles which she might very beneficially renounce, may be enumerated the preposterous doctrine that real estate cannot be conveyed by a will; or the theory that a defendant out of the country is sufficiently advised of the institution of a suit against him by an entry made in a book kept in a public office in Edinburgh. Of the second class of cases in which assimilation is advantageous, those in which either nation has found its own laws unsuitable to its needs, we have fortunately of late years had not a few instances. England, satisfied of the need for a

reform in her law of bankruptcy, of divorce, of bills
of exchange, has, in all these departments, approached
nearer to the law of Scotland than she was before ;
while Scotland, finding the time to have arrived when
her law of entails, of evidence, of relief of the poor,
was inconsistent with modern ideas, has adopted, in
whole or in part, the more advanced principles of
the English code. In such cases assimilation is not
merely possible, but may be of the highest advantage.
It is a reciprocal benefiting by the results of the
experience of the sister country which gives to the
nation which adopts it the security of results already
effected under circumstances at least exceedingly
similar, and protects from the liability to error
which would attend efforts for reform in a wholly
untried path. But such experience is only properly
available when a remedy is spontaneously sought for
admitted defects, and when it may serve to point
out the remedy most desirable. It certainly gives
no support to any scheme which would involve the
abandonment by either nation of a system which has
given it contentment, for the sake of embracing one
of which all that is known is, that it has given like
contentment to a race substantially different in many
points of character and custom.

Nor even within the useful though humble range
of assimilation thus suggested, are there wanting

indications of the need for anxious care and caution.
So much are the whole laws of a nation interwoven ;
so closely are all their provisions dependent on each
other, and on the practice of the people by which they
are interpreted, that in attempting to transplant them
there is the greatest risk of either destroying their spirit
or of bringing with them some unforeseen evil. Two
instances of this result may be culled from the recent
legislation of Scotland. The assimilation commissioners of 1853 recommended the abrogation, in
Scotland, of the old law of sale, under which the
property in goods sold was not transferred till delivery
took place, and the adoption of the English rule, which
transfers the property at the moment of completing the
bargain. The change was effected by a statute in
1856. But the legislature, in passing it, forgot that
in consequence of their rule of sale, the English had
found it necessary to establish the further rule, that no
secret bargain of sale should injure the rights of
creditors, and that, where the property was not
delivered, the bill of sale must be registered to make
it effectual. The omission of this safeguard against
fraud has already, in Scotland, led to inconvenient
results. The other instance is still more curious.
When England introduced the divorce law into her
practice, she conferred on the paramours the privilege
of intermarriage after the divorce was obtained. In

this respect she followed the spirit, though not the letter, of the Scottish law;—for though the Scottish Act declares, that the offending spouse may not marry the paramour "named in the sentence of divorce," the rule was evaded in practice by not naming the paramour in the pleadings, so that he could not be named in the sentence; and very high authority had declared that, if not so named, the subsequent marriage was valid. But in 1861, it was decided to import the rule of the English Court, which requires that the paramour shall be in all cases made a "co-respondent." The result is, that he must now be named in the pleadings; and, apparently, as a necessary consequence, in the sentence. Here, then, by a side door, the old statute forbidding marriage between those so named is brought into operation; and the practical effect is to make illegal in Scotland marriages of a character which, till then, were valid, which the legislature had no intention to interfere with, and which are at this day valid in England.

But since it is true that little inconvenience is experienced from dissimilarity, and that the cases are comparatively few in which assimilation would work other than evil, whence, it will be asked, arises the cry, which certainly has been loudly enough upraised, for assimilation in all respects? The answer is, that it originates with lawyers only, and among them from two very different classes of motives. There are, firstly, the scientific law reformers. Such men as these look upon law in the abstract. They are apt to refer every enactment to the ultimate principle, whether it be of innate morality, of pure reason, or of utility, which they have adopted as their theory of legal direction. They would bring each local custom to this standard, in the belief that there is a fixed rule of right and wrong in all human affairs, and in the hope that, when it is demonstrated, all men will willingly conform their conduct to it. But they forget that, in the vast mass of transactions between man and man, while reason, and morality, and utility (expressions, after all, which lead to the same result) ought to regulate the motives of the parties, and be the object of their dealings, yet they have very little whatever to do with the manner in which the object is effected. Thus, to recur again to the simple question adduced as an illustration, every theory of ethics will concur in establishing the propriety of adhering strictly to the terms of a bargain once made ; and in this, every theory of law will agree with morality. But ethics throw no light upon the question whether this result will be best attained by requiring the bargain to be expressed in writing, or by leaving it open to the incertitude of oral proof. Nor does reason here succeed any better : for reason cannot tell us beforehand whether a certain set of people are careful and guarded in their language, cautious in arriving at a mutual understanding, accurate in memory, and conscientious in testimony, in which case writing is plainly superfluous; or whether they are overwhelmed with business, a little, perhaps, addicted to speculation, hasty in assertion, or inaccurate in habits of thought, in which case writing may be a very needful check and test of their true intention. Obviously, there can, in such a case, be no universal rule of law applicable with equal advantage to both cases. Nevertheless, this is precisely one of the most common instances in which scientific lawyers urge the enforcement of one common and invariable rule. I cannot but venture to protest against such "science falsely so called." I venture to claim, on behalf of common sense and civilization, deliverance from this Procrustean idea of legal amendment, and to insist that, in matters in which no true rule save that of convenience, as ascertained by practice, can possibly be laid down, we shall not be required to sacrifice it to the ideal beauty of a symmetrical perfection.

But far less worthy of respect is the origin of the assimilation cry, as it comes from the self-styled "practical men" among our lawyers. These are commonly attorneys or writers, barristers or advocates, as the case may be, who, finding occasionally a point to arise in their practice which requires a knowledge

of different principles from those they have studied,
incontinently denounce the rules of which they are
ignorant as worthy only of barbarians, and call on the
legislature to sweep away at once such anachronisms
from our statute book. Happily the legislature, repre-
senting the interests of all the community, is not apt
to give much heed to the interests of so very small a
body. And to those whose only motive is annoyance
at being obliged to confess that their knowledge is
not universal, or mortification at the loss of some
possible profits, it were waste of time to address
argument or instruction. They must be left to their
own noisy declamation, and allowed to learn from time
the truth that lawyers were made for law, and not law
for lawyers.

Carried away to a certain extent by the demon-
strations of these two classes of professional men,
there is undoubtedly also a small section of the
mercantile community who give their support to the
doctrine of assimilation. It may have happened to
them,—but we have seen how rare is the occurrence,
—to have been put to some measure of inconvenience
by having to adjust a transaction with a view to a
different form of law from that to which they are
accustomed; or to have been disappointed in not
finding afforded, by the courts in which circumstances
compel them to sue, the same remedy as that which

the courts of their own country would have yielded.
These are, indeed, nearly the sum total of the inconveniences which can possibly arise from the discrepancy
of law; and few as they are, we may readily sympa-
thize with those individuals on whom they fall. But
ere they permit themselves to be led away by the idea
that what has happened to themselves must be of
frequent occurrence, and therefore give their ears
to the lawyers who proclaim so loudly that it is a
monstrous grievance that such things should ever
occur, let me ask them to consider the evidence which
has been adduced, as to the singularly slight measure
of annoyance actually produced in international dealings
by such a cause, and the suggestions which have been
offered as to the trouble and danger involved in a
forcible attempt to change the settled law of great
communities. No London merchant, we may be persuaded, who reflects on these consequences, will desire
that, for his occasional ease or security, the customs
of trade of a thousand merchants in Glasgow should
be overturned; nor will any Glasgow shipowner, who
finds that, in some particular case, the verdict of a
Liverpool jury might be more favourable than the
judgment of the Court of Session, invoke the prodigious
disruption of the social system of Scotland, which
would follow from the wholesale adoption of English
law in that country.

But even if these small and isolated sections of the public still adhere to their desire, there can be little store set by demands of persons who have neither reason nor authority on their side. Claiming to be pre-eminently practical, they are, in truth, the rejectors of practice in favour of theory; claiming credit for breadth of view, they are, in truth, the most narrow-minded; claiming to represent great interests, they are, in truth, opposed to every interest but their own. All that they can justly ask, the legislature should be ready to give. Whenever the rules of law are found inconvenient by those among whom they are in use, it should gladly seize the opportunity to import the neighbouring system if it seems preferable. Wherever the substance of law has, by the action of time, become identical in both countries, it should be ready to sweep away the fictions which still maintain the memory of ancient discrepancies. But, save in such cases, no one need take shame to confess himself in this matter honestly conservative. Such a conservatism is at least not founded on prejudice; for it frankly admits that it is hard to decide which country might most profit by accepting the system of the other in such matters as, subject to the doctrines above enumerated, admit of assimilation. But while in operation such principles are conservative, they are, in source, essentially liberal: for they accept, in the best sense, the *vox populi* as the *vox Dei;* they take the will of those who are to be chiefly affected by forms of law as the best test of their suitableness; they oppose themselves to that unreasoning and hurtful tyranny which would make the convenience of the few, or the so called scientific theories of still fewer, obtain a predominance over the advantage of the many, and the tested experience of nations.

CHAPTER IV.

THE LAW OF MARRIAGE IN ENGLAND AND SCOTLAND.

ONE of the most remarkable, and undoubtedly the most important, of the instances of discrepancy between the legal systems of England and Scotland is to be found in the laws relating to marriage. The appointment of a Royal Commission, now sitting, to inquire into the subject with a view to the assimilation of the law, recognises, but does not supersede, the concern of the public in this question. For it is not one on which the decision can be left to any body of lawyers, however learned, or of laymen, however respected. It touches the personal and domestic ties of all too nearly, it involves too much the happiness and the morality of the community to admit of being finally settled without wide discussion, or by any process save the agreement of general conviction. But discussion to be useful must proceed upon accurate knowledge, and unanimity of conviction can only come after a full examination of the principles involved. At present, however, such knowledge is unfortunately not common. Very few persons in Scotland are acquainted with the English law of banns and licences, or with that of marriage by a registrar. Still fewer in England understand the real nature or the ordinary forms of marriage in Scotland. It is not unusual to see in respectable English newspapers the statement that men and women may in Scotland be married without their knowing it. And a personage so eminent and learned as Dr. Lushington declared, before a Committee of the House of Commons in 1849, that " he supposed it is but rarely that marriage in Scotland is had in what is called in England *in facie ecclesiæ.*" Some service, therefore, may be rendered to the consideration of the question by explaining briefly the points of difference on which so much mutual ignorance prevails. And when the principles are understood which lead to such divergence of forms we shall be better able to judge which of them is most consonant with convenience, reason, and morality, so as to deserve adoption by the whole of the community.

For in such a matter as this it is incumbent on us to lay aside all national or educational prejudices, and to seek only for that system which intrinsically approaches nearest to perfection. It is true that we must at best be content with something short of that

standard. No human provisions can in every case
measure out absolute justice ; none can always protect
virtue and punish wrong, and under the forms of all
human systems will fraud and vice find cover and even
aid. But while this is the necessary condition of all
our institutions, the regulations which affect marriage
are open to especial dangers, and demand from us
peculiar care. It might be hard, perhaps, to point
out which class of social directory laws has been
productive of the greatest sum of misery ; but there
can at least be no doubt that the sharpest and cruellest
pangs are those which have been inflicted by the flaws
in our marriage code. The contract which it regulates,
divine in its origin, mystic in its nature, holy in its
obligation, becomes, by its subjection to human ordinances, tainted with human imperfection. Applying
to the dearest relations of life—involving all that is
most precious in our honour, our happiness, and our
hopes—touching most closely those whose sensibilities
are tenderest, whose affections are most devoted, and
whose weakness is least defended—the errors and
defects of the laws by which it is construed pierce
instantly to the heart. And the instinct of public
sympathy is not slow to acknowledge this truth.
Fiction adopts the mischances that arise from the
marriage laws as the most unfailing means of exciting
profound interest. The incidents, a thousand times

20—2

repeated, of an elopement, a marriage by a false priest, the destruction of a marriage certificate, never pall upon the reader's attention. They yield, indeed, in attraction only to the romance of fact. The whole kingdom is agitated with sympathy, with compassion, and with disgust, when, in the reports of a court of justice, there is unrolled before us some tale of villany that has made the marriage law its stepping-stone to success. Yet these are but rare and chance disclosures of sorrows such as at this day embitter many a bosom. Only the doctor, the clergyman, or the lawyer, power- less depositaries of so many secrets of cureless wrong, can guess at the multitude of cases in which a momen- tary neglect of caution, an inadvertence to, or ignorance of, statutory requirement and judicial interpretation

> " Takes off the rose
> From the fair forehead of an innocent love,
> And sets a blister there, makes marriage vows
> As false as dicers' oaths."

And only those whom accident enables to follow the history of such cases beyond the moment of agony when the knowledge first comes that all that is most dear has been perilled, and has been irremediably lost, can tell how far descending is the heritage of misery that takes its rise in deception under legal forms, or in an honestly conceived misapprehension of what is required by law to make the nuptial contract binding.

It is therefore not strange that the adjustment of doctrines on which so much depends should have occupied the frequent attention of the greatest lawyers and statesmen of this country. Nor, perhaps, is it wonderful that in the two parts of the island there should have resulted a difference of law in a matter in which neither could be expected to sacrifice its own ideas of what is right to the mere desire of uniformity. But not the less is the existence of such a state of things to be deprecated. For without doubt the discrepancy in the law affecting marriage is a more serious source of evil than the discord in any other branch of our jurisprudence. In other matters subjection to a different legal system is an accident arising from the locality in which the contract is naturally completed, and it is generally provided for by taking local advice. But in the case of marriage the fact of a different law being in force, is sometimes the reason why the contract is entered into in one country rather than the other. And where resort is had to a foreign law merely because it is foreign, and in a matter in which lawyers are less likely to be consulted, because it is being conducted clandestinely and away from home, in which, at all events, it is almost certain that one of the parties trusts to the assurances of the other, or to an indistinct popular idea of what the law is, there cannot fail to result an evil beyond any which accrues when the transaction is conducted in its natural place, and through the intervention of persons versed in the local law.

And in this case, happily, there does not exist at least that obstacle to assimilation which has been so fully pointed out in a preceding chapter, as one which must above all be taken into account in legislating with such purport. There is no essential and fundamental difference in the ordinary practice of the people of England and Scotland in regard to the form of contracting marriage. With all deference to Dr. Lushington, it may indeed be safely asserted, that marriages in the face of the church are even more customary in Scotland than in England, for there are in Scotland no registrars' marriages, and what are called irregular marriages are exceedingly rare. In Scotland, it is true, marriages are not solemnized within the walls of the church, (except when the parties are of the Episcopal communion,) but all regular marriages must be preceded by banns, and must be celebrated by a clergyman, in presence of witnesses. Hence, while the question whether the ceremony should be within a church, and according to a liturgical form, as in England, or in a private residence, and merely by the joining of hands and the clerical benediction, as in Scotland, must, as involving points of religious dogma, be still left to national choice, there could be no difficulty in enacting that the main elements of the ceremony, the publication of banns in church, the solemnization by a clergyman, the presence of witnesses, and their signature in the registry, nay, if desired, the restriction to canonical hours, should be the same imperative conditions of legality in both countries. And as it is not more the habit of minors to marry without consent of parents in Scotland than in England, it would be open to the legislature, without any shock to national customs, to lay down a general rule on this head also.

But the fact that the law could be thus assimilated does not answer the inquiry whether it ought to be assimilated on these terms. For in no case of legislation does mere facility stand as equivalent to wisdom of enactment. Nor does the fact that a general practice prevails, establish that it ought to be made compulsorily uniform. And the law of marriage is a matter that needs more wary and delicate adjustment than any other department of jurisprudence, since it involves considerations that need not elsewhere be taken into account. Other contracts affect only property, marriage affects morality. A difficulty imposed by law in the way of constituting other contracts is only an inconvenience to trade or to some pecuniary transaction; placed in the way of marriage, it is a stumbling block to virtue. The motives which lead to disregard of

strict legal form in other contracts are of comparatively little strength or urgency, they are seldom really
more than mere haste or convenience; but those which
sometimes suggest a departure from ordinary practice
in regard to the contract of marriage, arise from the
over-mastering sway of the affections. In other contracts
the parties are generally able to acquaint themselves
with all the legal formalities that ought to be observed;
they meet on equal terms, and if fraud has interposed,
the law gives a sufficient remedy, either in damages or
in the annulling of the bargain. But in the contract
of marriage, one at least of the parties is always
ignorant of legal rules; if deceived or mistaken, pecuniary damages afford no relief, and the remedy of
nullity would often be more terrible than the error
itself.

It is evident that in presence of such conditions
mere simplicity of rule is not sufficient to establish its
propriety, and the fact of general accord in a certain
practice does not entitle us to impose it in every case
by means of penalties in its breach. It must be a
large and clear gain to general morality which can
alone justify the establishment of forms which, in
certain instances, however few, must, if they take
effect at all, have an effect contrary to that which
morality would prescribe.

It is however obvious from these considerations that

the problem how best to settle the laws of marriage contains for the sole element of inquiry, the question how to arrange it so as best to promote the general morality.   This principle, vague though it seems, enables us at once to get rid of some irrelevant arguments of frequent occurrence, and to lay down some further doctrines of necessary application.   It is, for instance, clear that mere symmetry or analogy with other branches of law, cannot be regarded in dealing with the law of marriage.   So it is idle to listen to declamation about allowing a contract so important to be proved by evidence which would not be admitted in the sale of an estate or a bale of goods.   A particular species of evidence, a particular stamp on a document, may be regarded as, for the sake of conveniency, essential to such transactions, and its absence may be punished by forbidding the most conclusive proof otherwise to prevail.   But obviously this is not a course that is necessarily consistent with morality when applied to the contract of marriage.   On the other hand, though simplicity of rule is not an advantage which should supersede higher considerations, it is undoubtedly a more than usually important condition of any satisfactory settlement of the law on this matter.   Thus, though nothing could be more simple than the enactment that no marriage should be valid save such as are solemnized by a clergyman, it was found in this country to be objectionable because it did not regard the case of those who had conscientious or other objections to such rites, and the complication of marriage in a registrar's office had to be introduced for remedy. But again it is obviously essential that the rule actually established should be so plain and easy, encumbered with so little of formality or nicety, that men and women of every rank, and of every grade of intellect or education, shall know exactly what is necessary to make marriage valid. We must therefore be careful to interpose on the one side no difficulty of expense, or prejudice, or conscience, for the sake of mere simplicity; on the other, no obstacle of obscurity or complexity for the sake of reconciling an unsuitable general rule to the exigencies of particular cases.

In dealing, then, with a matter surrounded with so many difficulties, and where abstract reason can only point out some few leading principles, leaving the application of them to be proved and guided by experience, it is in truth a great advantage that we are able to compare two systems, existing side by side, of a nature so essentially different as those of England and Scotland. The characteristic of the former is that of demanding as the sole admissible evidence of marriage, compliance with certain legal formalities. The characteristic of the latter is that of admitting every species of evidence by which real intention of contracting marriage can be proved. The former aims at sustaining morality by laying down a fixed rule, transgression of which is known to carry the penalty of nullity. The latter seeks to obviate immorality by allowing no defect of form to vitiate substance. No one could *a priori* pronounce which system would best attain the common end of both. And we must therefore examine closely their actual operation in order to enable us to decide which of the two principles is proved by experience to be most successful in achieving its object.

In this view, the history of the successive changes which have been made by statute in the marriage law of England, since it was first taken under statutory direction, is highly instructive. There is a higher wisdom than legislative wisdom, and the influence of the public opinion of a civilized country, formed out of the experience of generations, is more powerful to discover and enforce true principle than the emphatic declarations of the most exalted legal authorities. Let us, then, ere we enter into the comparison between the present state of the English and Scottish law, briefly review the enactments on which the former is founded, and examine the modifications which the mere necessity of circumstances has engrafted on a system the most eminent jurists and statesmen had exhausted their skill in framing.

Down to the year 1754, the original marriage law of England was in its main respects similar to that which still subsists in Scotland. It was, indeed, far less clearly defined; and even where it was ascertained, it was subject to some singular inconsistencies. A striking instance of the former peculiarity occurs in the fact that it is only twenty-one years since it was decided that, by the common law, prior to the Marriage Act of 1754, solemnization by a clergyman was necessary to make matrimony complete. The poets and novelists had, indeed, perhaps faithfully reflecting the common opinion, settled the point long before. The invalidity of a marriage celebrated by a pretended priest is the foundation of many a plot of the romances of the first half of last century. Yet many great lawyers, among whom it is enough to cite the names of Coke, Blackstone, Holt, Kenyon, Ellenborough, Mansfield, Stowell, and Story, laid it down that the mere consent of the parties, without any ceremony, constituted in law true marriage. This was, in fact, the general law of Europe anterior to the Council of Trent, and the decrees of that council were never accepted in England. At last, however, in 1844, in the Queen v. Millis, the point was brought to solemn argument in the House of Lords. It was an appeal from a conviction for bigamy in Ireland, where the first marriage had been one of mere consent without ecclesiastical ceremony. And as the old English law was still in force in that country, the validity of the first marriage depended on the question, whether by that law the intervention of a parson was requisite. The English judges were called in, and acknowledging that the point was full of difficulty, inclined to the affirmative. With them agreed Lords Lyndhurst, Cottenham, and Abinger, while Lords Denman, Campbell, and Brougham supported the negative. The House being thus equally divided, the decision was, according to the rule in such cases, to affirm the judgment appealed against. And thus it is now settled that, prior to the Marriage Acts, solemnization by a priest was requisite. Yet it is curious to reflect that, had the decision in the Court in Ireland been different, the equal division in the Appeal Court would, by the same rule of practice, have settled the disputed point in a diametrically opposite way. But whether or not con-sensual contracts unsanctified by religious rites ever amounted in England to complete marriage, it is certain that they always created obligations not much inferior in force. Neither party could withdraw from them, and either might at any time, even after a regular marriage with another person had supervened, apply to the Ecclesiastical Courts to compel the cele-bration of the ceremony. So, too, the mere living together as husband and wife, not under a present consent, but following on a promise to marry, was either marriage, or a contract to marry, which the law would enforce. So, too, there were cases in which no evidence of any ceremony could be given, but in which evidence that the parties had for years acknowledged each other as husband and wife was held sufficient to support the fact of legal marriage.

But there was one material point in which the law at that time was more defective than that of Scotland has been for two centuries past. The general practice in England then, as it is in Scotland now, undoubtedly was to celebrate marriage by the aid of a clergyman, and subject to the notices and the ritual prescribed by the Church. But while in Scotland, by the Act 1661, c. 34, not merely the parties to a marriage in which these formalities were disregarded were subjected to penalties, but the celebrator was made liable to punishment, no such provision had found its way into the English statute book. The consequence was a state of things the like of which has never existed in Scotland. The sanctions of religious ceremonies, and of the blessing implored or bestowed by a clergyman, were profaned to the most indecent and fraudulent purposes.

The class of "Fleet parsons" sprang into active employment and rich emolument. These were degraded and disgraced clergymen, who, nevertheless, according to the theory of the Church, having been once clergymen were always clergymen, and who, within the purlieus of the Fleet Prison, or in whatever other place they might be wanted, and could venture to be seen, were ever ready to perform the nuptial rites without inquiry and without scruple.   Thence arose a perpetual series of violent abductions of heiresses, completed by the intervention of a Fleet marriage ; of fraud upon fraud, as in the case of Beau Fielding, who, intending to repair his fortunes by clandestine marriage with a rich widow, was imposed upon by the substitution of a woman of the town, while the marriage, notwithstanding the *error personæ*, subjected him to the penalties of bigamy   on his entering into a second marriage with the Duchess of Cleveland ; of seductions perpetrated under the guise of marriage by a clergyman, where the known facility with which a real clergyman could be had made it easy for a villain to deceive his victim by procuring some one to personate the clerical functionary.   These scandalous abuses loudly called for a legislative remedy.   A remedy might have been found, as it had been in Scotland, in the imposition of civil penalties on the guilty ; but while this was done with ample severity, a further punishment was enacted, which, in many instances, fell with crushing weight on the innocent and the honest.

The Statute 26 Geo. II., c. 33, drawn and carried through Parliament by Lord Chancellor Hardwicke, declared, that for the future, any marriage had without prior publication of banns in the churches of the parishes to which the parties might belong (unless in virtue of a licence obtained from the proper party), or which should not be celebrated in one of such parish churches, should be void. The licence here spoken of is not the special licence, which only the Archbishop of Canterbury can grant, and which dispenses with the requirements of law in respect of place and time, but the ordinary licence, in the name of the bishop of the diocese, obtainable, at a fee of about 3l., from any of the numerous "surrogates" in the diocese, which dispenses only with the publication of banns. But before such a licence could be had, Lord Hardwicke's Act required, that one of the parties should have resided in the parish for four weeks. To the validity of the licence, and of the marriage following on it, the consent of the parents or guardians was made essential, if either of the parties was a minor. No provision was made for the case of any incapacity or refusal to consent on the part of the father, if he were in life; but if he was dead, and the mother or guardian was unable to give, or unreasonably refused, permission to marry, the impatient lovers were offered an appeal to the sympathizing · bosom of the Chancellor himself. A marriage by banns—if that were the course resorted to—did not require the express consent of the parents of a minor; but the notice was to be read three times, on three successive Sundays, in the middle of the morning service, and if the parent or guardian then declared his objection, it avoided any marriage which might follow. The marriage—supposing these preliminaries were duly performed—was to be solemnized only between the hours of eight in the morning and 12 noon; it was to be in the presence of at least two witnesses; an entry was to be immediately made and signed by the parties and the clergyman in the parish registers, and any falsification of such entry was declared punishable with death.

Such were the essential principles of the measure. They amounted to this, that no marriage of a minor could be valid without the consent of his parents or guardians; and that no marriage of any one could be valid unless celebrated by a clergyman in a church, after due notice given in the parishes in which the parties had resided. But these principles, spite of the eating cancer of the Fleet scandals, and of the superlative authority by which the remedy was suggested, met with no very favourable reception in the country or in Parliament. Mr. Macqueen, the author of a standard work on the law of husband and wife, in

England, thus describes the feelings which experience of the bill excited :—

"About a quarter of a century after Lord Hardwicke's enactment, Mr. Fox, in June 1781, brought in a bill to repeal it. On that occasion, delivering one of his greatest orations, he described the New Marriage Law as ' tyrannical, unjustifiable, oppressive, and ridiculous.' He was followed by Sir George Yonge, who, painting in strong colours the mischief of all restrictions upon matrimony, denounced the measure of Lord Hardwicke, after the experience had of it, as a ' very disgraceful and pernicious law, not only impolitic, but wicked.'

" Mr. Fox's bill was read a second time, by a majority of 90 to 27. It was read a third time, passed, and carried in triumph to the House of Lords, where, however, it was rejected on the second reading ; since which time the people of England, more obedient than the Scotch, have come, under the tuition of the Legislature, to look upon clandestine and consensual marriages as things, not only illegal here, but of very questionable morality in those countries where they are still allowed. So that what Englishmen viewed with abhorrence seventy-five years ago—what Mr. Fox and Sir George Yonge pronounced ' tyrannical, unjustifiable, oppressive, ridiculous, disgraceful, pernicious, impolitic, and wicked,'—the Scotch are now held up as wilfully blind and obstinate for not adopting, at the recommendation of those very neighbours who so recently entertained and so furiously expressed such opposite opinions."

So thoroughly well, however, as a legislative draftsman, had the great Chancellor done his work, that for seventy years no lawyer dared to think that he could amend what was there set down. But it must not be supposed that the rules, simple, brief, and accurately penned as they were, succeeded in excluding difficulty of interpretation in every case. There was more litigation on the subject of the validity of marriages than ever, for the litigation was now no longer confined to the question of fact, whether or not there had been real consent—it further dealt with questions of law. There had to be settled, in the innumerable instances in which accident, mistake, or design had led the parties to deviate ever so little from the statutory requirements, whether or not such deviation was a fatal error. Thus, while it was held that publication of banns in the Christian name of William only—whereas there were two Christian names, William Peter—invalidated the marriage, it was in other cases held that the rule was not so strict as regards accuracy in licences as in banns, and so that the writing the surname as Ewen, in a licence, instead of the true name Ewing, did not invalidate the marriage. It is obvious what a field for hair-splitting distinctions lay between these two examples. So, too, there were questions as to what was celebration in a church, and what was a church; questions as to whether consent of parents might be implied, and what amounted to implied consent; whether, when given, it might be recalled, and what amounted to recall; whether it was essential if the marriage took place out of England, the decision on which being, after some fluctuations, in the negative, gave rise to Gretna Green marriages. Then there were questions as to who might institute suits to declare the nullity of a marriage; whether the party through whose fault or fraud it had occurred; whether the relatives of one or other; whether those interested in the property of either; and so on *ad infinitum*.

But by the time that the Act had been cleared, or darkened, by abundant judicial interpretation, the forebodings of Fox became evidently truths; and it was felt by all, that the lawyers of the last century had, in this matter, laid a burden on men's shoulders too heavy to be borne. It was acknowledged that it could not be the true principle on which a marriage law should rest, that an unwitting blunder in a technical point should have the effect of setting the parties loose from their bond, and of irremediably bastardizing their issue. As Dr. Lushington puts it, " void marriages became at last so exceedingly numerous, that it was absolutely necessary to apply a legislative remedy." So the 3 Geo. IV. c. 75, repealed the provision which made consent of parents requisite to a marriage by licence, in every case in which the parties had cohabited, and no proceedings had, before the Act, been taken to set the marriage aside. But the wording of the Act presented an unhappy contrast to the elegant precision which distinguished Lord Hardwicke's; and ere a year was out, an ominous crop of litigation sprang from its fertile soil. Next year, however, Lord Hardwicke's Act was itself repealed in full; and a new statute, 4 Geo. IV. c. 76, undertook to regulate the whole law relating to marriage, with full appreciation of the experience which had at such cost been accumulated.

The main principle of this statute (which forms, with some amending Acts, the existing authority on the matter of marriages *in facie ecclesiæ*), is, while retaining almost unaltered the machinery and provisions for order and publicity suggested by Lord Hardwicke, to restrict the extreme penalty of nullity of the marriage to the cases where *wilfully*, and with the knowledge of *both* parties, the marriage was solemnized without licence or banns, or not in a church or licensed chapel, or by a person not in holy orders. The publication of banns is regulated as before, and

may be made void by an objection stated by the parent
or guardian of a minor; but a licence is now obtainable
on a fortnight's general residence of either party in the
parish, and on an oath that the parent or guardian of
a minor consents; though a false oath does not affect the
validity of the marriage. Nullity is therefore no longer
the penalty of marriage of minors without express
consent of parents, nor of a marriage procured irregularly in any way by fraud of one of the parties, without
the knowledge of the other. These breaches of rule
are still punished; but the punishment is made to
consist in fine or imprisonment, or in forfeiture of
property, which would otherwise have accrued through
the union.

But important and salutary as these alterations were,
they still left serious defects, for which the legislature
was called on to find a remedy. The first was in
principle. There are many persons who object from
religious scruples to be married in a church; perhaps
there are still more who are somewhat indifferent
whether their union be in the eye of law a marriage or
not, and who are even deterred, by the very respectability of a church and a clergyman, from proffering
themselves to secure the benefit of such respectability.
To meet these very different cases, the Act of 6 and 7
Will. IV. c. 85, was passed. It abandoned altogether,
in favour of those who might choose to avail them-

selves of its provisions, the ecclesiastical and religious element of matrimony. It authorized marriages to be celebrated in the office of any district registrar of births, marriages, and deaths, by mere declaration of consent made by the parties in the presence of the registrar: It embodied provisions as to previous notice, intended to be equivalent to the provisions of law applicable to márriages *in facie ecclesiæ*. In place of banns in church, the notice of marriage was to be read at three successive meetings of the Board of Guardians for the poor of the parish. Instead of a licence from the bishop's surrogate, a licence might, on an oath to the like effect, be had from the superintendent registrar. The marriage in the registrar's office must take place between 8 and 12 o'clock, with open doors, in the presence of two witnesses; and, as a matter of course, it is instantly registered. These things so done, the marriage is to all intents and purposes valid; and only wilful and fraudulent deception by both parties, in reference to the essentials of the form, can avail as a ground for setting it aside. This statute has been amended by some subsequent Acts, but its leading principles remain unaltered.

But even the restriction of nullity to the single case where both parties are aware of misrepresentation on an essential point, has not been found under these

Acts to render the proof of marriage always either easy or certain. Still questions perplex the courts with reference to the interpretation of the words on which so much hangs. Still it is often needful to institute suits to learn what amount of wrong spelling of names in banns, how far the omission of one of several Christian names—what use of the name of common repute, instead of that of baptism or descent, or *vice versâ*, what evidence of knowledge of such errors by both the parties,—will be sufficient to turn a marriage ceremony into so many idle words. Still it becomes frequently necessary to ascertain who is a clergyman, and what is a church or chapel. A remedy to these doubts is sought in fresh statutory definition. Since the commencement of the present reign there have been about twenty such statutes passed, some retrospective and special, some prospective and general. It may readily be conceived how perplexed the code is growing; and it may be imagined what a mass of incertitude must exist, when parliamentary action has been invoked to such an extent, to set palpable doubts at rest. For it must be remembered that each statute probably applies to many cases, and yet that probably many more cases of doubt must exist which no statutes have settled. For it is only when the doubts have arisen in cases where the interests at stake have caused inquiry, or where the difficulty has been palpable, that an appeal to the legislature is likely to be resorted to.[1]

It must also be kept in mind that the solemnization of an English marriage, even when in a church, does not exclude the inquiry, whether the parties were really competent to enter into that particular contract. Thus the marriage of the Earl of Portsmouth, solemnized in London in 1814, was in 1828 declared *ab initio* null, though the parties had lived together till 1822, had had children, and had been recognized as married by the earl's relatives. The ground taken by the Court was, that the earl had all his life been, if not of unsound, at least of weak mind, that he was timid and passive of character, that in such circumstances he might possibly contract a valid marriage, and (for he was in fact a widower) that his first marriage might be

---

[1] In the present session there has been, for example, the "Marriages (Lambourne) Bill," for the purpose of declaring to be valid the marriages celebrated in a church that had been consecrated, but not licensed, and in which was introduced, on the precedent of an Act of 1861, a clause declaring that all prior marriages in any church so circumstanced should be valid. But the clause was objected to, and struck out, and it was observed that the proper course was, if the Registrar-General should discover such cases, to pass separate bills for each. The Bishop of Oxford declared that there are many such cases, and that the clergy are not versant in the law. Lord Derby thought the Act of 1861 was notice enough of the law to persons about to marry.

very capable of being supported; but that his second
marriage being with the daughter of one of his trustees
who had entire influence over him, and in whose house
he was living at the time, could not be permitted to
stand.   So in a recent case evidence was admitted
to prove averments, with a view to annul an English
marriage, that it had been procured by the persuasion
of the parents of the man, taking advantage of the
tender years and inexperience of the woman, and of
her being at the time in their house, away from the
advice of her natural protectors.   And many such
cases are found in the books.   They make it clear
that the strictness of external form does not always
exclude fraud or coercion, and that they cannot
prevent courts of justice from entertaining and giving
effect to such objections, at whatever cost of uncertainty
in similar cases.

Such is, in brief outline, the legislative history of
the existing English marriage law.   The statute book,
and the reports of judgments by which the statutes are
interpreted, thus establish, on the highest possible
evidence, three points.   The first is that it is not
possible in modern society to maintain a solely
ecclesiastical form of contracting marriage.   The
system was fairly tried; at last there was found to
be an absolute necessity of allowing an alternative
in the shape of means for constituting a purely civil

contract. The second is, that if any special formality is made indispensable, there are sure to arise a large number of cases in which there is a question whether it has been accurately observed or not, or whether, if not quite accurately observed, the inaccuracy is so serious as to be fatal. The third is, that these elements of uncertainty do not solely arise where the parties know that they are treading on dangerous ground, that they are adopting a course unusual and therefore hazardous, but often also arise where the fullest intention was to do everything correctly, and where years have elapsed before any suspicion is suggested that what was believed to be marriage has only been concubinage.

The law of Scotland on the subject of marriage has no legislative history like that of England. It has always remained as part of the common law, and except in the instance referred to, of the punishment of persons celebrating a clandestine marriage, its main principles have been unaffected by statute. Under it, as already observed, the contract depends wholly on the consent of the parties, that consent being of course free, advised, and deliberate. The fact of the consent may be either proved, or inferred by the law from certain circumstances. The various methods of proof (or what are commonly called the methods of contracting marriage) fall into the following divisions :—

1st, *Regular marriages*, celebrated by a clergyman, after due proclamation of banns.

2nd, *Clandestine marriages*, celebrated by a clergyman without proclamation of banns, or by a layman using religious forms, in which cases the marriage stands good, but all the parties are punishable.

3rd, *Irregular marriages*, in which there is no pretence of religious ceremony, and which are subdivided into :—

[*a*] Those in which consent ("consent *de præsenti*,") is signified by declaration in words, proved by two witnesses, or in writing.

[*b*] Those in which consent is inferred by the law from the facts of a written promise to marry, or a verbal promise admitted by the party on oath, in either case followed by cohabitation ("promise *de futuro, subsequente copulâ*.")

[*c*] Those in which the consent is inferred by the law from the fact that the parties had, during a long period, represented themselves to their neighbours as married, and had been universally understood to be married ("habit and repute").

In every one of these cases the point considered is the identity of the persons, without any regard to the names they had assumed, and in all but the *b* and *c* cases it is immaterial what the secret intention of one of the parties was, provided the other really believed that marriage was intended, while in these two cases it does not even appear that the intention on the part of either to constitute marriage is material, the law holding that in the circumstances the intention ought to have existed if it did not.   The reasons for this will be pointed out hereafter.   For the present it will conduce to simplicity if we regard the law of Scotland as recognizing a marriage on any sufficient evidence of real intention, without question whether religious ceremony or other formality has been used or not.

The first question to be considered in comparing this system with that of England is that which, in the case of the latter, its history has already enabled us to estimate, viz. the degree of certainty of legal proof which is attainable.   It is generally alleged by those who have not made careful investigation that on this head the law of Scotland is grievously, if not barbarously, deficient.   But there is this primary distinction to be noted, that the cases in Scotland in which uncertainty has been shown, by the institution of a lawsuit, to exist, have been isolated, and that it has never been found necessary, as in England, to pass a statute to cure uncertainty in a whole class of cases. And with regard to such isolated cases it may be said in round numbers that their average total does not exceed the number of amending or correcting or explanatory statutes, which, in a series of years, are found necessary in England. But a very important distinction is also to be found in regard to the character of the cases in which uncertainty ever exists. In England, as we have seen, it may arise in regard to marriages intended and believed to be solemnized with the utmost accuracy. The want of due consecration or licensing of a new church or chapel may be fatal, and remain undiscovered for years, the omission of one of several Christian names, or the use of a name of custom instead of the real name, may give rise to the most distressing doubts or fatal certainties. In Scotland no such error can affect the contract. The marriage may be in any place, witnessed by any person, solemnized under any name or *alias*, it will still be valid if only the evidence of consent is adduced, and the identity of the parties under the names they adopted is proved. Thus, while in England error may vitiate the most honest intentions, or very natural ignorance (such as if a woman allows her banns to be published in the name of Mary instead of Mary Ann) may enable the dishonest to triumph ; in Scotland, those who mean honestly can by no possibility suffer under a moment's doubt, and the dishonest must resort to far more marked and unusual devices if they would escape being caught in the snare they try to set.

It may also be observed that the doubts in England always go to unsettle a marriage which had been ostensibly valid. In Scotland, when they exist, they tend to set up as marriage a connection not formally legitimate. Nobody in Scotland can, while adhering to usual practice, have an instant's hesitation that the contract is valid. The only instances in which doubts occur are where the parties, one or both, have endeavoured to avoid the forms of marriage, but where they have used expressions or done acts which imply marriage in the eye of the law when spoken or done with such meaning. In the whole range of Scottish legal reports no case will be found of doubt thrown upon a regular marriage, except, of course, in the one or two instances that have occurred where, as in the Earl of Portsmouth's case, mental weakness has had to be considered. But had none but regular marriages been allowed, then not only all that have been duly contracted in an irregular form, and which have never come before the Courts because clearly legal, must have been bad; but those which, being irregular, have been so far open to doubt as to call for legal investigation, must have also been esteemed bad. Restriction to one form of proof, or to one indispensable ceremony, can never avail to convert concubinage into marriage; but the admission of every species of proof will sometimes establish as marriage what on a narrower view might have seemed to be a less honourable arrangement. Of course it may be argued that this result is not always to be desired, and the argument will deserve consideration when we come to deal with the moral aspects of the two systems. But at present we are only considering the comparative certainty they offer, and the character of the cases in which the uncertainty is to be found.

It may, no doubt, also be observed, that it is only the permission of irregularity that suggests its existence, and that if these looser forms were not allowed, the parties would adopt the stricter. But this argument leaves quite untouched the introduction of uncertainty by the enactment of forms in which default may be made. And it is opposed to the results of experience, even in the class of cases to which it does apply. There is in Scotland a very strong motive to adopt the regular method of marriage by a clergyman. Its non-observance, if not visited by civil penalties, calls down ecclesiastical censure and the reprobation of society. The irregular forms of marriage are, in a word, esteemed disreputable. The motives, then, for avoiding the regular form must be of the strongest character whenever an irregular form is resorted to. Is it conceivable that, being so strong as this, they would often be overcome by the mere circumstance of an irregular marriage being impracticable?

On the whole, then, startling as the conclusion may be to those who have never before fairly reviewed the facts on both sides, it appears indisputable that there is more uncertainty in the English than in the Scottish law of marriage.   The former, making specific ceremonies essential, lets in doubts, affecting often a multitude of cases, whether the ceremonies have been duly observed.   The latter, taking evidence of the real intent of the parties, admits no doubt where the intention, on one side at least, has been honest.   The uncertainties in the former tend to annul marriages believed to be good, in the latter to establish as marriage arrangements ostensibly different, but really intended to be marriage.

Such being the legal, we have now to turn to the moral and social aspects of the question.   And, in this regard, the charges which are brought by the advocates of statutory forms against the admission of mere proof of consent, seem reducible to the following heads: 1st, that it permits of marriages being entered into hastily, and without notice to the natural advisers of the parties, or to those interested in their proceedings ; 2nd, that it give facilities to the designing for the perpetration of fraud.

No doubt can exist that each of these classes of possibilities ought, as far as is in our power, to be

22

provided against. But we may observe that they are nevertheless of a materially different nature. Fraud ought in all cases to be punished; but it cannot be said that clandestinity ought in all cases to be forbidden. The law of France, far more imperatively than that of England, makes the marriages of minors, without consent of their parents, invalid; and it cannot be said that it thereby tends to promote the morality of the young of either sex. We may discourage as much as we please alliances formed at an early age without parental sanction; but it is too dangerous to declare that every such alliance must inevitably be concubinage. Somehow or other, the law must allow a safety-valve for the vehemence of youthful yet virtuous passion. Even Lord Hardwicke allowed such a safety-valve, in the form of an appeal to himself, whenever any authority less sacred than that of the father presumed to offer an impediment. A more effectual one was, however, adopted in the Gretna Green recourse. So necessary had been found this mode of evading the harshness of Lord Hardwicke's law, that it had been resorted to by an Archbishop, a Chancellor, and a Lord Privy Seal, all at one time in the councils of that pattern of connubial propriety, King George III. These runagate marriages are now, indeed, nearly abolished by Lord Brougham's Act, the 19 and 20 Vict. c. 85,

which requires three weeks' residence in Scotland by
at least one of the parties; but it may be doubted
whether outward respectability did not gain more by
the change than morality. Indeed, if morality has
not actually suffered, it has been simply through the
preceding change in the law, by which the penalty
of nullity affixed by the earlier statute to a minor's
marriage without consent, had been modified into a
pecuniary, or at the most, a personal punishment.
The fervour of true and honourable affection is seldom
subdued by such a risk; and to permit the lawful
union of such minors as choose to submit to it, is
evidently a sounder course, than to bar them from any
remedy save that of an elopement over the Scottish
border. But the question of principle is not to be
confined to the case of minority, although to such
cases the penalties of English law are confined.
Secret marriages, whatever the age of the parties,
are always to be deprecated; but it is beyond doubt
that the alternative often lies between a secret marriage and an arrangement which is not marriage.
It may indeed be said with tolerable accuracy, that
wherever a secret marriage takes place, a union of
a different nature would probably have been consum-
mated, had marriage in secret been impossible. And
the matter for us to weigh, therefore, seems to be,
whether it is least detrimental to morality and the

22—2

interests of society, to allow of alliances innocent in themselves, though objectionable, because through their privacy they may hereafter become a snare and occasion of falling to others ; or to brand them at once and for ever as illegal, in order that none but the parties concerned may suffer through them.

There is a semblance of justice in the latter course ; but it is a thin covering of deeper injustice. Obviously, it is a doing of evil that good may come. It is a deliberate placing of a stumbling-block in the way of virtue, on the pretence of preventing a future, a possible, and a less serious mischief. For it is the presenting, in every case to which it may apply, a temptation to two persons to live in sin, who, had there not been this " forbidding to marry," would have lived in purity. True, had they been privately married, it is within the limits of possibility that either might have taken advantage of the fact being unknown, to enter into like engagements with another. But of this, the sin would have still lain only at the door of the guilty party ; the innocently deceived would have been free from guilt. Miserable in an earthly sense is the fate of a woman so deceived ; but at least she has not sinned. It is, then, beyond dispute, that the worst evils from the permission of secret marriages would be temporal, secondary, and distant ; while from their prohibition comes, far more frequently, sin, deadly and immediate. Can we hesitate in our choice between the legal principles, whose operation leads to such opposite conclusions ?

But, treating the question as one not of principle, but of practice, we shall find enough to absolve us from the necessity of pondering such arguments. The fact is, that by no practicable system can secret marriages be prevented. For it matters nothing to the question of secrecy whether they be constituted in absolute solitude, as they may be in Scotland, or whether they be contracted in the presence of hundreds, if not one of the hundreds knows who the parties contracting are. And this may with the greatest ease be effected in England. Leaving aside altogether the operation of the licence to dispense with banns, which may be obtained by any one who can swear, or who will swear, that he or she has been resident in the parish for fifteen days, and that both are of full age, or if minors, have the consent of their parents, let us look at the real operation of the publication of banns, in its strictest sense. In the middle of the divine service, when all the congregation is present, but when, it may be hoped, the minds of some are lifted to higher things than the matrimonial intentions of their neighbours, there is read out a list of those who, " of this parish," have a purpose of marriage with certain persons of the same or another

parish. That name and designation must be odd and
striking indeed, which, in the long list of a large city
parish, catches the attention of any in the congregation
as having a peculiarly familiar sound. But if such
risk should exist, the means of obviating it are easy.
It needs only that the parties should take a lodging
in some town or rural district, where no chance of
recognition exists. They have then a right to have
their banns published in the parish church, and the
ceremony performed by the parish clergyman. None
is wiser for the event ; and they may return, without
fear of discovery, to the bosom of the families which
they have united by so close yet unknown a tie. Nor
need they both resort to the same parish to procure
the matrimonial conveniences. While the lady visits
her aunt at Brighton, the gentleman may reside in his
shooting box on the Yorkshire moors. While the
dairymaid takes service in the next market town, the
shepherd may engage himself to a farmer ten miles
off. The rich can afford the means of escaping with
greater art their more numerous acquaintance ; the
poor pass beyond recognition, by an easy and inex-
pensive change of abode. These, and a hundred
other simple devices, are all perfectly consistent with
the law ; but it scarcely needs suggestion, how enor-
mously they are capable of increase, by the adaptation
of a little of that ingenuity which may be called

fraud, but which cannot in practice be punished as fraud.

In a matter so obvious to common sense, we need the less regret the impossibility of adducing direct evidence of its occurrence. The earlier law-books of both England and Scotland contain a record of many secret marriages effected irregularly, because, in the former country, secrecy, under certain circumstances, avoided the marriage, and the question was therefore sometimes worth trying in court; while, in the latter, it had not yet been determined how far such secrecy was compatible with *bonâ fide* intention to marry, and consequently there was also room for forensic . disputation in each case. But, in both, such reported cases are now more rare, merely because the law assures the validity of the marriage in question when known, and consequently suggests no plea on which to bring them before any court. The relative actual number of such marriages can therefore be only vaguely surmised, even by those who have some acquaintance with the habits of both countries. But, judging from the facts which occasionally come for an instant to the surface in the gossip of the day, or in reports of the Divorce Court, the inference may be safely drawn, that the abolition of Gretna Green facilities has not diminished in England the practical facilities for eluding parental control, and that the necessity of the publication of banns, and of solemnization by a clergyman, or by a registrar of births, marriages, and deaths, seems in no very appreciable degree to impede the ease with which marriage may be contracted *incognito*.[1]

There is indeed one species of evidence which might be of some weight in determining the comparative number of secret marriages in the two countries. One of the principal objections to their being permitted at all, is the possibility of their forming no difficulty in the way of the commission of bigamy. Now, as bigamy, by the recent practice of the Scottish Courts (disregarding the principles laid down by some writers), is held to be committed though the first marriage was irregular, we might expect, if there was an unusual resort to secret marriages in that country, to find the crime more prevalent than in England. Such, however, is not the case. In 1863 (the last year of which the statistics are published), there were tried for bigamy in England 97 persons; in Scotland, 7 persons. The average of the preceding five years was in

---

[1] Thus, only a few months ago, a young English peer of the highest rank, was married in a London church to a lady, affianced at the time to another gentleman, the relatives on both sides being utterly ignorant of what was being done, and the lady making her way to the altar while her carriage was left standing at the door of a shop, through the other entrance of which she made her escape.

England, 91; in Scotland, 11. Of the five years before that, in England, 85; in Scotland, 11. The increase of this crime in England keeps pace with the increase of the population, in Scotland its frequency is rather diminishing; but taking the population of England as about six times that of Scotland, it is greatly less frequent in the latter country than in the former. Evidently, therefore, the simplicity of the Scottish marriage system does not lend itself to enhance the dangers to the peace of families which arise from the contracting a second marriage, while the fact of a prior obligation remains concealed.

Finding, then, that clandestine nuptials are in no perceptible degree encouraged by the principles of the Scottish law, and that the law of England now shares with it the praise of interposing discouragement only, and not insuperable difficulty, in the way of those whose ardour leads them to dare the reproach attendant on a private union, it remains for us to consider to what extent the northern rules afford convenience to the perpetration of virtual fraud, to the inveigling into a mésalliance the unwary, who, were time for reflection allowed, would shrink from the suggested union. And on this head it must first be remarked, that the laws of neither country afford any protection to those who endeavour to make use of them for the purposes of imposition in essential particulars, or who take undue advantage of the weakness of persons subjected to their influence. It is true that in neither country is mere error or mistake as to the worldly position of the parties a good ground for setting aside the contract. There are several cases in the English books, in which a marriage, held to be binding, had been procured by misrepresentations on the score of rank or estate. The rule is laid down by Lord Stowell, that " though a man should represent himself of superior condition or expectations, it will not of itself invalidate a marriage, as the law asserts that parties should use timely and effectual diligence in obtaining correct information on such points." In cases of such error, the Courts of both countries hold that the choice of the persons is that which the law regards, and not the external circumstances of either. But the case in both is different, where the facts indicate that true personal consent to the engagement was not given. The cases of the Earl of Portsmouth, and others which have been before referred to, show that in neither country can fraud on weak-minded persons be wholly prevented, even by the utmost solemnity of ritual, but that in neither will the Courts support a marriage discovered to have been so procured.

But it is conceivable—and the possibility of the occurrence must be considered because it has been strenuously urged by some members of the House of Peers—that a lad of rank may, in Scotland, rashly utter a declaration, or sign a document, which may make him in law the husband of a woman of low birth or degraded character. In Lord Brougham's Committee of the Lords, in 1844, the following question was put to the then Lord Advocate, now the Lord Justice General :—

" Suppose a young nobleman of fourteen is trepanned into a marriage by a woman of bad character of thirty or thirty-five, and he says, in such a way that it can be proved, 'I take you for my wife,' and she says, 'I take you for my husband;' at this moment would that be a valid marriage, and carry a dukedom and large estates to the issue? *Ans.* It would do so if it were a deliberate interchange of present consent, for the purpose of constituting the relation of husband and wife."

Nothing could better illustrate the true nature of the apprehension entertained than the question ; while certainly no words could more aptly express the true principles of the law of Scotland than the answer. The dread is, that rank and wealth should be degraded by a poor or a dishonouring alliance : the law declares that even rank and wealth must abide by the consequences of its own deliberate promises. What consolation shall be offered to reassure the peers against

the terrible imagination of a dukedom and large estates
involved in such a catastrophe ?   May we dare to
remind them that the only noblemen who, "at this
moment," have fallen under the fascinations they
contemplate with such terror are English peers whose .
nuptials were solemnized by English clergymen ? May
we dare to recall that English marriages also are legal
at fourteen years of age, and are perfectly valid though
parental or legal consent has been evaded ; and that
the only recorded cases of such infantile marriages in
the peerage have been English cases.   Thus Lady
Shaftesbury became the origin of a " leading case "
in Chancery, by instigating the secret marriage of her
son, the earl, whose age was fourteen, and whose
guardian was the Lord Chief Justice of England.   But
the suggestion of the Peers' Committee still remains,
as regards Scotland, a hypothetical danger.   Nor need
we waste time in giving other answer to such appeal
for further protection to the descent of dukedoms and
large estates.

For the truth of the matter is this, that whatever
the inconveniences, and too often the wretchedness
consequent upon hasty and ill-assorted unions, we
cannot dare to prevent them by the expedient of annulling every marriage in which a certain time has
not elapsed between the declaration of the intention
and the solemnization of the ceremony.   The most

prudent are not always masters of the circumstances
that determine their lot. Many things may occur in
a life that will not allow of a fortnight's pause. A
regiment may have a sudden order to march, a ship
to sail, an emigrant may have a sudden opportunity
to make his voyage, a sudden commercial necessity
may despatch a mercantile man for years to the anti-
podes. On such a call of duty, Lord Clyde was ready
in three days to start for India; but what if he had
been engaged to marry, was going on a service likely
to absorb the best years of his life, and was too
poor and friendless to have his bride sent out by a
following ship? Shall we say that, in all such cases,
men and women must be condemned to a life of
celibacy, or that they must start on their journey
together, unmarried, awaiting the hour when a legal
form can sanctify their union, in order that we may
preserve inviolate a rule contrived for the security of
the reckless? Shall we say even that with those
living at home no urgency may occur which demands,
in the highest interests, that no delay shall be interposed in ratifying a legal union? We shall at least
fail to find authority for such a course in the existing
provisions of the law of England. While a fortnight's
notice, and the publication of banns on three Sundays,
is its rule, it meets exceptional cases by the grant of
a licence which may be obtained, as matter of right,

by any one on the very morning of the proposed wedding. Reducing thus, by a most salutary and needful privilege, the time for deliberation to a few hours, it seems scarce necessary to inquire further into the distinctions between the principle here admitted and that enunciated by the Lord Justice General, that marriage in Scotland is constituted by the deliberate interchange of present consent, for the purpose of constituting the relation of husband and wife. For the imperative demands of the public moral sense have broken down the hedge of forms by which Lord Hardwicke strove to secure the inviolability of his restrictions. The registrar may fill the place of the priest; a false priest will do as well as a real one, if believed to be a real one by only one of the parties; the licence is not void though obtained by perjury; the residence requisite to obviate perjury may be *incognito*; the consent of parents need not be asked when the ceremony can be accomplished without their cognisance. What is there remaining that forms a difficulty to the designing, or a safeguard to the imprudent? Absolutely nothing. While yet the forms that do survive are of sufficient force, many a time, to convert those who have honestly misinterpreted them into paramours merely, and to leave them to the late mercy of statutes " for declaring valid certain marriages heretofore solemnized in the church of —— ;" but bearing the customary proviso, that no such marriage shall be validated, if proceedings at law have already been commenced to set it aside!

To the objection so often urged ignorantly in the South, that in Scotland a man may frequently not know whether he is married or not, a very brief answer may be made. Nowhere can an honest man be so certain how that fact stands as in Scotland; for it is in no way dependent on the consecration of a church, or the true apostolic succession of a clergyman, on the construction of statutes, or the spelling of names. It depends solely on the question, whether the parties truly meant to marry each other. This is what every man must know who chooses to deal honestly with his own conscience. For those who " palter in a double sense," who use words to conceal thoughts, who have a reserved meaning different from that which they express, who seek to shelter vice under the outward semblance of virtue, to deceive the public or deceive their victims, who shall demand sympathy? If they are caught in their own snare, it is well; if they have been astute enough to keep clear of furnishing legal evidence of what they seemed to intend, we can only regret that the law must proceed by fixed rules, and that the only retribution that will fall on them will be the scorn of all who count virtue in woman and truth in man of higher esteem than large estates or ducal

descent. And if any, by using such arts, bring themselves into the position of being really uncertain how
far they have bound themselves, all honourable men
will congratulate Scotland, that, in her courts at least,
there is a chance of justice having its course; and that
the cry of the betrayed and forsaken will not be met
with the reply that, ere they trusted and were lost,
they should have studied the 4 Geo. IV. c. 76, or, at
the least, the 5 and 6 Will. IV. c. 85.

It may be observed, however, as forming a curious
anomaly in the administration of law, that Englishmen
are not wholly to blame for denouncing the Scottish
law of marriage as depending on a loose species of
evidence, seeing that in English courts it often happens
that a Scottish marriage is proved by evidence which
would be insufficient in a Scottish court. For in
Scotland the rule of evidence is, that a single witness
is not enough to establish the case alleged by the
suitor. But it is a principle of international jurisprudence, that courts of justice, though they judge of
a contract by the law of the country in which it was
entered into, yet apply to the suit their own forms of
procedure and rules of evidence; and as a single
witness is sufficient in England, it frequently occurs
that, in the courts at Westminster, the consent to
marriage, which, in deference to the Scottish law,
they accept as marriage, is proved by testimony which,

in the Court at Edinburgh, would be rejected as inade-
quate. A forgetfulness of this rule appeared, in the
Yelverton trial in Ireland, to lead to an apparent
discrepancy between the evidence of two Scottish advocates as to the law of Scotland. The one, called on
behalf of the alleged Mrs. Yelverton, correctly stated
the law, and properly left the Court to apply it to the
case as proved. The other, called for Major Yelverton,
stated the Scottish principles of law as affected by the
Scottish rules of proof, with which the Irish Court had
no concern, and of which it could not take cognisance.
But if any other lady in the like case of Miss Long-
worth, succeeds in England or Ireland in proving
herself to have been lawfully married in Scotland,
while, at the same time, she fails in Scotland to make
out her right, we must remember that the result
follows, not from the laxity of the Scottish law of
marriage, but from the less strictness of the law of
evidence by which in England the question is judged.

Having thus dealt with every objection that has
been urged against the great Scottish principle of
consent being the one essential in matrimony, I may
now touch very briefly upon the two cases in which
the law does not require a present consent, in words,
to be directly proved, but infers its existence from
certain facts. These are, indeed, mere corollaries
from the leading doctrine; but they are corollaries

23

signally illustrative of the genuine justice, and true
spirit of Christianity, by which, on the whole subject,
the Scottish law is distinguished.

The first case is that in which a woman has been
seduced under promise of marriage. Though a mere
promise, referring only to the future, is not the present
consent required to constitute marriage, yet, where
seduction follows upon a written or admitted promise,
the law holds it as fulfilled; and the marriage, consequently, as completed. That this principle should
be especially repugnant to those who complain that
they are in doubt whether they are married or not, is
very easy of comprehension; but it will probably
commend itself to the approval of those whose approval
is of value. It is indeed a practical embodiment of
the common sentiment, that if such persons are not
married, they ought to be; and it is only an adaptation to Scottish legal forms of the rule which, prior to
Lord Hardwicke's Act, prevailed in England, under
which a seducer could be compelled to marry the
woman, whom, by a promise of marriage, he had
induced to trust him. A significant indication of its
influence upon morals is afforded by a comparison of
the trials for seduction in the two countries. Scotland
may not, indeed, so far as statistics prove the case,
boast of comparative purity of manners; but bad as
she may be, it will be granted that the evil would be

many times increased if, to other temptations to the
frail, the law permitted a promise of marriage to be
added.[1] But though there is in that country no technicality which forbids a woman to bring an action for
her own seduction, it is of the rarest possible occurrence to find one brought, in which a promise to marry
had been used to procure her fall. In England, on
the other hand, it is notorious that such a promise is
proved in the majority of instances; and how numerous
these are may be inferred from the fact, that though
the law only permits such actions to be brought where
the woman's services to her father or her master are
capable of pecuniary estimation, and though 98 per
cent. of all actions brought are settled before they
come to trial, yet, in 1863, there were 11 actions for
seduction actually tried, or, on that proportion, 550
actions brought. There were also 39 actions of breach

---

[1] The effect of the law of legitimation *per subsequens matrimonium*,
which subsists in Scotland, makes it impossible to draw from the
statistics of illegitimate births any conclusion as to the comparative
ante-nuptial morality of the two countries. In England, if marriage
is ultimately intended, it must be solemnized before the birth of a
child, or the child is irremediably bastard, but when it has been
solemnized the child is registered as legitimate, and no trace appears
of a prior lapse from virtue. But in Scotland marriage legitimatizes
previous offspring, hence there is no motive to solemnize the marriage
before the birth, and the child is registered as illegitimate at birth.
In the rural counties on both sides the Tweed a large proportion of
the immorality is of a character to which these remarks apply.

of promise of marriage tried, equivalent to nearly 2,000 brought. That system can surely not be reprobated which takes from the dishonourable the most powerful enticement which he can suggest, the temptation to which, if any yield, it is those who are most near to virtue, and who would be most strong against all less honourable lures.

The second exceptional case is that of marriage by reputation, or, in Scottish language, 'habit and repute.' This is, indeed, truly a marriage by declaration, for it is founded on the statements and the acts of the parties which have led their neighbours for years, and without exception, to believe them husband and wife. The peculiarity in this case, then, rests in the fact that, when such a result has followed, the parties are not allowed to give proof that their statements were from the beginning false, and their conduct meant only to deceive. The law holds that this is a just and necessary restriction of the rule of consent ; and as they have, in fact, been joined together, it forbids, in the interest of public morality and decency, that they should put each other away, by so simple a bill of divorcement as the assertion that they never meant to be joined. Here, also, none can have a doubt respecting their position in the eye of the law, save those who have, by a long dissimulation, drawn the doubt upon themselves. And, on this principle, the English law, in every case in which the question of a marriage is not directly in issue, permits it, however momentous the consequences, to be proved by reputation only. Such is often the evidence given in tracing descent to the largest properties. The Scottish law, in like manner, does not admit reputation as sufficient in a criminal case; but it has unquestionably much of reason on its side, in holding, in civil cases, that what the common sense of mankind accounts sufficient proof of marriage shall constitute a marriage in law, and that such a connection shall not, to the scandal of all who have so accepted it, be declared by the parties never to have been aught more than a convenient cloak to vice.

Having thus passed in review, so far as space permitted, the theoretical arguments and the experience of facts bearing on the policy of the marriage law which subsists in the two extremities of our island, it may now be permitted briefly to summarize the results of our investigation. We have seen that the principle of consent, independent of formal ceremony, was the original law of both countries, as it was that of all Europe, and as it seems, from the absence of any specific injunction of ceremony, to be that intended by the Divine Founder of the institution of marriage. We have seen, however, that the natural and commendable introduction of a religious ratification of so

solemn an engagement, led, in both England and
Scotland, to profane abuses; that these were eradicated
in Scotland by rules, providing that, where religious
sanction was at all invoked, it should be done in an
orderly and decent manner; but that in England they
were dealt with by enactments making the marriage
itself void, save where a duly performed religious
ceremony intervened. We have seen that in England
advantage was taken of the opportunity to declare the
marriages of minors void, when without parental
consent; and the marriages of all others void when
not preceded by due and formal publication of the
intention. We have seen that these impediments,
endured for three quarters of a century, were at last
thrown off by the outraged moral sense of the nation ;
that now religious ceremony may be, and is as often
dispensed with in England as in Scotland; that minors
may evade parental control, and secret marriages may
be contracted, with equal ease in the one country as
the other; that on no defect of form does nullity
follow, unless it be in an essential point, and the
error had been known to both parties. But we have
seen that, though the English system is thus reduced
to little more than a rule affecting evidence, it is, as
such, productive of the very evils it professes to
remedy; that the question, how far a mistake in law,
or deception known to both parties, is so essential as

to avoid the marriage, is of constant recurrence ; and that other questions of law, utterly beyond the foresight of the parties, are frequently arising to throw doubt upon the most solemn and deliberate unions. We have seen, on the other hand, that in Scotland no doubt can exist, save where essential dishonesty has existed ; that the inquiry, where it does arise, is not into the correctness of forms, but into the reality of facts ; and that where the fact is that a marriage, whether regularly or irregularly contracted, has been really in the view of the parties, there is no power in either party to evade the obligation, nor any possibility of subsequent doubt emerging as to whether it was legally constituted.   Finally, we have seen that, while in the majority of instances the English rules admit of doubts which could have no existence in Scotland, they gain any certainty which, in isolated cases, they can boast over those of the sister realm, by the process of declaring unquestionably adulterous, an intercourse which in Scotland might very possibly have been declared, on a consideration of the real meaning of the parties, and having regard to the principle that no one shall be allowed to take advantage of his own wrong, to have been truly and legally marriage.

I do not think that there is any possibility that those who candidly consider these facts will propose

that the marriage law of England, as it stands, should
be extended over the whole of the United Kingdom.
But the inquiry remains whether there may not be a
middle course found, in which simplicity shall be
combined with uniformity, in which the evidence of
marriage shall be defined, while yet no obstacle of
form is placed in the way of any who wish to contract
matrimony with the least amount of external ceremony.
To this question, though it is at present merely hypothetical, no such system having yet been propounded,
I shall devote a few observations.

We must in the first place keep clearly before our
minds that if any such system is adopted, it must be
under the sanction that if the prescribed form is not
observed the marriage is null. For if the marriage is
good in spite of non-observance of, or error in, the
form, then we are thrown back on other evidence of
consent, *i.e.* on the Scottish principle. And this
would be the case whatever the penalty (short of
nullity) that we laid upon the irregularity. For,
after the penalty was inflicted, there would still
remain the question, was the marriage good or bad,
and obviously it could be held to be good only on
general evidence of other facts than the form, which
in reality was disregarded. Hence it is clear that
there is no middle course, as regards evidence of
marriage, between a form which is to be exclusive

and indispensable, and a form which is not to be imperative at all.

But the moment we try to frame a form which is to be indispensable, we are met with the difficulties which English experience has so fully illustrated. Let us, for the sake of example, suppose as the simplest conceivable form, the entry of the names of the parties in the marriage register. Nothing can apparently be more easy than such a rule. But then the question will rise, what are the names? Is it to be a void marriage if one of the parties is entered under a false name? Is it to be void if the spelling is inaccurate? Is it to be void if the spelling would give the correct sound, though really a different name? Is it to be void if the Christian name is wrong, or one Christian name is omitted, or a name of usage is substituted, or a name of baptism is given instead of the name of christening? Such inquiries must be endless, for they may rise out of a perfectly infinite diversity of circumstances. All lawyers know that, in whatever department of law a signature by the true name is required, such doubts have sprung up. But how much the more if the unspeakably important question of marriage or not marriage is to depend upon the legal decision in each case?

But if we attempt to solve the difficulty by enacting that the marriage shall be good whatever the pecu-

liarity of signature, if only the identity of the parties
be ascertained (*si modo constet de personâ*), then we
open the door to an evasion of the whole system.
If we allow an entire *alias*, then there is gone all
the virtue of publicity, and certainty. If we allow
names that on the whole resemble the true names,
we only call into play a little ingenious spelling
sufficient for disguise, and more than sufficient to
make the ultimate proof of the marriage tenfold
more difficult than if only evidence of consent were
demanded.

This, also, is but one class of doubts. But if the
signatures must be in the proper register, then there
may be questions whether the book is a proper register.
And if no other evidence is admissible, then what is to
be done in the case of an entry showing marks of
erasure or alteration ? Then if the attestation of the
registrar, or witnesses, be requisite, there are the
questions about what is due attestation, or how far
a blundered attestation is fatal. All these questions
are common enough and painful enough when they
occur in the case of wills or affidavits, but sure to
be more common and more terribly painful when the
legality of marriage is in question.

I do not think that any form can be framed which
shall not be open to such questions. English jurisprudence has striven for above a hundred years to

do it, and has confessedly failed. It has at last abandoned the attempt in every respect save that requiring the ceremony of marriage to be in a church under the true names; to all appearance the simplest and most universally understood requirement that could be asked, and yet such is the infinite diversity of circumstances to which social arrangements give rise, that every year people make mistakes about what is a church, and brides and bridegrooms make mistakes about what are, in law, their true names. I earnestly wish a form could be devised not subject to such risk of misapprehension, but I cannot imagine any, and I can scarcely hope that the Royal Commission of 1865 will be more ingenious and sagacious than Lord Hardwicke, and the statesmen and lawyers of three generations.

Precisely the same difficulties, too, attend the question of consent of parents or guardians. If such consent is to be made essential (which it is not at present in England), the condition must annul a great number of marriages, and introduce doubts into many others where it has been rather evaded than violated. If it is, as at present, not to be essential, but delay and publicity are to be interposed in order to allow parental objections to take effect, then we are placed in the dilemma of either forbidding marriages where such delay is, from the circumstances of the parties, impossible, or of allowing a licence to dispense with delay to be purchased, as at present, on an oath, which may be false, that consent has been obtained. And in either case we introduce a variety of complex conditions which entirely destroy the simplicity essential to a good system of marriage law.

It seems to me, therefore, that no course is tenable save that of allowing proof of the real intention of the parties to establish marriage, no matter in what form such deliberate intention is signified. Scottish experience is here useful in showing that it is very rarely, indeed, that any doubt arises on such a question, far more rarely than on the question whether a statutory form has been observed.

There can, of course, be no objection to our supporting the force of public opinion by imposing penalties, not amounting to nullity of the marriage, on all who do not resort to the statutory form. But the force of public opinion is itself a very strong sanction, and those who are prepared to brave it will seldom be checked by the possibility of fine or imprisonment in the event of discovery. And if the statutory penalty were made so sharp and certain as to be a more potent detriment, I confess I should greatly fear evil results. For, considering the powerful motives which are in operation on both sides, considering the youth, the inexperience, the blindness of passion, the confiding trust, the sanguine hopes which agitate the minds of those who contemplate secret marriages, because they dare not at the time contract marriage openly, it cannot be thought that a penalty, so severe as practically to forbid such contracts, would enforce separation, and prevent illicit union. And surely, even in this age of mammon worship and reverence for outward respectability, there will not be found any to argue openly that improvident marriages ought to be forbidden at the cost of encouraging, or rather almost enforcing, arrangements of seduction and concubinage.

It may, therefore, be feared that there is small hope at present of any proposal being successful which shall have for object the assimilation of the marriage law in England and Scotland. Although in the former country it has undergone great modifications since the first statute that was passed, and every modification has brought it nearer to the original system, still maintained in Scotland, it is not probable that the English public, and still less that English lawyers, will be found prepared to abandon the remaining shred of imperative formality. On the other hand, the Scottish cannot be asked to renounce their own doctrines, which the experience of both countries has thus confirmed. If a common meeting ground were possible, Scotland might indeed, for the sake of uniformity, abandon one of the developments of that doctrine.

The marriage " by habit and repute " is not essential to morality ; it is chiefly a sacrifice to public decency, and with the object of obtaining a compromise; it might, without serious evil, be given up. But the remaining forms of irregular marriage, that by actual declaration and that by promise, followed by cohabitation, are essential to morality and admit of no compromise.

I trust I may be pardoned if, before concluding, I add a few words respecting the changes in my own opinions on this subject. It would be natural to suppose that my preference for the Scottish doctrine is partly due to the prejudices of nationality, or to those imbibed through prior study of the law of Scotland, and such a suspicion would naturally and properly weaken the effect of the arguments I have adduced. But the reverse is the truth. When I was acquainted with only the Scottish law, its apparent want of definition, and its occasional difficulty of application, shocked me, and what seemed the simplicity in legal principle of the English rules led me to desire that they should be extended to Scotland. I felt strong interest in the measure which the late Lord Rutherford, one of the very ablest lawyers whom Scotland has ever produced, repeatedly strove to carry through Parliament with the view of substituting an official record for all looser forms of contracting or proving matrimony. But when, after being called to the English bar, I had an opportunity of examining carefully the nature and operation of the system I had admired, my opinions underwent a slow but irresistible change. I could not disregard the evidence furnished by the statute book and the reports, that these fixed rules made marriage uncertain in England in an incomparably greater number of instances than those in which it is doubtful in Scotland. I could not help perceiving that the restriction to evidence of an imperative ceremony often gave room for doubt even where the intentions were honest, while the admission of any evidence of purpose made all those safe where the purpose, on both sides or on one, was honest. I could not avoid seeing that secret marriages were as easy and as common in the one country as the other, and that the only effect of such fixed rules as had in England survived parliamentary alteration, was to give aid to the seducer, or to enable one of the parties, when weary of the tie, to dissolve it by taking advantage of a latent illegality in its constitution. On these grounds I could not but change my preconceived opinions. And I have striven fairly to set down the facts and arguments which brought me to this conclusion, in the belief that those who have hitherto looked at the question from only one side, will be induced to compare both its aspects, and so comparing, will be brought to the like convictions as myself. For here, if anywhere, we are bound to throw aside prejudice, and to search candidly and honestly for the right course. And here, above all, where not only the deepest human, but eternal interests may be at stake, we are bound to renounce the pride of human theories, and to submit ourselves humbly to the law of God, the broad principles of which are revealed to us in his Word, though many a time it happens that their due application to human circumstances is taught to us only by the consequences of our human errors.

APPENDIX.

APPENDIX.

*(REFERRED TO AT PAGE 31.)

————◆◆◆————

IT is to be observed that in the following draft Bill some necessary matters of detail and technicality, which the parliamentary draftsman will readily supply, but which seemed not required for the clear perception of the means intended to be employed, have been left out.

The draft at present applies only to England, but the principle of the measure could easily be adapted to the slightly different machinery existing in Scotland and Ireland.

DRAFT OF A BILL FOR EXTENDING THE FRANCHISE TO PERSONS WHO CAN READ AND WRITE.

I. Every male person of the age of 25 years and not subject to any legal incapacity, who shall obtain, in manner hereinafter mentioned, a certificate of sufficient education, shall be entitled to be registered as a voter, and to vote in the election of a member or members for the county or borough within which such person shall have resided for a period of six months previous to the date of his claim to be registered. Provided that no such person, though duly registered, shall vote at any election if in receipt of parochial relief at the time or within one year prior thereto.

II. The Committee of Her Majesty's Privy Council for Education shall, as soon as may be after the passing of this Act, appoint a sufficient number of persons to be Examiners under this Act, and shall assign a district to each such Examiner, each district containing a population of not more than   persons according to the last census, and may from time to time appoint additional Examiners for each district, or alter the limits of any district, as may be found necessary.

III. The persons appointed Examiners shall be (*qualifications which may be thought desirable*), and shall be removable at the discretion of the said committee, and shall be paid a salary of   *l*. per annum out of the Consolidated Fund.

IV. Each Examiner shall notify his appointment to the Clerk of the Peace of every county, and to the Town Clerk of every borough which shall be within the district for which he is appointed.

V. Each Examiner shall, once during every year, in the period betwixt the 1st day of October and the 20th day of July immediately following, hold a sitting in each borough within his district, and at each polling place in a county, not being a borough, within his district, for examination of persons desirous of obtaining a certificate of education under this Act.

VI. Every person desirous of obtaining such certificate shall give or send to the Town Clerk of the borough, or to the Clerk of the Peace of the county, as the case may be, in which the place where he desires to be examined is situated, a notification of such desire, setting forth his name, residence, and trade or profession, which may be in the form of Schedule A.

VII. Immediately after the 20th July in every year a list of the persons who have so notified their desire to be examined, subsesequently to the 20th July preceding, shall be made up and transmitted to the Examiner for the district, by the Town Clerk of every borough and by the Clerk of the Peace of every county situated within such district, and in such list, in the case of counties, the persons who have applied to be examined at each polling place, not being a borough, shall be distinguished.

VIII. The Examiner shall give one month's notice, in writing under his hand, to the Town Clerk of the borough, and the Clerk of the Peace of the county, respectively, of the days on which he will hold sittings for examination under this Act in such borough, and at each polling place, not being a borough, in such county.

IX. The Town Clerk and Clerk of the Peace respectively shall provide, by hiring or otherwise, a suitable room in, or as near to as may be, each such place, for holding the sittings for examination on the days so appointed, and shall provide suitable furniture for such room, and the room shall be of such size and the furniture of such description as shall be specified by the Committee of Her Majesty's Council for Education.'

X. Three weeks before the day fixed for such examination in each place the Town Clerk of the borough, or Clerk of the Peace of the county, as the case may be, shall advertise the place, days, and hour fixed for the same, in two of the newspapers published or of principal circulation in such borough or county, and shall intimate the same by notice transmitted to the overseers of every parish in such borough, or to the overseers of every parish within the district of the county at the polling place of which such examination is to be held, as the case may be, and the overseers shall publish such notice in the manner in which they are required to publish notices under the Act passed in the sixth year of Her Majesty, cap. 18.

XI. During the sitting for examination one agent for each Member of Parliament, as well for the county as for the borough in which such sitting may be held, and also one agent for each candidate at the last preceding election, and for each person who may have by printed address announced his intention to be a candidate at the next ensuing election for such county, or borough, shall be permitted to be present ; the fact of such agency being proved by production of a certificate in writing purporting to be signed by such Member of Parliament or candidate, and the fact of any person signing such certificate having been, or intending to be, a candidate, being proved by the production of a newspaper containing his printed address to the electors.

XII. The Examiner may in his discretion permit any persons not being such agents to be present during the examination, and may at any time require them to retire if inconvenience arise from their presence; but the examination shall in no case proceed unless there are at least three persons present besides the Examiner and the person under examination.

XIII. No person shall in any manner interfere with the examination, or speak or make any noise while it is proceeding; and no person shall during the examination be nearer than a distance of six feet from the Examiner and the person under examination.

XIV. The examination shall consist in the reading aloud, by the person under examination, of a passage, of not fewer than fifty words, pointed out to him by the Examiner in any book, not being the Bible, Book of Common Prayer, catechism, or articles of religious belief of any religious denomination; and in the writing to dictation of not fewer than ten words: and the Examiner may require any further passage to be read, or words to be written, and may put any questions he may think proper to enable him to judge whether the person examined understands what he has read.

XV. If the Examiner is satisfied that the person examined can read with understanding, and can write so as to be generally understood, he shall give to him a certificate under his hand in the form of Schedule B.

XVI. Any person who has failed to obtain such certificate may make a new application to be examined in any subsequent year.

XVII. Any person who has obtained such certificate shall, within three years after he has been for the first time registered as a voter in virtue thereof, be liable to be objected to by a registered voter for the same county or borough, on the ground that such certificate ought not to have been granted, and notice of such objection must be served on such voter personally, before the 20th of July in any year: and at the revision of the register of voters in the year following that in which such notice has been served, the name of the voter may be struck out of the register, unless he shall, when the objection is heard, produce a second certificate of education obtained under this Act; but no such objection shall be valid if served after the lapse of the said three years, or after such second certificate has been produced.

XVIII. Examiner may require attendance of constables to preserve order, and may order the removal from the room of any person guilty of contempt or disturbance.

XIX. Town Clerks and Clerks of Peace to be reimbursed for outlays out of borough or county rates.

XX. Persons not to be liable to be dismissed from service for absence for the purpose of being examined, if the place where they are examined is the nearest to their place of service, but to suffer a proportionate deduction from their wages for the time of actual absence.

XXI. On applying to be registered as a voter in virtue of a certificate under this Act, the applicant shall produce a certificate of identity and of residence, signed by one of Her Majesty's Justices of the Peace, or by a Clergyman in the form set forth in Schedule C, and which certificate shall be dated within one month prior to the date of the applicant's claim to be registered.

XXII. Claims to be registered as a voter in virtue of a certificate of education, and notices of such claims, and objections thereto, and objections to such voters remaining on the register on the ground of a change of residence, to be made in the same manner as in the case of other voters under the 6 Vict. cap. 18.

XXIII. Penalties on personation, &c. (*as in existing Acts*).

SCHEDULES.

A.

I, A. B., residing at

profession), desire to be examined at

of being registered as a voter.

(Date)

(*trade or*

for the purpose

(*Signature of Applicant.*)

B.

I certify that A. B., residing at   (*trade or profession*), has been examined by me at   this   day of   , and that he is possessed of sufficient education to be entitled to be registered as a voter under the provisions of the Act of the   reign of Her Majesty, cap.   .

(*Signature of Examiner.*)

C.

I, C. D., Justice of the Peace for the County of (*or* Rector of the parish of, *or* Minister of the church or chapel of, *as the case may be*), certify that A. B., now and for the last six months residing at   (*trade or profession*), is known to me to be the person named and designed as A. B. (*add residence and trade given in Examiner's certificate*) in an Examiner's certificate dated at   the   day of   , 186 , and signed (*state signature of Examiner.*)

(*Signature of Justice or Clergyman.*)

London : Printed by Smith, Elder and Co., Old Bailey, E.C.